DOING BETTER

DOING BETTER

Improving Clinical Skills and Professional Competence

Editors

Jeffrey A. Kottler
W. Paul Jones

Brunner-Routledge
New York and Hove

Published in 2003 by
Brunner-Routledge
29 West 35th Street
New York, NY 10001
www.brunner-routledge.com

Published in Great Britain by
Brunner-Routledge
27 Church Road
Hove, East Sussex
BN3 2FA
www.brunner-routledge.co.uk

Brunner-Routledge is an imprint of the Taylor & Francis Group.
Printed in the United States of America on acid-free paper.

Cover design by Mark Lerner.
Cover photo: Courtesy of Jeffrey A. Kottler.

10 9 8 7 6 5 4 3 2 1

Library of Congress Cataloging-in-Publication Data

  Doing better : improving clinical skills and professional competence /
Jeffrey A. Kottler & W. Paul Jones, editors.
        p. cm.
  Includes bibliographical references and index.
  ISBN 1-58391-329-7 (pbk.)
  1. Mental health counseling—Practice. 2. Psychotherapy—Practice.
  I. Kottler, Jeffrey A. II. Jones, W. Paul.

  RC466.D65 2003
  362.2′04256—dc21

                                                    2003002046

CONTENTS

PREFACE

Doing Better is designed to help practicing therapists and counselors, as well as students of these professions, to explore more fully and systematically their own processes of self-improvement in their clinical practices. Although self-supervision is hardly intended to replace traditional forms of professional development in the form of advanced training, supervision, or personal therapy, it does provide a framework—and a process—for monitoring one's own strengths and weaknesses and taking steps to improve excellence across a host of domains.

In the chapters that are included in this book, readers are introduced to a wide range of methods for initiating and maintaining self-development and professional development activities. Attention is directed to the natural stages of development in a clinician's life, including those critical incidents that can help to make a good therapist even better and the role played by licensing boards in support of continuing professional development. Readers are encouraged to develop more effective critical self-monitoring skills that can be used to measure effectiveness, assess strengths and weaknesses, and improve their efficiency and therapeutic influence. Help is provided for dealing with the thorny issues of boredom and routines as they arise in sessions. You are encouraged to deal with personal adversity because it affects not only your own life but also your work with clients. You are urged to confront personal biases and prejudices that may compromise your work. Finally, additional chapters describe ways that you can do better professionally and personally with tools borrowed from other fields such as medicine and sports performance and with assistance of technological resources, including the Internet/WWW. When all is said and done, this book provides you with innumerable ways that you can take greater responsibility for improving your own clinical skills and professional competence. This is not intended as a substitute for other forms of training and supervision, but as an adjunct to them.

This book will help any practicing counselor and therapist improve professional skills and competence. It may also be used as a text in a variety of beginning and advanced level clinical courses in counseling, psychology, social work, family therapy, psychiatry, nursing, human services, and allied mental health disciplines, or as a resource for continuing education independent study.

Although the chapters in this book are both scholarly and solidly researched, we have tried to emphasize throughout the practical applications of the concepts to your daily life as a clinician. It is by taking a more proactive stance on behalf of your own continued growth and development that you not only can become increasingly effective in your work, but also more energized and excited about what you do and how you do it.

We are grateful to the constructive reviews by the following individuals who helped us to shape the content of these chapters into a coherent treatment of self-care and self-supervision: Dr. Fred Bemak, Dr. Margaret Miller, and Dr. David A. Spruillo.

We are also indebted to Emily Epstein Loeb, our editor, for her flexible, caring, and supportive style helping us to "do better" as writers and editors.

Jeffrey A. Kottler
Fullerton, California

W. Paul Jones
Las Vegas, Nevada

THE EDITORS

Jeffrey A. Kottler is Professor and Chair of the Counseling Department at California State University, Fullerton. He has authored over 50 books including: *On Being a Therapist, The Imperfect Therapist, Compassionate Therapy, Travel That Can Change Your Life, Theories in Counseling and Therapy, Learning Group Leadership, Doing Good, Making Changes Last, Bad Therapy,* and *One Life at a Time.*

Jeffrey has been an educator and psychologist for 25 years. He has worked as a teacher, counselor, and therapist in preschool, middle school, mental health center, crisis center, university, community college, and private practice. He has served as a Fulbright Scholar and Senior Lecturer in Peru (1980) and Iceland (2000), as well as worked in dozens of countries as a consultant and trainer specializing in multicultural issues.

W. Paul Jones is Professor of Educational Psychology at the University of Nevada, Las Vegas, a practicing clinician with more than 50 articles in refereed professional journals and two books: *Deciphering the Diagnostic Codes: A Guide for School Counselors,* and *Educational Psychology: The Teaching-Learning Process.*

Paul's 40 years of professional experience include teaching and counseling at the public school, community college, and university levels, and full-time practice as a therapist. He is a licensed psychologist in Nevada and New Mexico, a registrant in the National Register of Health Service Providers in Psychology, and a Fellow in the American Academy of Clinical Sexologists.

THE AUTHORS

Michael K. Altekruse is Chair and Professor in the Department of Counseling Development and Higher Education at the University of North Texas. He has taught counselor education for over 30 years and is a past president of the Association for Counselor Education and Supervision.

Leah Brew is an Assistant Professor at California State University, Fullerton. Her primary interest and research areas include supervision, culture, group, and career. She is coauthor of the book, *One Life at a Time*.

Jesse Brinson is a Counselor Educator in the Department of Counseling at the University of Nevada, Las Vegas. His teaching and research interests include multicultural issues in counseling, group work, and issues with minority adolescent substance abusers.

Laurie Carty is a Professor of Mental Health Nursing at the University of Windsor (Canada). She is editor of the journal *Guidance and Counselling* and a researcher in the area of peer group counseling.

John A. "Jack" Casey is Professor and Coordinator of Educational Counseling Programs at California State University, Bakersfield. He has served as a school counselor for 8 years and a counselor educator for 15 years in Nevada and California.

Joseph M. Cervantes is an Associate Professor at California State University, Fullerton. He specializes in ethical issues, spiritual issues, and work with Latino and indigenous populations.

David D. Chen is a Faculty Member in the Division of Kinesiology and Health Promotion at California State University, Fullerton. He teaches and does research in the areas of motor behavior and sports psychology.

Dana L. Comstock is an Associate Professor and Graduate Program Director in the Department of Counseling and Human Services at St. Mary's University in San Antonio, Texas. She also has a part-time private practice.

Thelma H. Duffey is an Associate Professor and Graduate Program Director in the Counseling Program at Southwest Texas State University, San

Marcos, Texas. Her research interests include family therapy, gender and multicultural issues, and the uses of creativity.

Shirley Emerson is Emeritus Professor of Counseling at the University of Nevada, Las Vegas. She served as President of the State of Nevada Board of Marriage and Family Therapists for 12 years.

Matt Englar-Carlson is an Assistant Professor at California State University, Fullerton in the Department of Counseling. His areas of scholarly investigation include the psychology of men and masculinity and the conceptualization of social class as a multicultural variable.

Robert L. Harbach is an Associate Professor of School Counseling at the University of Nevada, Las Vegas. He has published in the area of family issues and relationship skills.

David Leary is the Director and Senior Counsellor at the Come In Youth Resource Center at Paddington in Sydney, Australia, where he works with homeless and marginalized youth.

Gerald Monk is a Faculty Member and Director of the School Counseling Program at San Diego State University. He has written in the areas of narrative therapy and mediation.

Gloria Morrow is a Licensed Clinical Psychologist in private practice. She works as a community activist and co-pastor in the African American community in Pomona, California.

Kathy O'Byrne is Executive Director of the Center for Experiential Education and Service Learning at the University of California, Los Angeles. She maintains a private practice in Pasadena.

Maryam Sayyedi is an Assistant Professor of Counseling at California State University, Fullerton. Her professional and research interests focus on anxiety and mood disorders of childhood. She works as a psychologist within the Persian community of Orange County.

Carol Scott is a Chartered Psychologist in private practice in Calgary, Alberta, Canada, where she specializes in sex therapy.

David Shepard is Assistant Professor of Counseling at California State University, Fullerton. He is also a therapist in private practice specializing in clients with mood disorders and in couples counseling.

Stacey L. Sinclair is a Nationally Certified Counselor and an adjunct professor at San Diego State University. Her interests include social constructionist and postmodern feminist epistemology, and the cultural constructions of gender, ethnicity, sexuality, and the body.

Sherrill Wiseman is a Chartered Psychologist in private practice in Calgary, Alberta, Canada. She is a Faculty Member at City University Seattle, Washington and is the Psychological Consultant for The Calgary Prostate Cancer Center.

CHAPTER 1   Jeffrey A. Kottler

When Therapists Supervise Themselves

On the surface of things, the whole idea sounds pretty ludicrous: a therapist supervising him- or herself is sort of like trying to see the back of your own head—without a mirror. Even if a reflective object was available, the whole enterprise is so awkward, the angles so limited, the view so restricted, that it hardly seems worth the effort . . . unless, of course, there is nobody else available who can tell you that there is some unflattering indentation.

Therapists attempt to supervise themselves sometimes out of choice, but more often out of necessity. When there is nobody else around, when there isn't the option of waiting until the next scheduled supervision session, we may have no other choice except to try and work things out on our own.

Needless to say, there are limits to what one can do on one's own. For instance, it is difficult, if not impossible, to recognize and work through characterological problems on one's own; believing you can do so might be evidence of its' own form of personality disorder (Shub, 1995).

☐ The Role of Supervising Oneself

There have been times in my career when I have worked with a supervisor I trusted fully, a mentor with whom it felt safe to share aloud my fears

1

and insecurities, but that has been the exception rather than the rule. In most of the clinical settings in which I've worked, my supervisors were evaluators as well as consultants. They were the ones who decided if I got licensed or promoted. They wrote reference letters testifying to my competence. They decided if I was good enough, and their judgment might very well affect my whole future career. There was no way in such situations that I was ever going to talk about how little I really understood about what I was doing.

In case conferences, my fellow therapists and I would only bring up those clients with whom we already had a pretty good idea about what was going on. Although we were encouraged to present those clients and families with whom we were struggling the most, the actual consequence of doing so was that we would have most likely been skewered alive, ridiculed for our ignorance, and held out as examples of poor training and judgment. Group supervision was absolutely the *last* place in the world where we would have thought about being frank and honest about where we needed help most.

Even in individual supervision, I was reluctant to bring up my deepest fears of inadequacy, although I might very well do so during the times I consulted my own therapist to work on these issues. It was one thing to tell a therapist I trusted that I felt like a fraud, that most of the time I was faking it, pretending I knew so much more than I really did. But alas, the supervisors who controlled my workload would never have been those to whom I could reveal my greatest vulnerabilities.

I hope I am among the slimmest minority in this regard because I would hate to think that my own supervisees feel the same toward me, or that the majority of practitioners out there in the world are merely going through the motions in their own supervision. Unfortunately, based on my own research on the subject, I know that I am hardly alone in my caution. There are many of us just going through the motions with our supervisors, just doing what is expected in order to meet the minimal requirements.

Over the years, I have heard so many therapists relate similar stories of "performing" for their supervisors, saying what was expected, presenting "safe" cases in which they could demonstrate their expertise, flexibility, and responsiveness to suggestions. "The last place I'd ever talk about a troubling case," one therapist admits, "is with my supervisor. Even if the guy could help me (which I often doubt), there would be repercussions at a later time."

"What sort of consequences?" I asked her, feeling both intrigued and disturbed by how casually she was validating my own experience.

"Oh, you know. The usual. Black marks in my record for being less than perfect. Paternal condescension in which I was expected to act like a needy child. Basically feeling vulnerable because I admitted I don't know what I'm doing all the time."

"So?" I asked again. "Where *do* you get help with your difficult cases?"

This therapist revealed that she talks to colleagues about her struggles, but sometimes that isn't all that helpful (or safe) either. So most of the time, she pretty much keeps things to herself, tries her best to look good in front of her peers, and then tries to figure things out on her own.

Such a strategy, of course, is not only misguided but also dangerous. Therapists are not only mandated to work continually on improving competence through various supervisory/educational experiences by qualified experts, but we *need* to do so in order to survive the uncertainty, ambiguity, and complexity of our jobs. If hierarchical supervision (with a designated supervisor) or peer supervision are preferred, the reality is that much of the time rather than consulting with others we try to work things out on our own. This may involve a variety of self-supervision activities, from solitary reflection, meditation, and journal writing to reading books, constructing narratives, reviewing audio- or videotapes, or journal articles (Lowe, 2000; Todd, 1997). At its best, self-supervision activities are highly rigorous and critical for continued improvement in clinical skills (Morrissette, 1999, 2002).

There are so many blind spots and dangers associated with trying to monitor our own progress; it flies in the face of the most sacred standards of our profession. Self-supervision is not intended to replace the formal instruction or structured supervision that is so critical for reality testing, accountability, and receiving constructive feedback. Rather, it is designed as a supplement for these traditional forms of professional improvement that involves training in specific skills (Donnelly & Glaser, 1992). Because therapists and counselors are in the rather unique role of facilitating positive changes in other people's lives, we are also perfectly positioned to make ourselves better as well.

☐ Realities of Practice

Most of the time I am doing therapy I feel lost, confused, or in over my head. Under such circumstances I would love to have someone (or several someones) whom I can consult with about these cases, and particularly to talk about my feelings of ineptitude, failure, and impending doom. I have been fortunate at various times in my career to have such opportunities, but often the timing isn't right.

For example, right now I spend most of my professional life teaching therapy in the classroom. Even though I have been doing this for almost 30 years, there isn't a class I live through that I can't think of at least a dozen confusing incidents that I didn't understand and twice that number of things I said and did that were less than effective. I leave each class flooded with thoughts about things I could have done differently, just as I do when I see clients. The amazing thing to me, however, is that faculty almost never watch each other teach and almost never seek or offer feedback to one another. Somehow, it is assumed that because we are supposed to be such experts, we no longer need such supervision. So we rely almost entirely on student evaluations that, although useful, offer us a limited view of our behavior.

During the last class I taught, I was working with a group of masters students in Hong Kong. Although the students are quite fluent in English, some of them feel some reluctant to express themselves outside of their native language, especially related to the kind of personal matters that often crop up in a group therapy class. More than I am used to, there is a tremendous fear of losing face.

The discussion about instances when leader intervention is required was going particularly well when, all of a sudden, one of the students became agitated and started speaking rapidly in Cantonese. I politely interrupted him and asked what was going on. He apologized and then did his best to explain what was happening, but it seemed the moment was lost. I wondered whether I should have just let him go, and desperately wanted to consult with a colleague about the matter, but there was nobody available at the time. As a matter of fact, I have no colleagues at all who work with me during these assignments abroad.

A few minutes later, there was another incident in which several students began speaking to one another in Cantonese; by the look of their agitation, they seemed to be in conflict over something. This time I decided to let things run their course; to my surprise, the whole class jumped in, speaking away in a language I couldn't understand. I leaned over and asked the person next to me what was going on, and whether it was safe to let things go. He ignored me and joined the discussion.

This, of course, was only one of a hundred things that took place during the day that puzzled me. I wished there was someone watching from behind a one-way mirror, or better yet, someone in the room with me. As a second choice, I would have been most grateful if I could have run down to a colleague or supervisor's office during the break to get some input. But the nature of these circumstances was such that it was a few weeks before I could debrief these incidents with my supervisor, who did indeed have several useful suggestions. By then, of course, I had been struggling on my own to make sense of what happened for dozens of hours. I thought to myself then, as I have many times before, I sure wish I was better trained in supervising myself.

There are many reasons why therapists don't make maximum use of traditional supervision opportunities: (a) Help isn't readily available when we need it. (b) Whatever resources are available are not offered at a time and place that are convenient. (c) It is not safe to be very open and honest with one's assigned supervisor. (d) The supervision available is not all that helpful. For these and a variety of other reasons, we often work things out on our own, sometimes intentionally and other times quite spontaneously. That, after all, is what we do—teach people to do their own therapy when we aren't around.

☐ Joys of Self-Supervision

When therapists are left to their own devices, several common themes are frequently reported. First of all, just as with our clients, there is often a high degree of emotional activation present that gets our attention in a way that can't be ignored. When therapists are disgusted with themselves— when they are afraid, frustrated, exasperated, and helpless—they are extremely motivated to find some sort of peace and resolution. If a supervisor is not readily available, then we do what we can on our own.

Because we work in such intensely interpersonal settings, sometimes the solution to our problems is not more discussion and interaction with others, but less. Solitude, and what it affords, gives us a chance to metabolize stress, debrief ourselves, lick our wounds, and then perhaps consult others at a later time. When self-supervision is integrated into all the other forms of the learning, feedback, growth, and critical evaluation that are part of any therapist's life, then we have a balanced blend of influence from without and within.

This can take many forms, depending on interests, style, and personal resources. Some therapists use hobbies or creative pursuits as a means to debrief themselves from work and process the difficulties they are experiencing. Others find that it is less the structured activity than the internal process they follow, whether that is during idle moments between sessions, driving home, going for a walk, or drifting off to sleep. This internal process can be systematically described in a series of logical, progressive questions (Table 1.1).

☐ Structured Ways to Do Better

Surely one of the most annoying, dreaded, and time-consuming assignments that any therapist could be asked to complete is the construction of

---

TABLE 1.1. Questions for Self-Supervision

How am I distorting or exaggerating what is going on?

How are the ways I am stuck with this client similar to other relationships that I have experienced?

What personal issues are being triggered by this situation?

What am I expecting or demanding of this client that he or she is unwilling or unable to do?

What have I been doing that has been most and least helpful?

Which ineffective strategies am I reluctant to let go of in favor of something that might work better?

How are issues of power and control getting in the way of progress?

How are my arrogance and sense of grandiosity complicating matters?

In what ways am I working too hard or taking on too much responsibility for the outcome?

How am I acting out my impatience toward this client for moving more slowly than I'd prefer?

What do my fantasies during sessions reveal?

How are my self-doubts and fears of failure being triggered by this situation?

If I am truly honest with myself, what mistakes and misjudgments have I made in the way I've handled things?

How am I blaming the client(s) for being uncooperative rather than looking at our shared responsibility for the impasse?

What do I need to do or order to reclaim my compassion?

How might my difficulties be part of a larger systemic dysfunction in my work environment or personal life?

In what ways is my unhealthy lifestyle contributing to the difficulties?

What am I avoiding by not bringing these issues up to a supervisor who could confront me or offer alternative viewpoints?

How could a colleague, supervisor, or therapist help me to work through unfinished business?

What is it about these questions that I find most threatening?

---

a typescript that represents a verbatim record of the exact conversation that took place, including an annotated commentary of all the things that were done right, wrong, as well as any new awareness and insights that have subsequently taken place. Of course, because nobody of sound mind would willingly undertake such a tortuous task unless assigned by a supervisor, one could make the case that this isn't really a form of *self*-supervision as much as an adjunct to regular supervision. I disagree.

Although there is some accountability in that, presumably, the instructor or supervisor will review the typescript and write his or her own comments, the very act of doing this on one's own promotes quite a bit of self-reflection and self-critical behavior that can be internalized afterward.

Let's take a look, for example, at a 2-minute excerpt from just such an assignment in which a student-therapist in an assessment and diagnosis course looks at her own performance with a critical eye.

Transcript	Commentary
Therapist: "Okay, so this was an experience of not handling a work situation that you always were able to deal with before. Things just seemed to go from bad to worse."	That was a pretty good summary, I think.
Client: "It went from being, you know, sort of, well, I guess depressed. I suppose anyone gets that way sometimes. But it's this anxiety thing that's got me worried. I can't remember feeling this way before."	Here I get a better clarification that he was experiencing depression before the anxiety attacks started. But I want to separate them out as they seem a bit fused together in his story.
Therapist: "They actually seem quite different to me—the anxiety and the depression. You haven't really said much about the depression. How does that fit in your life at the moment?"	I didn't realize until this moment that I said "depression" when I was thinking anxiety. I also note that he answered me as I meant it, not as I said it. It's like we were in tune with one another! I wanted to find out how the anxiety and depression were related.
Client: "Well, the depression seems. . . . Well, I feel alright at the moment. I'm not really coping that well with my situation at home, but I am seem to be getting by. The anxiety seems to hit first, then I feel depressed about losing control."	
Therapist: "So they are linked."	
Client: "Yeah, I guess they are. It feels kind of like a roller coaster. You know, like major lows, and then highs. I'm not sure what it's like to feel normal."	I am reminded here that he is an expert on his own experience. I forget that sometimes. I am very aware that I've never had feelings like he is describing so I need to take on the position of student, learning from him. I also want to find out what he thinks this is all about. Because he tends to intellectualize, I realize also that I should shift things to a more emotional level, using more empathic responses and few probing questions.
Therapist: "You've been tracking this for some time. I think you said earlier ever since you can remember."	
Client: "I guess that's true. I've always been rather logical about this whole thing."	

Some of what this therapist reports is insightful, and other things may be a bit off base, subject to consultation with others who have more experience. But it is this process of self-scrutiny that is so important. What this student learns to do while reviewing a typescript after the session, experienced practitioners do inside their heads throughout the interview, constantly making adjustments as things proceed. Under the best of conditions, this critical voice does not so much scold or shame us, but bring our attention to things in need of closer scrutiny and self-reflection. It is, after all, reflective activities that help us understand better what we are doing in our work, what works best, and what we can do to improve our effectiveness (Best, 1996; Johns, 1999; Moore, 2000).

☐ Informal Growth Opportunities

Some professionals use travel as a transformative experience, not only to recover from work, to rejuvenate and replenish themselves, but also to stimulate new growth through their journeys in novel environments. Ironically, significant changes most often occur *not* when under the "supervision" of a tour guide but when you have ventured off on your own. Under such circumstances, the pilgrim is more likely to solve problems in new ways, overcome challenges, expand horizons, face fears—do all the things we know lead to change in other settings.

In my research on this subject (Kottler, 1997, 2001; Kottler & Montgomery, 2000), it was surprising to learn how often that travel becomes most transformative after people get lost or face obstacles they must overcome. It is when you force yourself to do what is most difficult, when you get outside your comfort zone, when you immerse yourself in novel environments that require you to invent new ways to meet your needs, that growth most often occurs. Of course, that is the same lesson we teach our clients. This leads to the most important point of all related to our subject of self-supervision. If what we wish most for those we help is that they become self-sufficient in continuing their own therapy (with a little help from some family and friends), what better way to do that than for us to model this process in our own lives? It is through such efforts that we are able to show the world, and ourselves, that we can practice what we preach.

Doing Better is a book designed for those practitioners, both beginners and veterans alike, who are interested in improving their own professional competence. It is not intended to replace the formal instruction or structured supervision that are so critical for reality testing, accountability, and receiving constructive feedback. Rather, it is designed as a supplement to these traditional forms of professional improvement. Because therapists and counselors are in a rather unique role to facilitate positive changes in other people's lives, they are perfectly positioned to make themselves better as well.

Of course, we can all use some help.

☐ References

Best, D. (1996). On the experience of keeping a reflective journal while training. *Therapeutic Communities, 17*(4), 293–301.

Donnelly, C., & Glaser, A. (1992). Training in self-supervision. *The Clinical Supervisor, 10*(2), 85–96.

Johns, C. (1999). Reflection as empowerment. *Nursing Inquiry, 6,* 241–249.

Kottler, J. A. (1997). *Travel that can change your life.* San Francisco: Jossey-Bass.

Kottler, J. A. (2001). The therapeutic benefits of structured travel experiences. *Journal of Clinical Activities, Assignments, and Handouts in Psychotherapy Practice, 1*(1), 29–36.

Kottler, J. A., & Montgomery, M. (2000). Prescriptive travel and adventure-based activities as adjuncts to counseling. *Guidance and Counselling, 15*(2), 8–11.

Lowe, R. (2000). Supervising self-supervision: Constructive inquiry and embedded narratives in case consultation. *Journal of Marital and Family Therapy, 26*(4), 511–521.

Moore, B. (2000). The therapeutic community worker as reflective practitioner and the social worker as skillful dynamic explorer. *Therapeutic Communities, 21*(1), 3–14.

Morrissette, P. J. (1999). Family therapist self-supervision: Toward a preliminary conceptualization. *The Clinical Supervisor, 18*(2), 165–183.

Morrissette, P. J. (2002). *Self-supervision: A primer for counselors and human service professionals.* New York: Brunner-Routledge.

Shub, N. F. (1995). The journey of the characterologic therapist. In M. B. Sussman (Ed.), *A perilous calling: The hazards of psychotherapy practice.* New York: Wiley.

Todd, T. C. (1997). Self-supervision as a universal supervisory goal. In T. C. Todd & C. L. Storm (Eds.), *The complete systemic supervisor.* Boston: Allyn & Bacon.

2

CHAPTER

Jeffrey A. Kottler
W. Paul Jones

The Natural and Unnatural Evolution of Therapist Development

The concept of stage theory is near and dear to the heart of psychologically trained professionals. Sigmund Freud (1924) popularized the idea that human beings proceed through a series of orderly, invariant, sequential steps in their evolution. That he was basically misguided in the emphasis he placed on infantile sexuality doesn't change the fact that the structure he borrowed from biology and applied to psychosocial development was immeasurably helpful in both understanding and predicting behavior. If we can plot the natural evolution of the way most people evolve, regardless of their cultural and individual characteristics, then we have a pretty good idea of where they have been and where they're headed next.

Following Freud's lead, a number of other theorists have attempted to devise stage models to account for human development in a variety of areas, including cognitive development (Piaget, 1926), psychosocial development (Erikson, 1950), moral development (Kohlberg, 1969), ego development (Loevinger, 1976), cultural identity development (Sue, Ivey, & Pedersen, 1996), family development (Carter & McGoldrick, 1989), and gender development (Basow, 1992). It is not surprising that career development (Super, 1953) also can be plotted on a continuum of sequential stages, each of which implies different needs, abilities, and tasks implicit in each stage.

For our present subject, such developmental assessment is particularly important because therapists and counselors require different sorts of supervision and growth experiences depending on their current stage of

functioning. Someone early in her career might be hungry for more structured intervention, whereas a more experienced clinician might actually
profit from less structure. Among group therapists, for example, more
experienced practitioners enjoy certain benefits as a function of their expertise but they also fall prey to problems that would not likely trouble
beginners as much. Thus, experienced practitioners struggle with problems related to making overgeneralizations and holding invalid assumptions about clients, whereas beginners are likely to proceed too cautiously
and conservatively (Kottler, 1994). This is in marked contrast to beginning practitioners, who tend to struggle more with issues related to self-
confidence, feeling competent, trusting intuition, and setting limits
(Wallbridge, 1995).

☐ Developmental Stages of the Therapist's Development of Competence

If we look at one issue in depth that concerns therapists a lot, it would be
the ongoing struggle for competence. Whether this is framed as a fear of
failure, or the striving for mastery, most clinicians feel challenged throughout their careers to achieve a sense of personal and professional mastery.
The particular form this may take evolves over time and may be framed
in terms of a series of internal questions that may be plotted as sequential
stages (Kottler & Blau, 1989). Depending on the stage of development in
which a therapist may be currently functioning, supervision needs are
distinctly different, whether this help is self-administered or offered by
mentors.

What If I Don't Have What It Takes to Be a Therapist?

This is often a question asked in the very beginning of one's training and
is not likely to be spoken aloud, except among one's most trusted confi-
dantes. It is rare indeed that a student or intern would confide doubts
about one's fitness for the profession to a supervisor. This is one of those
fears that is often pushed aside, buried, denied, or perhaps whispered in
secret. It is typical of the kinds of professional and personal doubts that
are addressed internally and privately, and it is certainly one of the many
things they rarely addressed in training programs (Kottler & Hazler, 1997).
Examples of others that are rarely brought up to supervisors but nevertheless plague beginners in this stage are the following:

1. *Life isn't a multiple-choice exam.* Reinforced over and over again in school was the notion that the questions that plague us come down to choosing the "correct" answer among four choices. How disorienting to discover that when we're stuck there are actually unlimited alternatives, among which we can never be certain that there is a right answer, much less that we picked it. What this means during the early stages of training is that we tend to keep our mouths shut so that people—especially instructors and supervisors—don't find out how little we really know.

2. *Answers aren't found in books.* We worship books as students. Tucked somewhere on the neatly printed pages is "the truth," or at least someone's version of it. Hungry for answers, or at least direction, we stock our shelves with tomes that promise to deliver everything that we are missing. It is again disturbing to find that much of the good stuff we learn after graduation comes from our clients, who become our teachers.

3. *What you do is often absurd.* Let's face it: The job we do is pretty strange. People come to us in pain. They want answers. They want us to fix them. And they want quick relief. Unlike other health professionals, we have few tools at our disposal for diagnosis and treatment. Just imagine comparing our primitive assessment instruments to the CAT scans, biopsies, and MRIs that physicians can use. One of the reasons that a beginner might feel that he or she doesn't have what it takes to be a good therapist is because he or she doesn't yet realize how little we have to work with.

4. *Your family still won't listen to you.* It is seriously depressing to realize that after spending all the time and energy learning to be a therapist, your friends and family still won't accord you the respect and reverence you feel you deserve.

5. *You will never feel good enough.* There is a myth, an illusion, that somehow if you study hard and long enough, get enough degrees and supervised hours, gain enough experience, then finally you will know enough to feel totally competent. We're here to tell you (if you don't already know this) that it isn't going to happen. Yet as beginners, we still hold out that fantasy that some day, somehow, we'll finally get it, we'll finally understand the mysteries of how therapy works and how to do it perfectly.

6. *This job has negative side effects.* Being so busy proving you are worthwhile and worthy to join this profession, you rarely stop to consider the price that will be paid during this journey. All your relationships will change. Your whole interpersonal style will change as well, a consequence that many friends and family will not only fail to appreciate but might also resent. You will be subjected to the absolute worst in human depravity and see people who are so obnoxious to be around that therapists are the only ones who will listen. You will have nightmares about the horrible

things you witness and the stories you hear. You'll find yourself "catching" the symptoms of your clients, or at least feeling polluted by their pain. Furthermore, you'll be subject to codependent relationships, isolation, stress, compassion fatigue, burnout, isolation, suicidal threats, political squabbles, boredom, and the grinding daily battles of being overworked and underpaid (Kottler, 1993; Sussman, 1995).

7. *Who you are is as important as what you do.* Beginners are so worried about doing therapy right that they rarely stop to think about how important the personal dimensions of their work may be. Helping and healing are often not about what you *do* with clients, but how you *are* when you are with them. If, in particular, you don't feel good enough as a person (which few of us do), then you will naturally feel like you are letting others down.

Because most of the focus of our training is about learning new techniques, methods, and interventions rather than reshaping and refashioning ourselves into more personally effective individuals, there is always going to be a sense of unease.

8. *Some clients don't improve no matter what you do.* This last point is a reminder about the unrealistic expectations that beginners often hold for what they can do. It takes some time before you realize that there are definite limits on what you can do to be helpful, no matter how well-trained and experienced you are.

When you put all this together, what you've got during this first stage of initiation into the profession are a lot of self-doubt and fears of failure. In the next stage, these core fears take a more specific form.

What If I Don't Know What to Do with a Client?

It is a luxury to reflect on the bigger picture of what we do, and how we feel about it, once thrust into the trenches of seeing our first clients. Just on the brink of going into your first sessions (if you can remember), you were likely obsessed with hurting people. Even if you didn't help anyone, if you forgot everything you ever learned, if you froze solid and babbled for an hour, at least you didn't want to do further damage. There is an overriding fear that you might say or do the wrong thing in your ignorance, and before you know it, your client will jump out of the nearest window.

The really hard part is that you have to pretend you know far more than you really do. You might notice that many of your peers appear so much more poised and confident than you feel. You can't exactly confess to your clients about how unprepared you feel, nor can you admit fully to your supervisors that you are a fraud. So you walk around pretending that you know far more than you really do. Fake it long enough, you hope, and maybe you will start to feel like you know what you're doing.

If you're very fortunate, you might have the kind of supervisor to whom it feels safe to admit what you don't know. However, no matter how open this relationship might be, you will never confess all of your ignorance and ineptitude. You might also find comfort with a few trusted peers. Nevertheless, you will attempt to counsel yourself through the doubts and reassure yourself as best you can. After all, you know people who are a lot less talented and capable than you are and they seem to do okay.

The really tough part is when you spend time with clients who so desperately need your reassurance, your illusion of confidence. They plead with you to tell them that you understand what is going on, and more importantly, that you can fix them. Even though you might not have a clue, or not even be sure where to start, you still present yourself as a model of poise and expertise. "Sure I can help you," you lie through your teeth, already panicking inside as you wrack your brain for where to go first for help. Before there is the chance to seek consultation, supervision, or relevant literature, you first have to get along on your own. You will have to keep the client calm and persuaded that you can help him or her. Just as important, you have to convince yourself.

What If I'm Caught Making a Mistake?

In the next stage of development, you might not worry so much about how well you can fake that you know what you are doing; now, your main concern is being caught screwing up. Because there isn't a session that goes by that you can't think of at least a dozen things you could have done better, or at least differently, there is plenty of material available to worry about.

This is a stage of self-monitoring that is prone to worry and anxiety, sometimes verging on panic.

- What if my client kills himself? What did he mean when he said he might not see me next week? Did I miss something? I know I blew it. How should I write this up in my progress notes?
- I got a request to release my records on a client. Does that means someone is checking up on me? Am I being sued for malpractice?
- Why did I say that? I can't believe I said something so stupid! I must be a moron. Didn't I learn a damn thing? If anyone finds out about this screw-up, they'll laugh me out of the profession.
- Did I do the right thing? I'm sure I blew it. There are so many things I

could have done instead. I'm going to get skewered if I bring this up in supervision. How can I explain this to someone?

Obviously, this sort of negative self-talk is less than productive, but sometimes we can't just help ourselves. We are overwhelmed with the reality of all the things we don't know and don't understand, all the things we can't do nearly as well as we would like. It is so easy to second-guess ourselves, think of a dozen, maybe a hundred, different things we could have done instead.

This is a stage in therapist development that can be sheer agony. There is just enough confidence to take on more challenging, complex cases, but not nearly enough to delude ourselves that we are completely in control. Again, we are prone to keeping secrets from supervisors, peers, and even ourselves. We are still selective about what we bring up in supervision, still careful about presenting ourselves in the best possible light.

It is more than a little helpful to realize that failure is such an integral part of our work. If you are taking risks and experimenting with new strategies, if you are trying out your intuition and creativity, if you are pushing yourself (and your clients) to reach beyond what has been done before, then occasional failures are inevitable. In a study of the worst failures of the world's best therapists, the conclusion that many of these prominent theoreticians reached is that their lapses and mistakes were viewed as opportunities for further growth and learning (Kottler & Carlson, 2002).

What If I'm Not Really Doing Anything?

With further training, supervision, and experience comes a new stage in which we no longer fear screwing up quite so much. We can pretty much deal with whoever walks in the door. Even when we don't know what to do, we've got our routines down to the point that we can stall long enough until we can get a handle on things, find a way to begin. We even feel reasonably competent most of the time.

But then there are those doubts, whispers of a different sort altogether. No longer are we as concerned that something we might do will hurt someone; instead, we wonder if we are really helping anyone at all. This qualifies as a full-fledged existential crisis, questioning life's meaning, wondering if our life's work really matters. Maybe we are just kidding ourselves. Most likely, we have exaggerated our own sense of power and influence. We may even question whether our clients are really changing much at all, or whether these changes ever last.

Given all the huge problems in the world—poverty, violence, hate, racism, intractable mental illness, fatal diseases—what real difference are you really making in the world? If you think about it (and we know you would rather not), it's all a drop in the ocean. For every person you help, there are a million others who need you far more. For every client you *think* you assisted, there are others who were just pretending to change. They lied to you. They deceived you. They just told you want you wanted to hear.

Well, if you're not at this stage of disillusionment, or at least self-questioning yet, we apologize for giving away what's around the corner. That's a lie, too; we aren't sorry at all. In fact, it's our job to warn you, so you can better prepare yourself for what may lie ahead.

The fact is that, when we spend so much of our day with people who are questioning every part of their existence, challenging and pushing themselves to get into forbidden territory, asking themselves that which they fear the most, it is impossible for us not to do the same. Late at night, or during sleep, on long commutes, during idle time, sometimes even during sessions, we hear those infernal whispers: "Who are you kidding? Do you really think any of this matters? You're just wasting your time."

Thankfully, this is a stage that can't last all that long. You either work it through and move on, or burn out and leave the field. What sustains us most is the belief (or illusion) that what we do really does matter. Once we lose that, there is little left to keep us going. It sure isn't the lucrative salary and generous benefits.

Is There a Happy Ending to This Story?

A common theme in most stage theories is a movement toward a positive, if not optimal, condition. Piaget's model of cognitive development gets us to a stage of formal operations where all thinking modes are available for our use. Kohlberg's model of moral development directs us toward a level in which decisions are guided by ethics and moral principles. Is there anything comparable in the development of a therapist? Do we ever reach a level where comfort and confidence are more evident than distress and concern?

If there is some dream of reaching a stage in which effective clinical performance becomes simple and automatic, that dream needs to be reclassified as a delusion. It's not going to happen. Comparable to the continuing "butterflies" reported by performers on the stage and screen, there will, and probably should, always be some degree of apprehension before each and every therapy session. What we do, when all is said and done, is a science-based art. Great art is never routine, and great artists seldom, if ever, approach a new work with a feeling of total confidence.

Would it at least be reasonable to look forward to a stage of development as a therapist in which the distress is reduced to a tolerable level? The answer to this question has to be Yes. Otherwise, we have all made really foolish career decisions. Reaching this stage is contingent in part on successfully confronting the fears described in the following section, and another element may be influenced by accomplishing the reframing of a statement made at the beginning of this chapter.

As beginning therapists, we had to learn to abandon a quest for the one "correct" answer to the problems being presented by our clients. Earlier in this chapter we described this need with an assertion that "life is not a multiple-choice exam."

Attaining and maintaining the desired level of development as a therapist may be influenced by your ability to reframe this assertion as a template for your work. The practice of the therapist in fact may well be appropriately described as an ongoing series of multiple-choice tests (Jones, 1997).

An inconsistency between this assertion and the earlier one is not avoided by changing the word "exam" to the word "test." It comes instead by substituting "best of the available choices" for the illusive "correct" answer. Letting go of a quest for the "right" answer, being able to rapidly generate a list of plausible alternatives, and making instant informed decisions about the "best available" among those alternatives defines an experienced clinician.

This difference is more than just semantic. Clients come to us for help with problems. The complexity of human experience speaks strongly against any belief that there will be one and only one correct way to cope with those problems. Even if there were such a thing as a single correct response, the reality of our own limitations would make it terribly presumptuous for us to assume that we would have some mystical power to identify it. More reasonable, more accurate, and potentially just as helpful to our clients is to set our sights on helping the client identify the viable choices and to help them choose what appears to be the best from those available. There may be no "right" answer, but obviously there are choices that are better than others.

During the early stages of our clinical training, we delegate identification of alternatives and best responses to our supervisors. With experience, we learn to do this on our own; and with maturity, we come to recognize the importance of ensuring that the alternatives and selection among the alternatives must come from the needs of our clients, not from our own needs or those of our supervisors.

☐ Confronting Fears

The preceding stages of therapist development all highlight, in one way or another, the kinds of fears that we face and might be most reluctant to bring up in supervision. Instead, we live with them as best we can, or better yet, bury them as deeply as possible.

Under the best of circumstances, the fears are identified, owned, and dealt with in constructive ways. Some of the most common such concerns, listed in usual chronological order according to developmental stages, are listed in Table 2.1.

Fear of Rejection

As we mentioned, the very first concern that threatens beginners at their core is the belief that they will be found inadequate, wanting, or somehow not having the "right stuff." Like most fears, this one is not entirely unwarranted. The truth of the matter is that training in our profession has competitive elements that are indeed intended to weed out the less qualified. It is for this reason that newcomers often are confused with the mixed messages they receive: (a) Do your best and we will decide if you are good enough. (b) Be as authentic and disclosing as possible. Naturally, if one is truly as honest and open as supervisors say they want, the risk of rejection may be far greater. It appears much safer to do the same things that have proven useful throughout one's schooling: Figure out what the Powers That Be want, and then deliver it as well as you can.

TABLE 2.1. A Summary of Therapist Fears	
Fear of rejection	Not being allowed to do it
Fear of failure	Not being able to do it
Fear of ineptitude	Not doing it right
Fear of mediocrity	Not doing it as well as others
Fear of power	Hurting someone by lapse in judgment
Fear of limitations	Letting clients down
Fear of shattered illusions	Wondering if really helping anyone
Fear of losing control	Giving in to temptation
Fear of annihilation	Being consumed by clients
Fear of the predictable	Boredom setting in

It is often reasoned that in the short run it is better to play this game—to read accurately what teachers and mentors prefer and then mold one-self in that image. Later, after you get your ticket punched and are considered a legitimate member of the guild, then you can really express yourself the way you want to and talk about your doubts.

We've got some bad news: Although it is true that once you are li-censed you will no longer be held so accountable to conflicting masters who control your future, you will only trade one set of fears for others.

Fear of Failure

A new client walks in the door. She is polite, respectful, and deferential, but you can see how hard she is trying to keep things together. Her pos-ture looks stiff and her hands clenched. When you look closer, you can see whitish indentations in her palms from where she has been pressing so hard. She nervously brushes hair out of her eyes, which are flittering about the room as if she is searching each corner for an enemy about to pounce on her. She is wired so tight she looks like she is about to explode.

The anxious woman confides that she is at the end of her rope. She has been depressed, not sleeping much, and has been having serious thoughts about suicide. You can feel panic well up in your chest, and you start going through your mental checklist of all the things you will have to do to protect her from harm and protect yourself from making a terrible mistake. Before you can regain your composure, she starts sobbing un-controllably. She pleads, then begs you to help her. She tells you that she has all but given up; you are her last chance.

During the next moments of silence while you frame the best response, you understand clearly what is at stake. This client is reaching out to you like a lifeline, and if what she says is even half-true, you are one of the few options that might literally save her life.

As you continue to review options about the best way to proceed, and consider who you can go to for help with this desperate case, you are aware that you are feeling almost as helpless and overwhelmed as she must be feeling. You consider and reject a half-dozen things to say, all of which seem hollow and superficial. Finally, you just stare at her help-lessly, frozen in panic. You want to help her but you don't know what to do. You can't tell her this, of course, so you launch into the usual things you do: Reflect her despair and other feelings, collect some more back-ground information, offer hope and reassurance, exact a promise that she will not harm herself, and schedule the next appointment. When she finally walks out of the office, you feel like sobbing yourself.

The fear of failing clients, of not being able to do enough for them, or perhaps not being able to help them at all, is another quite realistic concern that has a definite basis in reality. It is certainly appropriate to bring this up in supervision and talk about it over and over again, especially because it is so universal among practitioners. However, this is also one of those issues that you will have to work on by yourself—every day.

Fear of Ineptitude

Similar to, and perhaps indistinguishable from, the fear of failure are obsessive ruminations about doing therapy "right." This is a more micro version of the more abstract, generalized concern about screwing up. In this version, therapists become uncomfortably aware of all the things they say and do, noticing how awkward, inadequate, and gracelessly they performed.

Sure, it was the intervention of choice to confront the client about his denial of responsibility for his troubles, but I sure could have been a little, okay, a LOT more sensitive in the way I brought this to his attention. And I can't believe that I stumbled around so much, instead of getting to the point. I'm sure whatever good could have come from this was neutralized by how awkward I appeared.

Get inside the head of any therapist at this stage of development, and the internal dialog is often filled with remorse, guilt, and self-criticism. In part, this is what self-supervision is all about: (a) becoming aware of things that could have been done better, or at least differently; (b) considering other options of what could be done in the future; (c) assessing the relative strengths and weaknesses of the intervention chosen; and (d) examining the impact of the intervention so as to plan the next therapeutic move. Forgiveness is the one thing missing in this process, however. What we mean is that, because it is inevitable that our actual helping behaviors rarely match our expectations, we are often faced with situations of facing and accept our limitations. This is not about surrendering to mediocrity but about demonstrating the same sort of self-acceptance that we hope to teach to our clients.

Fear of Mediocrity

Ours is not supposed to be a competitive business, but the reality is that in order to determine how well we are doing, humans tend to make comparisons between themselves and others. Therapists are no different.

It isn't that difficult to fool clients. We see consistent evidence all over the place of professionals we consider less than competent, even dangerous, who still manage to attract a following and apparently even help clients (or convince them they were helped). Sometimes, you've got to wonder why *you* have to continue to struggle to prove yourself. When will you have finally "made it"?

Deep down inside many of us is the fear that we are only ordinary, or maybe even a notch below that. Every time you see someone do something that you can't, or say something poetic or intelligent that you could never say, it reinforces this fear.

Depending on your supervisor and peers, consultation with others may only make matters worse. Every time something you missed, or could have done, or should have done is pointed out, there is a residual feeling that your own essential mediocrity betrayed you.

Fear of Power

Clients often choose a direction different from the one we think would be advantageous. We are supposed to avoid giving "advice," but the fact is that often that is exactly what we are doing, either directly or indirectly. Often, our "advising" appears to be for naught. We wonder why clients continue to come to see us when there is no evidence that anything we've said has made any difference.

The preceding is a problem, but it's not the real problem. In this stage, we begin to recognize and fret about the opposite outcome. That is, in fact clients sometimes do take our advice, going exactly in the direction they think we are recommending, and that is very frightening. Having that kind of influence over the life of another person brings with it the very thing we wanted to avoid, responsibility for things we can't totally control.

A female client is in an abusive relationship. The research literature and your own experience with other clients says clearly that she must get out of the relationship. It will not get better; it can only get worse. She comes to her next therapy session and informs you that she has taken your advice. Just as you suggested, she's kicked him out, and she's obtained a restraining order. How does that make you feel? Pleased, that she has taken what clearly would seem the best of her available choices; or frightened about the power you have just exerted? The answer for most of us is some combination of both pleasure and fear.

Mixed with your feeling of "good work" is often a series of troublesome questions. Did you really tell her to get a restraining order immediately, or was that just something that came out in discussion about things that might be necessary? Did you really have enough information about the total situation to make such a suggestion? What impact will this have on her immediate and extended family? Will she be safe? And, the big one, what if you were wrong?

The last scene in the play *Equus* should be required reading for all therapists. If you don't remember the play or the movie, it ends with a psychiatrist's reflections about the influence he has exerted on the life of a young man and is filled with self-doubt. As therapists we are often in a position to have major influence on the lives of others. As human beings, we wonder whether we should. We wonder if we will be able to use it wisely. We wonder if we really want it at all.

Fear of Limitations

There are times when you let others down, sometimes when you even hurt someone because of a lapse in judgment or the result of your own limitations. No matter how good you are at what you do, you can't possibly do everything as well as you'd prefer. Sometimes you bungle an intervention. You confront someone prematurely. You miss an important cue that you should have picked up on. You miscalculate what you believe a client really needs. You make a mistake. All of these occur because you are not perfect, because you have weaknesses that sometimes get in the way.

Right now, take inventory of what are your most significant weaknesses as a practitioner. Reflect on what gets you in trouble most often. What don't you do all that well?

I (JK) am impatient. I push clients to do things before they are ready. Because I get bored easily, I sometimes do and say things to be deliberately provocative, even though that may not be what the client needs at that moment. I don't pick up on more serious pathology that might be going on because I too often give clients the benefit of the doubt, remaining blind to self-destructive tendencies that have been in evidence. I like to explore issues that interest me, even when they are not among the client's major priorities. I have a look on my face when I concentrate that appears judgmental. Okay, I tend to be too critical and judgmental and sometimes I can't hide it.

I (PJ) am an excellent clinician. I know how to bring just the right balance of objectivity and sensitivity into my therapy sessions. I am bright, curious, and caring. Or am I? You see, I know these things partly because other people have told me. But what if they are wrong? They've never actually been with me in a therapy session. Come to think about it, they probably mostly think this because it's an image I have carefully cultivated and communicated. What if they knew how often I was totally at a loss during a therapy session, switching into a Rogerian mode because I had no idea what to do with this client? What if they knew how often I hoped for a no-show near the end of the day because I was simply tired of the whole process?

So, what about you?

Fear of Shattered Illusions

What I do really doesn't matter. Clearly, this is the most devastating feeling a human can experience. It is probably the single best predictor of intentional self-destructive behavior. Obviously, given a choice, we would all prefer "good" consequences to come from our actions, and we can learn to deal with "bad" consequences. What we don't handle well at all is "no" consequences.

We came into this profession, at least in part, because we had some desire to be of help to others. The same persuasive skills so important to effective therapy could just as easily have been applied in some form of marketing occupation. Had we done so, our incomes would probably have been larger, and the opportunities for direct feedback about our efforts would have been plentiful. That's not the choice we made, however, and with our choice comes the reality that we often really don't have the important ingredient of knowing the real effect of our work.

Consider that couple or family with whom you just know your work was exceptional. How do you know? They seemed very happy during the termination session. But, was that really because of your involvement, or were they just grateful that they were now going to have more time (and money) available because the therapy is over?

Assume it was the former. You did good work. You, however, in a Pavlovian sense, have also become and will remain a visual and verbal stimulus associated with some bad feelings. Your voice, your appearance, even your office setting are forever associated with a really bad time in their life. Is it really a surprise that some future meeting in another setting results in only a cursory bit of courtesy?

As with the other fears identified in this section, the fear related to whether you actually are helping anyone is not something that can be avoided. It goes with the territory; it is implicit in the career path we have chosen.

Creating or participating in outcome studies, arranging meetings with an external supervisor, building networks of supportive colleagues, and so forth, are not luxuries in our line of work. They are required ingredients if we are to maintain and grow the quality of our clinical performance. Without such ingredients, learned helplessness is an inevitable and devastating outcome.

Fear of Losing Control

There is a fantasy that we often hear clients express in therapy. It has many variations but basically sounds something like this:

> Whenever I stand anywhere near a balcony or open window in a high building, I feel this urge to just jump. I have no particular suicidal thoughts, nor do I wish to kill myself. But I am just scared of my own impulses. What if, in a single moment, I just jumped without thought? One second later, I would regret it, but by then it would be too late; I'd be on my way down. So I just prefer to stay away from those places.

Here is another variation:

> There are times I find myself attending a play or program with a large audience. As I sit in the crowd, I sometimes feel this urge to just walk up to the stage, climb onto the set, and sit down in an empty chair. I know this would be so humiliating. I would disrupt the play or presentation. It might even destroy my whole reputation, but sometimes I can get the urge out of my head even though I know I would never do it.

We include these rich examples not to provide you with fodder for making interpretations about the meaning of these fantasies. Most certainly they could reveal a lot about the person and provide lots of material to work therapeutically. We include them because they represent the kinds of impulsive thoughts that we often hear our clients speak. Similarly, we have our own impulses that occur during sessions and sometimes they are quite disturbing if not terrifying.

Who among us has not entertained the fantasy of slapping or strangling a client who we find pushes our buttons? Who has not wondered what an especially attractive client looks like without his or her clothes on? Who has not thought about telling a client all the things you really think or feel but dare not say? We have learned over time that this sort of internal activity is not only normal but often a valuable source of data about countertransference issues as well as indications about how others may react to the client. Yet in spite of how aware we might be that such fantasies and thoughts are unavoidable, no matter how clear we are about our ethical and moral responsibility, no matter how certain we are about our self-control, there is still the fear that, one day, or even one impulsive moment, we might give in to our most dangerous impulses. There are more than a few practitioners, just as strong-willed and responsible as you are, who somehow, some way, lost control of themselves. What makes you immune?

Owning and Confronting Fears

We have mentioned only a few of the common fears with which therapists live. There are, of course, many others. There is the fear of being consumed by clients, especially by those who are particularly demanding. There is the fear of losing ourselves totally in someone's story; some of those we hear are so poignant, so tragic, so overwhelming that we wonder how we can possibly metabolize what we've heard. There is also the fear of the predictable—that after so many years you will become just as wasted and cynical and burned out as other old-timers you've known.

Yet as Winston Churchill once said (or meant to say), it is not the fears themselves that are a problem, but rather how we live with them. In the next chapter about self-monitoring, as well as others that follow, you will have the opportunity to examine more closely your own fears and weaknesses, and to make a plan for dealing with them.

☐ References

Basow, S. A. (1992). *Gender: Stereotypes and roles*. Pacific Grove, CA: Brooks/Cole.

Carter, B., & McGoldrick, M. (1989). *The changing family life cycle*. Boston: Allyn & Bacon.

Erikson, E. (1950). *Childhood and society*. New York: Norton.

Freud, S. (1924). *A general introduction to psychoanalysis*. New York: Washington Square Press.

Jones, W. P. (1997). Counseling is a multiple-choice test. In J. K. Kottler (Ed.), *Finding your way as a counselor*. Washington, DC: American Counseling Association.

Kohlberg, L. (1969). *Stages in the development of moral thought and action*. New York: Holt, Rinehart, and Winston.

Kottler, J. A. (1993). *On being a therapist*. San Francisco: Jossey-Bass.

Kottler, J. A. (1994). *Advanced group leadership*. Pacific Grove, CA: Brooks/Cole.

Kottler, J. A., & Blau, D. A. (1989). *The imperfect therapist: Learning from failure in the practice of therapy*. San Francisco: Jossey-Bass.

Kottler, J. A., & Carlson, J. (2002). *Bad therapy: Master therapists share their worst failures*. New York: Brunner-Routledge.

Kottler, J. A., & Hazler, R. (1997). *What you never learned in graduate school*. New York: Norton.

Loevinger, J. (1976). *Ego development*. San Francisco: Jossey-Bass.

Piaget, J. (1926). *The language and thought of the child*. New York: Harcourt Brace.

Sue, S., Ivey, A., & Pederson, P. (1996). *A theory of multicultural counseling and therapy*. Pacific Grove, CA: Brooks/Cole.

Super, D. (1953). A theory of vocational development. *American Psychologist, 8*, 185–190.

Sussman, M. B. (Ed.) (1995). *A perilous calling: The hazards of psychotherapy practice*. New York: Wiley.

Wallbridge, H. R. (1995). Difficult issues for new therapists. In D. G. Martin & A. D. Moore (Eds.), *First steps in the art of intervention*. Pacific Grove, CA: Brooks/Cole.

David Shepard
Gloria Morrow

Critical Self-Monitoring

Nicole had begun her practice only a month ago as an art therapist. She was eager to build her practice and a little anxious about paying her overhead. The first referral that came in was from an HMO. The client was a 16-year-old girl who, for no apparent reason, had stopped talking. The extreme shift in behavior of the client troubled Nicole, as did the mother's description of her daughter as "acting crazy," but she rationalized the girl's sudden silence as probably a symptom of depression. Nicole took the case. After several weeks of getting nowhere in therapy, Nicole asked the mother to participate in the session. To Nicole's horror, her client began to pour out an incoherent stream of invective toward her mother. "Oh, my God," Nicole realized. "This poor girl is schizophrenic and I'm way over my head."

Richard was a seasoned therapist, specializing in cognitive therapy for mood disorders. After 20 years of experience and a long string of successful cases in treating depression, he had never felt more confident. When he began to work with a new patient, an African-American policeman, he proceeded with his customary approach, pointing out to the client the various ways he viewed the world through a prism of unrealistic beliefs. In the third session, the client jumped out of his chair in the middle of a dialog, declared he'd had enough of being treated like a child by his therapist, and stormed out of the room. He never returned.

Anne, a 70-year-old Jungian therapist, was struggling with cancer but determined not to let the stress of the disease and the chemotherapy side effects impede her work. She was particularly proud of how she had carefully processed her illness with her clients without compromising professional boundaries. In one session with a long-time client, the woman interrupted the conversation, and haltingly said, "This is so difficult for me to say, but it's like, you're not the same therapist you were. I guess I was afraid to hurt your feelings, but you've hurt me when you've clearly confused me with other clients." Anne felt like she'd been kicked in the stomach, and she could barely hold back from bursting into tears.

All three of these therapists had made clinical mistakes, but not out of incompetence—these were all well-trained, talented clinicians. The mistakes were made because the therapists were not sufficiently "self-monitoring," that is, engaging in a process of self-awareness that "serves the essential purpose of maintaining our bearings and avoiding self-deception" (Coster & Schwebel, 1997, p. 10). Nicole, in failing to monitor her fears about money, made a poor decision-to-treat choice and took a case outside her scope of competence. Richard did not monitor how he was becoming overconfident, failing to realize that utilizing a one-size-fits-all approach with all clients may not be effective. The result was his insensitivity to the cultural implications of proving to an African-American man in a "macho" career that the man did not know how to think realistically. Anne, afraid to take a hard look at the impact of her illness on her clinical work, deceived herself into believing that her memory was not being affected.

☐ The Purpose of This Chapter

The fact that clinicians *should* engage in some form of self-monitoring has been demonstrated by research and emphasized by a number of authors (e.g., Norcross, 2000; Sapienza & Bugental, 2000). The three vignettes with which we began this chapter illustrate three areas where self-monitoring is critical to effective therapy: decision-to-treat choices, cultural competency, and therapist self-care. But it is also important to ask: *How* can clinicians engage in a self-monitoring process? If clinicians are to incorporate reflective searching into their ongoing professional work, it would be advantageous to have some model they can follow. Moreover, we would argue that a truly useful model needs to include two components. First, it would be helpful to identify those moments—before, during, and after a session—that can serve as cues to signal the clinician that self-monitoring is needed. Second, a workable model should include a number of different self-monitoring strategies. Clinicians would then be able to choose strategies that best fit their particular self-reflective styles.

The purpose of this chapter is to present a comprehensive model of self-monitoring. In order to develop this model, we conducted in-depth open-ended interviews with six seasoned therapists, ranging in age from

40 to 60, and with 15 to 30 years of clinical experience. As coauthors, we also asked ourselves the same questions we put to our interviewees, and included our reflections in conceptualizing the model.

The interviewees covered a wide range of theoretical orientations (Gestalt, Object Relations, Humanist Existential, Cognitive Behavioral) and experiences with different populations. The interviewees were first asked to describe the significant cues they each experienced signaling the need for self-monitoring. They were then asked to describe their particular self-reflective processes. Each therapist shared poignant examples that demonstrated the necessity of paying attention to their inner voice. It is important to note that we are not attempting to generalize the findings of the six interviews to the entire population of therapists. However, the voices of those we interviewed, and hopefully our own voices as well, enabled us to develop a model for self-monitoring that may enlighten and enrich our capacity to grow as professionals.

☐ What Is Self-Monitoring?

A model needs to begin, of course, with a definition. The term self-monitoring most frequently appears in the cognitive behavioral literature, relative to the treatment of disorders such as depression, anxiety, pain management, and self-control (see Beck, Rush, Shaw, & Emery, 1979; Kanfer, 1970; Meichenbaum, 1977). In this context, self-monitoring is defined as the process of clients "observing the connection between external events and internal subjective responses" with the goal of increasing desirable and decreasing undesirable thoughts, feelings, and behaviors (Rehm & Rokke, 1988, p. 157).

In recent years, self-monitoring has appeared in the literature focusing on psychotherapist self-care (e.g., Coster & Schwebel, 1997; Norcross, 2000; Schwebel & Coster, 1998). However, the notion that therapists need to engage in some form of ongoing self-scrutiny appears in a number of research arenas, albeit using different terminology. For example, Skovholt and Ronnestad, in their studies of the characteristics of master therapists, used the term *reflective stance*, which means that the therapist is "consciously giving time and energy to processing, alone and with others, significant experiences" (Skovholt & Ronnestad, 1992, p. 509).

The counselor training and supervision literature has described the idea of the reflective practitioner. The reflective practitioner is a clinician who has the ability to continually reflect on the information he or she encounters in a therapy session (Nelson & Neufeldt, 1998). According to Neufeldt, Karno, and Nelson, the reflective process is characterized by an "intent to understand what has occurred, active inquiry, openness to that understanding, and vulnerability and risk taking, rather than defensive self-protection . . ." (Neufeldt, Karno, & Nelson, 1996, p. 8). The authors emphasized that reflectivity means a profound and meaningful self-questioning, focusing on issues that go to the heart of what the counselor believes therapy is about, its goals, and how it works.

Thus, there are several overlapping constructs that describe some form of therapists' looking inward. Based on the literature and our interviews, we are proposing: *Self-monitoring is a process of self-scrutiny where therapists reflect honestly and realistically on their values, limitations, cultural competence, countertransference issues, life stressors, or any other aspects of their personal and professional lives that inevitably bear on their clinical work.* We also use the term self-reflection interchangeably with self-monitoring throughout the chapter.

Regardless of the exact terms used to describe a process of self-monitoring, the importance of engaging in such a process has been demonstrated in research. Jennings and Skovholt, after interviewing 10 of the most widely respected therapists in a major midwestern city, observed that these master therapists "seem to be constantly striving to learn more about their work and themselves" (Jennings & Skovholt, 1999, p. 7). A similar study, based on interviews with 12 therapists with a mean age of 74, revealed that these senior therapists strongly value processing and reflecting experiences in all of life's arenas as crucial to professional development (Skovholt & Ronnestad, 1992). That veteran clinicians would place high value on self-scrutiny as a crucial component of being an effective practitioner should come as no surprise; the notion dates to the origins of psychotherapy. Freud, using the process of free association, conducted his own self-analysis, a scrutiny of his memories, dreams, concealed wishes, and emotions. In 1897, he wrote to his colleague, Fliess, "that the most important patient for me was my own person . . ." (Gay, 1988, p. 96).

The implication of Freud's missive and the results of these two studies is that self-monitoring is a characteristic of seasoned clinicians. Ironically, most of us probably did engage in frequent self-monitoring—during our novice years, when we began our graduate programs or clinical internships. Who can forget all those self-reflective take-home exercises in our counseling skills textbooks? Or how we lay awake nights when we first started seeing clients, wondering if we had what it takes to be a therapist? Actually, with all our exams, practica, and hours of supervision, we probably self-monitored more than actually necessary. However, then that memorable day came when our "Congratulations, you've passed the licensing exam" letter came, and the wonderful realization that after years of schooling, we would never have a teacher or supervisor looking over our shoulders again. To be sure, we recognized that there would be times when we would seek consultation, or even personal therapy if struck by a countertransference logjam too massive to unravel by ourselves. But nowhere in the ethical codes does it mandate that we become our own supervisors, that we make sure we are looking over our own shoulders. The message implied by Freud's letter and the research on master therapists is clear; it is when we become independent practitioners that self-monitoring becomes a critical process if we wish to "do better" as therapists.

☐ How Do We Know When to Self-Monitor?

The need to self-monitor tends to be precipitated by a variety of internal cues (Table 3.1). "There are a number of specific signals or red flags to which therapists should pay particular attention to as they work to enhance their sensitivity to their own feelings and those of their clients" (Moursund & Kenny, 2002, p. 35). Moursund and Kenny further suggested that a therapist's body posture, failure to attend to the client, and the mismatch between the tone of the voice and body language all signal that it is time for the self-monitoring process to begin.

When we were going through the training process, we were taught the importance of identifying and recognizing the client's internal/external and verbal/nonverbal cues in order to understand what the client was thinking and feeling, and to explain her or his behavior. Therefore, as professionals it may be equally important for therapists to identify and recognize the cues that come up prior to, during, and after session with a client.

In order to understand more about the internal cues that may signal the need to self-monitor, we asked our interviewees to describe the internal cues they experience. They identified the following three categories of cues as the most salient in bringing to awareness the need to engage in the self-monitoring process: behavioral, affective, and cognitive cues.

TABLE 3.1. Internal Cues

Cues	Examples
Behavioral	Acting out in session demonstrated by a lack of empathy, genuineness, warmth, and respect
Affective	Feelings of anxiety, boredom, and failure
Cognitive	Intrusive internal debate

Behavioral Cues

Behavioral cues can be important in signaling to therapists that something is going wrong in the session. Sometimes, therapists may begin to "act out" in response to issues that come up in session. Watkins (1983) identified five categories of acting out behaviors in therapists: attentional failures, empathic failures, aggressive behavior, sexual and seductive behaviors, and logistical failures. Because our behavioral cues also may be apparent to the client, it is even more critical that we acknowledge these cues and begin to self-reflect on why we are acting out.

Rogers (1951) underscored the need for therapists to demonstrate empathy, genuineness, and unconditional positive regard for clients in order to develop a healthy therapeutic relationship that is critical to enhancing client change. When therapists exert power over the client by taking total charge of the session, fail to allow clients to complete her or his sentence, or demonstrate the ability to be attentive to our clients, they are "acting out" and their behavior suggests that they may be experiencing some level of discomfort. Further, that behavior is a warning sign that the therapist needs to understand more about the underlying cause of her or his actions.

> (*Gloria*) As a young therapist, I began to act out in a session when the client reached a therapeutic impasse. Because of my discomfort and impatience with the client, I found myself behaving in ways I otherwise would not have behaved. I began to bombard the client with questions, and I attempted to coerce her into responding to my interventions, even though she was not ready to do so. My behavior was a clear indicator of the need to self-monitor, and the need to make sense of what I was thinking and feeling about sitting in silence with the client. Unfortunately, I did not stop myself in the session, but while writing case notes, I was forced to reflect upon how I exerted power over the client, and how my excessive talking and questioning may have shut down the therapeutic process.

When an intern, it is sometimes easier to recognize the behavioral cues through watching videos in class and in supervision, and enacting role-plays in the presence of instructors and/or supervisors. However, it may be more of a challenge to detect behavioral cues when no one is watching. It is critical that therapists maintain an awareness of tone, speaking patterns, and nonverbal behaviors. All of these can be signals that countertransference or other treatment-obstructing issues are emerging for the therapist.

Case Example: Frances

Frances, a licensed marriage and family therapist for 15 years, discussed the importance of paying attention to behavioral cues in session.

(*Frances*) I was treating a 32-year-old female client suffering from depression. When exploring the client's history of abuse, the client revealed a long history of domestic violence by her live-in partner. During one of the sessions, I found myself talking over the client, rarely allowing her to complete a sentence. Initially, I justified this behavior by asserting that the client was having difficulty expressing herself, and it was my job to help her speak clearly. After one of our sessions, it dawned on me that perhaps I was the one "acting out." My tendency to interrupt her was a cue that I was having difficulty respecting this client because she was not taking care of herself. Fortunately, I was able to take a hard look at my negative reaction towards her. If I hadn't done so, she certainly would have begun to feel wounded by my disrespectful attitude.

In this case example, as well as in Gloria's, behavioral cues signaled negative countertransference reactions toward the client, and initiated self-reflective processes that prevented damage to treatment. Thus, failure to attend to cues may result in self-denial of countertransference issues that we must work on throughout our professional and perhaps personal lives. Our willingness to take responsibility for our acting-out behaviors is critical to "doing better" with clients.

Affective Cues

It is not uncommon for therapists to experience intense emotions when working with clients. However, there is a difference between the experience of empathy, sadness, and compassion as the client shares his or her story, and the affective cues such as anxiety, fear, anger, and guilt, that come up to warn us that something does not feel right. In this section, we will focus on three important affective cues that emerged for our interviewees: feelings of anxiety, boredom, and failure.

Anxiety

Perhaps the most common affective cue indicating that something does not feel right is the experience of anxiety, before, during and/or after a session. I (Gloria) work as both a clinical psychologist and pastoral counselor, and my work with a man suffering from gender-identity disorder provoked such strong feelings of anxiety that I considered leaving the profession.

(*Gloria*) I was assigned a 37-year-old African-American male who had been previously diagnosed with schizophrenia and a depressive disorder. He also had a long history of suicidal ideation as well as a recent suicide attempt. Case notes from the screening clerk described the client as odd, which was not unusual for schizophrenic clients. However, there was nothing in the case notes to prepare me for the client's unorthodox appearance. The client finally arrived for his intake; and when I went into the reception area to escort him back to my office, I could hardly believe what I was seeing. I found myself face to face with a rather unattractive, short, medium-built man, wearing a pink dress, with a blonde wig, heavy make-up including red nail polish, and totally adorned in jewelry. It took everything in me not to walk past the client and pretend I was there to greet another client. Certainly, someone had made a huge mistake, but I would have to play this out since the client was staring me in the face. When I asked the client about his presenting problem, he stated: "I want to have a sex change and they refuse to let me. After all, I am a woman trapped in a man's body, and I want to be set free." Further, he stated, "I would rather be dead than to live like this the rest of my life." I remember thinking to myself as the client rambled on about his desire to die, not only am I being asked to treat a population I have never treated before, but this individual may actually kill himself.

As he talked, I could feel anxiety on every level—my heart beating, my mind racing, even a warm sensation moving throughout my body as my anxiety level became intensified. The more he talked, the more anxious I became, and I was convinced I could do nothing to help him. Although somewhat daunting, I was fully prepared to deal with the client's clinical issues and current crisis, but I was far less prepared to deal with the apparent gender identity issues. I sensed that I needed to look at why gender confusion caused me so much distress that I was losing confidence in my ability to sit with this otherwise kind man.

This case example highlighted the need for me to pay attention to my reaction, (countertransference) I had toward this client. The ability to acknowledge my level of anxiety afforded me the opportunity to conduct a personal check-up, and to also consider how the client may have been reacting to me. Failure to acknowledge those feelings would have been detrimental to the therapeutic alliance, because the affective cues signaled the need for me to reflect on the personal biases, values, and beliefs I had around transgendered individuals, and perhaps even homosexuality.

In the next example from my (David) clinical work, anxiety became so intense, it merged into an experience of pure dread.

(David) I work a lot with clients suffering with mood disorders. I was seeing a 35-year-old woman [who was] complaining of vague feelings of depression and discontent with her life. From the beginning, she announced she was skeptical of therapy, but thought she "might as well give it a chance." Although a successful career woman, working with her was like doing therapy with an angry, sullen teenager forced to visit a shrink by her parents. She responded to my probes with the briefest possible answers, offered nothing of her own to break silences, and glowered at me throughout the sessions, as though somehow I were preventing her from doing something more important with her time. She was doing everything possible to make me dislike her. At the end of each session, she would icily tell me that she may or may not come back; yet she did return faithfully each week, and for weeks I persisted in exploring interventions that might help her open up.

The main cue that I needed to self-monitor was that I realized I dreaded seeing her. Right before going into the waiting room to get her, I would feel my body tighten, and force myself to take a relaxing breath. When she would occasionally cancel, I actually felt delighted. For a while, I simply ignored the cue, denying to myself that this dread was something I needed to look at in myself. The self-deception didn't work—in one session, she actually talked about her fear that I disliked her. Now I had to look at what issues this client was stirring up in me, lest her initial childhood trauma of parental rejection be reenacted in treatment. So, my dread reaction was a strong indicator it was time for some serious self-reflection.

I suspect I am not the only therapist who has dreaded working with particular clients. However, this case taught me that an intense anxious feeling needs to be understood, that dreading seeing a client means I have unresolved issues that are affecting the treatment. Initially, I dismissed the feeling as a normal reaction to a difficult client who devalued me; it would have been a profound clinical mistake to continue to minimize this kind of reaction. By looking inward at the meaning of the dread, I was eventually able to release it, and in the process understand more deeply the suffering of my client.

Boredom

Anxiety, whether experienced cognitively or affectively, is a hard-to-miss cue that self-monitoring is needed. Twisting sensations in the pit of the stomach or a racing mind are palpable symptoms. A less pronounced, but perhaps also common sensation experienced by clinicians is boredom. Psychotherapist boredom has been well described in the literature (Rule, 1998) as an existential issue (Kottler, 1993) and as a manifestation of countertransference (Flannery, 1995; Geller, 1994). Because boredom is an absence of intensity, it may be easier than anxiety to ignore. Nevertheless, it can be an equally important self-monitoring cue.

Michael, a successful clinician and postdoctoral supervisor, described boredom as the feeling that

> . . . I'm just hanging out or marking time, and I find myself asking myself, "What I am doing here?" First, I rule out pathology, whether my boredom is reaction to a dynamic of my patient. I also check for countertransference, and whether I need outside consultation, or perhaps more psychotherapy for myself. But if it's not countertransference and I still feel too cozy and

lazy with the person, what I realize is that I've lost a sense of what I'm doing as a healer and with the healing process.

As we shall see later in this chapter, Michael uses boredom as an opportunity to recharge the treatment. The key, of course, is that Michael is keenly aware of his experience. Rather than either denying the feeling completely or rationalizing it as an inevitable byproduct of a busy practice, he remains highly attuned to the sensation of boredom, and responds to it with a self-reflective strategy.

Feelings of Failure

Perhaps the most painful of all internal cues that self-monitoring is needed is the experience of failure. It is inevitable that some clients will terminate prematurely or that our best efforts will not help to resolve a presenting problem. Some therapists may interpret a poor treatment outcome as an occasional fact of life in our business; however, for some of us, it can represent a personal failure. Although the literature on treatment failure is limited, we can all relate to these feelings. Feelings of failure can derive from cognitive distortions, such as "If the therapy fails, this means I'm an incompetent therapist," or "Failure is unacceptable" (Persons, 1989). Nonetheless, when we feel we have failed, self-monitoring is essential, not only to regain perspective, but also to sort out true therapeutic mistakes from a blow to our narcissistic self-esteem.

Case Example: Janice

Janice has been doing psychotherapy and running workshops in creativity and dream analysis for 20 years. She also specializes in working with the chronically or terminally ill. She reported how she was working with a man who was suffering from cancer, and wanted to know he could emotionally support himself through this ordeal. After 8 months of therapy, she continued to feel that she was missing him, that there was something about him she could not get. Finally, he told her in a session that he was quitting therapy.

Janice reacted by taking the failure personally, convinced she was responsible for his premature termination and guilty about not having relieved his internal suffering. The self-monitoring she engaged in, as we shall see later, ultimately led not only to her understanding the cause of the termination, but, more importantly, to an underlying core issue of her own that she needed to address.

Cognitive Cues

Similar to other cues mentioned in this chapter, the interviewees reported experiencing cognitive cues alerting them to the need to self-monitor. We believe that most therapists can recall participating in "internal debates" regarding treatment decisions, legal and ethical dilemmas, and value and worldview issues. Sometimes, that internal debate is resolved quite easily, and we are able to rely on our knowledge and experience base to help us to make the correct decision without much thought. However, there are times when the debate continues while driving home, or even when we go to bed at night. It is as though we were being "haunted" by thoughts about our client—a sign that something is happening in treatment that needs to be attended to.

For example, John, an interning drug counselor told the story of working with a 40-year-old Hispanic woman who was an outpatient at the drug and rehab center. He described how he became sucked into her trauma, which is not hard to do when working with trauma victims. John stated: "While trying to make the right decision for the client, I felt haunted by the constant thought of what I should do in this situation." John reported symptoms that were similar to other therapists suffering from a "compassion fatigue." In the context of this chapter, "compassion fatigue," a term closely related to the terms "burnout" (a topic that is discussed elsewhere in this book) and secondary traumatic stress, refers to therapists' reactions to their work and continual interaction with counseling survivors and trauma work (see Beaton & Murphy, 1995; Figley, 1995; Fox & Carey, 1999; Ranier, 2000; Sexton, 1999).

Case Example: John

I was co-leader of a life skills group, and I found myself relating to this client in a very special way because of similarities in our family history and life story. Further, she had experienced serious trauma in her life, as she was a rape and incest survivor. I had been bombarded by clients who had suffered from incest over the past few years and I also related to their stories. She had been clean and sober for 60 days and was doing very well in her program. I was very proud of her, but somehow she mistook my pride in her accomplishments as a sign of affection, and responded to my praise by becoming seductive towards me in sessions. The problem was, I didn't notice her changing behavior. I didn't see the seductiveness, nor how her process was becoming increasingly odd and, in retrospect, psychotic.

But when I went home, I couldn't get her out of my head. I found myself distracted, thinking about her when I was watching TV, taking a shower, or reflecting on other clients. I was stuck; caught up in her drama. I noticed her behavior toward me change. [But] by the time I faced the fact that my preoccupation with her was an important red flag, it was almost too late. She somehow found my home telephone number and address, and I eventually had to get a restraining order to protect me from her. The client ended up incarcerated because she attempted to kill another counselor who refused her advances.

This case example clearly illustrates what happens when we fail to resolve the inner debate by engaging in the self-monitoring process. It was apparent that John had become exhausted not only because of his empathic engagement with the client, but also because of his inability to put the internal debate to rest, which severely hampered his ability to make better decisions. According to Miller (1998), the very nature of the emotional entanglement therapists engage in with clients makes them vulnerable to impairment. In this case, however, self-monitoring may not have been enough to help John make the appropriate decision to protect both the client and himself. The limits of self-monitoring are discussed later in this chapter.

According to the scant literature on this topic, along with the voices and experiences of the interviewees, attending to one's internal cues may serve as a vital first step in the self-monitoring process. However, the next step in the process is identifying appropriate strategies to enhance treatment outcome, as well as our own self-development. In the next section, we look specifically at four examples of self-monitoring as discussed by our interviewees. In addition, they describe in their own words how self-monitoring impacted treatment outcomes, as well as their personal lives.

☐ How Do We Self-Monitor?

Our interviewees identified four strategies of self-monitoring: self-talk, journaling, imagery/visualization, and using the unconscious (Table 3.2). All of the strategies that emerged are supported by the cognitive-behavioral and psychoanalytic literature. Indeed, cognitive-behavioral therapists have taught numerous clients to use self-talk to counteract maladaptive thinking (Maultsby, 1984), and Meichenbaum (1977) introduced imagery as a technique to assist clients in the self-monitoring process. In the classical psychoanalytic camp, journaling was used by patients as a method of self-analysis (Freud, 1954). Journaling continues to be a popular activity in graduate training programs to help students to get in touch with their inner thoughts, feelings, and processes (Baird, 2002). Freud's concept of the unconscious is paramount to psychoanalytic theory, and therapists of this persuasion strive to help clients to bring their repressed material into the conscious realm (Freud, 1949).

TABLE 3.2. Self-Monitoring Strategies

Method	Description	Key proponents
Self-talk	Internal self-dialogue	Maultsby; Ellis
Journaling	Written record of thoughts, feelings, and processes	Freud; Jung (psychoanalytic/Jungian)
Visual imagery	Technique used in psycho-therapy to elicit insight and feelings associated with past experiences	Michenmaum; Beck; Ellis; Reyher
Unconscious	Bringing repressed memories, thoughts, and feelings into awareness	Freud; Jung

Self-Talk

Perhaps the most common form of self-monitoring is self-talk, some form of internal conversation. Engaging in an internal dialog gives therapists the opportunity to engage in a rational discussion, with the possibility of ruling out maladaptive and distorted thinking. Therapists are not immune to debilitating thoughts and beliefs that come up because of low self-esteem, and propensity toward self-criticism, "a common pattern of mal-adaptive thinking" (Persons, 1989, p. 104). Kottler (1993) suggested that "talking to ourselves as we would to clients is the most direct and effec-tive cure" (p. 219). Self-talk, a strategy borrowed from cognitive theory, is useful for disputing the irrational quest for perfection (Ellis, 1984), and is beneficial in helping therapists to make better clinical decisions. The conversation can be an interior monolog, an imaginary dialog with a former supervisor, or Socratic questioning. One of our interviewees explains the utility of self-talk in the case example that follows.

Case Example: Lolita

Lolita, a licensed family therapist in private practice for 10 years, describes the self-questioning process she utilizes.

> When working with a male child using sand tray therapy, he would dump loads of toys into the sand tray. We would simply toss a plastic ball over the sand tray since it was impossible to work within the sand tray. Eventually,

he created an interesting scene in the sand tray. When I began Gestalt questioning, he picked up a zebra and plowed through the scene, destroying it. I began to experience anxiety because the client destroyed the scene, and made quite a mess. So I asked, does the zebra want to put everything back? It was as though he sensed my intolerance (which I did not notice in myself until later), and he put everything back. I thought, this child has no consideration, no concern for other people's things. Some time between the end of this session and the next, I began the internal self-monitoring process.

I began to think about the session and how everything played out. I thought, I did not carve out a way for him to find his way back, once he acted aggressively with the zebra. Had I done the right thing? Was I judgmental and intolerant? Had I destroyed the possibility for a therapeutic intervention? I asked myself, why did it go this way? This internal process of self-reflection finally led to my creating a plan to correct my mistake.

This error may have created missed opportunities for a therapeutic breakthrough, especially since he had moved from avoiding the sand tray to working with it in his own way. Intolerance can shut down the therapeutic process. However, I learned to be more tolerant and to rely on the self-monitoring process earlier in the process. During the next session, when playing in the sand tray, the client remarked: "He (the zebra) may want to tear it all up again." This time I said, "That's fine with me." After receiving my approval and acceptance, the client told me, "I don't think he wants to tear things up today."

Lolita described the importance of therapists' ability to listen to her or his inner voice. In order to participate in this process, we must acknowledge and trust the validity of that voice. When we fail to trust our own instincts and/or fail to pay attention to what our inner voice has to say, we leave ourselves vulnerable and open to making unnecessary mistakes.

Self-talk need not become self-inquisition, but can be an organized Socratic dialogue, which tends to be somewhat gentler on the spirit than listening to one's inner prosecutor. By engaging in self-dialog, my (Gloria) personal values and beliefs about a schizophrenic man seeking a sex change were significantly challenged.

I (Gloria) started out asking myself questions such as, "What in the world is this? What am I supposed to do with him? How can I help someone like this? What about my Christian values?" These questions were most certainly influenced by my level of anxiety, my own personal values and biases, and my fear of failure that makes self-monitoring a necessary component of my everyday life. As I began to respond to these and other questions in my head, the more rational my inner questions became. I began to wonder, if this client was not a transsexual, what strategies would help him? Then the questioning became more personal, and I thought:

Am I responding to the client this way because of my own personal values and biases, and if so, what am I really thinking about the client? As I continued with this process I finally asked myself the question, what Christian principles could I use to help this client regardless of his presentation and preferences?

This was an example of an opportunity for reactive self-monitoring, where I had very little time to pay attention to my inner cues, and make decisions based on a well-thought-out plan of action on behalf of the client. Fortunately for the client and myself, I was able to focus on my core values and beliefs, which include respect and dignity for all humankind. I began to focus on the task at hand, and I realized I possessed the necessary empathy and unconditional positive regard to connect with the client, and the critical skills to assess and assist the client during his crisis. I also discovered I was equipped to make a determination as to what resources I needed to connect the client with (e.g., psychiatrist, support groups, etc.).

The self-monitoring process may be even more effective as an ongoing process, and while I was writing my case notes and visualizing my experience with the client, I continued to explore and self-evaluate my personal biases as it relates to homosexuality. I began to ask myself whether or not I would be able to adequately treat the gay and lesbian community. It was only after that open and honest self-dialogue that I determined I would be able to assist gay and lesbian clients, but that it may be beneficial to base the decision to treat on a case-by-case basis. In this case, the client and I determined that it may be in his best interest to continue to see the psychiatrist for medication, and to connect with a transsexual group for support, and to work with an individual therapist who has expertise in working with transgendered individuals. However, the ability to self-monitor during the early stages of that traumatic session assisted me in providing the highest level of care and concern for the client, which may have impacted his decision to seek help from other mental health professionals.

Journaling

Another popular self-reflective strategy used by the interviewees was journaling, also referred to as "expressive writing." Expressive writing, where the individual writes without self-censorship about inner thoughts and feelings, has been shown to reduce psychological stress (Lepore, 1997) and increase physical health (Smyth, 1998). James Pennebaker, a psychologist who has done extensive research on the benefits of journaling, described why writing can foster problem-solving in general. According to Pennebaker, writing forces us to focus our attention on a problem longer than if we just think about it. It also slows our thinking down because the process of writing requires us to consider each idea fully before we go on to the next sentence (Pennebaker, 1997). One way to write expressively is to journal, and in the following David describes how journaling has become for him an effective tool for self-monitoring.

> (*David*) Earlier in this chapter, I described my dread at seeing a certain client in the waiting room. Journaling was the self-monitoring tool I used to deal with this dilemma. As part of the journalizing process, I also incorporated Jung's notion of the shadow, "the negative side of the personality . . . the unpleasant qualities we want to hide . . ." (Jung, 1946, p. 540).

I start with automatic writing; just letting my mind go where it wants to, helps me get to a core feeling or insight that tells me what's going on that needs to be addressed. But I do use a process of asking specific questions to help prime the writing process. For example, with this client, the first thing I did was ask myself, "What are my feelings about this woman?" I let myself spew out all my negative feelings about her, and then the negative feelings she made me feel about myself. In this case, the main feeling that came up for me was a sense of inadequacy, that I was missing something that other therapists would probably see. I went into why I disliked me. OK, now I knew I needed to do some inner work on why I would feel inadequate after 10 years of doing therapy, with many successful cases.

My next question usually is: How is the client my shadow? Am I dreading a client because he or she mirrors some part of me that I have disowned? With this client, I realized that she reflected my own fear of life, my own sense that "doom" is around the corner. I realized that the difference between her and me was that for me, the sense that life would inevitably disappoint me was a feeling I knew to be irrational and stemming from family-of-origin experiences. But my client literally believed she was doomed to suffer.

When I realized how the two of us were alike, I could ask myself: Well, if you were the client, what would help you? The answer was, I needed consistent reassurance, the way a 6 year old needs a parent to remind him there are no monsters in that tree outside the window. I could be the reassuring parent with this client by maintaining a therapeutic attitude that conveyed the message that whatever the client did to devalue me or the therapy, I believed in the process.

I decided that my only job with this client was to show up, welcome her with a smiling face, and not get rattled by her negativity. We could explore her negativity or not, but my attitude would be remain hopeful. Knowing that this approach would be helpful truly relieved the dread I would feel before seeing her. One day, she smiled at me, and said, "How can you possibly be so optimistic when I tell you all these things?" She was signaling to me that she appreciated my refusal to agree with her sense of life as doomed. It gave her hope.

Visual Imagery

In working with clients, therapists often utilize visual imagery to enhance and encourage personal insight (Esplen & Garfinkel, 1998). Esplen and Garfinkel state, "A relaxed state is viewed as a necessary condition for self-reflection" (p. 111). Replaying key moments in therapy through visual imagery, recalling the sound of the dialog, even the feel of the chair can be a helpful trigger to self-understanding.

Jane, in her work with the chronically ill, engages all her senses when she needs to self-monitor. In the following case example, she describes the self-monitoring process she used when her cancer-stricken client terminated prematurely.

Case Example: Michael

My self-monitoring process is to visualize the first two or three sessions and the most recent five or six. As I run through these sessions, I then begin to hear some of the dialog. And in hearing the dialog, I begin to get in touch with feelings. When I reflect on these feelings, I usually discover that one of my core issues had been activated in the therapeutic relationship. So, you can see, for me self-monitoring is a kind of gestalt experience. Although it begins as a kind of play in my mind, it involves all my senses.

So I engaged in the self-monitoring process. First I visualized some sessions, then I could hear his voice. I could hear him ramble continuously, and I recalled how I hadn't prevented him from doing this. I then realized that he was looking for me to give him practical advice about dealing with his illness—something as I rule I don't do in the way I work. I should have seen he needed this from the beginning of our work together, and that his need and my therapeutic approach were not a good match. But I had persisted in working with him anyway.

Ultimately, my self-monitoring took me to my underlying feelings—in fact, a very old feeling for me—the belief that I could work with anyone. Which of course is not true. I had hoped that I had finally worked that through, but apparently not completely. I had been telling myself, "Okay, I can do this, I can help him," when he was just one of those people I wasn't right for.

Using the Unconscious

When we are stuck on a clinical issue, and determined self-scrutiny is not facilitating a solution, tapping into our unconscious may be a useful strategy. This process may require that we first get into a quiet, meditative-like state and allow information we need to come into consciousness. This is certainly not a new idea. The psychoanalytic technique of free association presumes that when a client relaxes on a couch and lets the mind drift, important memories and thoughts can emerge into awareness (Rychlak, 1981). A more recent example is Gendlin's focusing technique, in which the individual tunes into the vague bodily sensation associated with a particular problem and patiently listens for the body to communicate a solution (Gendlin, 1981).

Our interviewee, Michael, developed his own method for exploring his unconscious to help him with a clinical dilemma. He calls it, "searching for the healing image." The process is essentially a form of meditation, involving both a quieting of the mind and an allowing of information to emerge, rather than actively seeking answers through self-talk. Michael reported two cases in which this search led him to more profound understanding of the core need of his clients.

Case Example: Michael

What I do is sit with myself and go into a meditative place. Specifically, I meditate on the person who is my client—not the "case," or the dynamics of the case. First, I get in touch with a visual image of the individual, and then I try to get in touch with what I call a "healing image." The healing image reconnects me with what is wounded with the person. It reminds me of why they came—for some process that is healing, even though we've lost our way with that process in our work.

First, let me describe how the healing image meditation works. Recently, I had a mother who came to consult about her 8-year-old daughter. The child had come to the attention of the school because of behavioral problems. The girl had difficulty controlling her impulses, couldn't sit with them, and would end up, metaphorically, bouncing off the walls. Not surprisingly, her mother had similar issues, perhaps some borderline personality traits. The mother tended to move from town to town, was in an out of relationships, etc. So, there was a reflected situation between mother and child.

I went into my meditative place, searching for a healing image. Then, I got this really strong image of myself with embracing arms. The image helped me understand what I needed to do with this family. I needed to help the child feel embraced, safe, and held within the therapeutic relationship.

This would help her feel relaxed with her emotions, instead of having to act on them. I shared my image with the mother, so that she could imagine the same image—herself embracing her child and helping her feel safe and able to relax. This became helpful and healing for her. And it became healing for me, too.

Here is another example when I had to self-monitor. I was working with a woman who made herself busy all the time; she had a frenetic personality. We would try to look at her frenetic-ness in therapy, but that would go nowhere. She was unable to look at it. We had explored her childhood early in treatment, but that didn't seem helpful. In the ensuing months, she would tell me the same stories about her work problems over and over again, without any movement or growth; and as the therapy progressed over time, I got that "boredom" feeling.

I meditated and waited for a healing image to surface. I remember getting a strong image of a little girl, all alone in a dark closet, feeling very cut off. It was clear to me that this image had a connection to her childhood material, material we had covered a long time ago in therapy. I knew this image was not a literal thing that had happened. But the image made me see that she had a hunger for connection, but no skill for getting it. Her mother was an impatient woman who never taught my client how to connect with other people. So it was understandable that her attempts to connect were frenetic.

When I connected to the image, I realized that I had become impatient with my client, just like her mother been impatient with her when she was a little girl. By getting in touch with the healing image, I relaxed and re-connected to my own sense of patience.

Michael's story illustrates the power of trusting the unconscious as a resource for learning both why a treatment is off-track and what is needed to move it forward. As Michael explained to us, when the therapist experiences a clue that self-monitoring is needed, it may be that the therapist has lost connection with what the client is really seeking. The therapist's task is to rediscover the core need of the client, information that was communicated in the very first sessions and somehow got lost as treatment progressed. Michael's technique seems particularly striking because a single visual image communicated by the therapist's unconscious—an image as simple as a lonely girl in a closet—may be all that is needed for the therapist to reconnect with the client.

☐ Knowing When Enough is Enough

It is important to point out that we can also engage in too much self-monitoring. The cognitive behavioral theorist, Jacqueline Persons, has pointed out that therapists can find themselves preoccupied with a client situation or personal issue stirred up by their work. When therapists start obsessing about a client or personal issue related to treatment and when thoughts about a therapy-related problem become intrusive, therapists are not self-monitoring; they are ruminating (Persons, 1989).

Ruminating is as unproductive for us as it is when our clients do it. For one thing, it has been demonstrated empirically that rumination reduces the likelihood of solving a problem (Lyubomirsky, Tucker, Caldwell, & Berg, 1999). Moreover, ruminating is psychologically unhealthy. Several longitudinal studies have suggested that ruminating on a problem is linked with anxiety and depression (Nolen-Hoeksema, 2000; Nolen-Hoeskma & Davis, 1999; Nolen-Hoeksema, Larson, & Grayson, 1999). Thus, the last thing clinicians want to do is self-monitor themselves into a state of paralysis and unhappiness.

The first thing we need to do when we find ourselves engaging in excessive self-monitoring is simply try to stop. A therapist we know recalled a conversation with his father, who tried to pass on a piece of hard-earned wisdom. "Son, a man needs to take a good hard look at himself every 7 years." The therapist thought as he heard this, "I look at myself every 7 minutes!" That's probably overdoing it.

However, sometimes we find ourselves unable to stop ruminating. When this happens, we need to ask ourselves three questions.

1. *Do I need outside help with this case?* Sometimes, our deepest self-reflection will fails to discover solutions because we are dealing with something outside our scope of competence. In effect, we are banging our heads against the wall unnecessarily when what is called for is the additional knowledge and perspective that an expert can provide us.

2. *Is this case triggering in me an issue from my life that I need to look at in my own therapy?* For example, I (David) once worked with a young man who activated my need to rescue people. The client unconsciously reminded me of my younger brother, whom, during our childhood, I had failed to protect from our father's wrath. The need to rescue and protect that I developed from this experience was stirred up by this client, and I found myself excessively and inappropriately worried about him in between sessions. Rumination may thus be a sign that the therapist is reliving an unresolved family-of-origin situation.

3. *What is it about this client that I think about him or her all the time?* Is it a diagnostic clue about the dynamics of the client? It has been observed, for example, that borderline clients "tend to get under our skins and to stay with us in a way that is different from that which we experience with other patients" (Berkowitz, 1983, p. 406). It is also possible that the therapist cannot stop thinking about the client because of feelings of attrac-

tion. Such feelings are certainly not unusual in clinical work; a major 1986 study of therapist sexual attraction revealed that 95% of male therapists and 76% of female therapists had been sexually attracted to their clients, and 63% felt anxious or confused about their attraction (Pope, Keth-Spiegel, & Tabachnick, 1986). In this case, unhealthy self-monitoring is a sign of countertransference that requires us to seek the counsel of another professional.

☐ Limits of Self-Monitoring

Finally, it is important that we keep in mind that in order to "do better" as therapists, we must constantly be aware that sometimes self-monitoring is not enough. We must be willing to consult with other professionals and our own personal therapists when situations, events, and feelings become excessive and out of our control. Each of the therapists interviewed for this chapter told us there are times when they needed consultation, when their meditations, internal dialogs, and journaling failed to quiet the internal cues that something was amiss with a case. Knowing the limits of self-monitoring is surely as important as appreciating its value as an ongoing part of our work.

☐ Summary

Based on the interviews we conducted, and our own experiences as therapists, we propose a model for self-monitoring that includes the following three components.

1. Identify and attend to behavioral, affective, and cognitive cues that can serve as red flags to signal the need to engage in the self-monitoring process.
2. Utilize self-talk, journaling, visual imagery, and the unconscious as strategies for engaging in the self-monitoring process both in response to our inner voice, and as an ongoing practice.
3. Evaluate the impact of self-monitoring on our work with clients, as well as our personal lives.

In each of the stories in this chapter, the need to pay attention to one's internal voice and responding by participating in the self-monitoring process was underscored. The ability to acknowledge that we are flawed beings, in constant need of self-supervision, may be difficult for some to accept; but that recognition is entirely critical if we are going to "do better" professionally and personally. We must continue to ask ourselves, "Why did I do that?" "Why am I responding to this client in this way?" "Why did the client prematurely terminate?" Even when it appears the client should bear some responsibility for not showing up, we must ultimately be willing to look at our role in the client's decision to not return again.

Most of our interviewees began the self-monitoring process in response to an event or situation with a client. However, the goal is for therapists to build on a continual process of self-monitoring on an ongoing basis. Checking in with ourselves is probably the most important act we can engage in, because this process can be important for good decision-making practices at every level.

Therapists can have an enormous amount of power over clients; therefore, we must avoid the temptation to exert that power simply because we have made the conscious decision to ignore our potential for making mistakes. "Doing better" involves taking risks by becoming open to the possibility that we do not know everything, and that lifelong learning is an asset, not a deficit. Relying on our own inner resources can be somewhat daunting, especially if we do not have sufficient ego strength to celebrate our strengths and to confront our limitations. Therefore, it may be useful for us to intentionally create the time and space for ongoing self-reflection activities. We may find that not only will we minimize making clinical errors and avoid missed opportunities in the therapy session, we may enhance our own creativity and skill and promote inner peace.

☐ References

Baird, B. N. (2002). *The internship, practicum, and field placement handbook: A guide for the helping professions* (3rd ed.). Englewood Cliffs, NJ: Prentice-Hall.

Beaton, R. D., & Murphy, S. A. (1995). Working with people in crisis: Research implications. In C. R. Figley (Ed.), *Compassion fatigue: Coping with secondary traumatic stress disorder in those who treat the traumatized*. Philadelphia: Brunner/Mazel.

Beck, A. T., Rush, A. J., Shaw, B. F., & Emery, G. (1979). *Cognitive therapy of depression*. New York: Guilford Press.

Berkowitz, M. (1983). Know your borderline: Countertransference as a diagnostic tool. *Psychotherapy: Theory, Research and Practice, 20,* 405–407.

Coster, J. S., & Schwebel, M. (1997). Well-functioning in professional psychologists. *Professional Psychology: Research and Practice, 28,* 5–13.

Ellis, A. (1984). How to deal with your most difficult client—you. *Psychotherapy in Private Practice, 2*(1), 25–34.

Esplen, M. J., & Garfinkel, P. E. (1998). Guided imagery treatment to promote self-soothing in bulimia nervosa: A theoretical rationale. *Journal of Psychotherapy Practice and Research, 7,* 102–118.

Figley, C. R. (1995). Compassion fatigue as secondary traumatic stress disorder: An overview. In C. R. Figley (Ed.), *Compassion fatigue: Coping with secondary traumatic stress disorder in those who treat the traumatized.* Philadelphia: Brunner/Mazel.

Fox, R., & Carey, L. A. (1999). Therapists' collusion with the resistance of rape survivors. *Clinical Social Work, 27*(2), 185–201.

Flannery, J. (1995). Boredom in the therapist: Countertransference issues. *British Journal of Psychotherapy, 11*, 536–544.

Geller, J. D. (1994). The psychotherapist's experience of interest and boredom. *Psychotherapy: Theory, Research, Practice, Training, 31*, 3–16.

Freud, S. (1954). *The origins of psychoanalysis.* New York: Basic Books.

Freud, S. (1949). *An outline of psychoanalysis.* New York: Norton.

Gay, P. (1988). *Freud: A life for our time.* New York: Norton.

Gendlin, E. T. (1981). *Focusing* (2nd ed.) New York: Bantam Books.

Jennings, L., & Skovholt, T. M. (1999). The cognitive, emotional, and relational characteristics of master therapists. *Journal of Counseling Psychology, 46*, 3–11.

Jung, C. G. (1946). *Psychological types.* New York: Harcourt, Brace.

Kanfer, F. H. (1970). Self-monitoring: Methodological limitations and clinical applications. *Journal of Consulting and Clinical Psychology, 35*, 148–152.

Kottler, J. A. (1993). *On being a therapist.* San Francisco, CA: Jossey-Bass.

Lepore, S. J. (1997). Expressive writing moderates the relation between intrusive thoughts and depressive symptoms. *Journal of Personality and Social Psychology, 73*, 1030–1037.

Lyubomirsky, S., Tucker, K. L., Caldwell, N. D., & Berg, K. (1999). Why ruminators are poor problem solvers: Clues from the phenomenology of dysphoric rumination. *Journal of Personality and Social Psychology, 77*, 1041–1060.

Maultsby, M. C. (1984). *Rational behavior therapy.* Englewood Cliffs, NJ: Prentice-Hall.

Meichenbaum, D. (1977). *Cognitive-behavior modification.* New York: Plenum.

Miller, L. (1998). Our own medicine: Traumatized psychotherapists and the stresses of doing therapy. *Psychotherapy, 35*, 137–146.

Moursund, J., & Kenny, M. C. (2002). *The process of counseling and therapy* (4th ed.). Englewood Cliffs, NJ: Prentice-Hall.

Nelson, M. L., & Neufeldt, S. A. (1998). The pedagogy of counseling: A critical examination. *Counselor Education & Supervision, 38*, 70–88.

Neufeldt, S. A., Karno, M. P., & Nelson, M. L. (1996). A qualitative study of experts' conceptualization of supervisee reflectivity. *Journal of Counseling Psychology, 43*, 3–9.

Nolen-Hoeksema, S. (2000). The role of rumination in depressive disorders and mixed anxiety/depressive symptoms. *Journal of Abnormal Psychology, 109*, 504–511.

Nolen-Hoeksema, S., & Davis, C. G. (1999). "Thanks for sharing that": Ruminators and their social support networks. *Journal of Personality and Social Psychology, 77*, 801–814.

Nolen-Hoeksema, S., Larson, J., & Grayson, C. (1999). Explaining the gender difference in depressive symptoms. *Journal of Personality and Social Psychology, 7*, 1061–1072.

Norcross, J. C. (2000). Psychotherapist self-care: Practitioner-tested, research-informed strategies. *Professional Psychology: Research and Practice, 31*, 710–713.

Pennebaker, J. W. (1997). *Opening up: The healing power of expressing emotions.* New York: Guilford Press.

Persons, J. B. (1989). *Cognitive therapy in practice: A case formulation approach.* New York: Norton.

Pope, K. S., Keith-Spiegel, P., & Tabachnik, B. G. (1986). Sexual attraction to clients: The human therapist and the (sometimes) inhuman training system. *American Psychologist, 41*, 147–158.

Ranier, J. P. (2000). *Compassion fatigue: When caregiving begins to hurt.* Sarasota, FL: Professional Resource Press.

Rehm, L. P., & Rokke. P. (1988). Self-management therapies. In K. S. Dobson (Ed.), *Handbook of cognitive-behavioral therapies.* New York: Guilford Press.

Rogers, C. R. (1951). *Client-centered therapy: Its current practice, implications, and theory*. Boston: Houghton Mifflin.

Rychlak, J. F. (1981). *Introduction to personality and psychotherapy: A theory-construction approach*. Boston: Houghton Mifflin.

Rule, W. R. (1998). Unsqueezing the soul: Expanding choices by reframing and redirecting boredom. *Journal of Contemporary Psychotherapy, 28,* 327–336.

Sapienza, B. G., & Bugental, J. F. T. (2000). Keeping our instruments finely tuned: An existential-humanistic perspective. *Professional Psychology: Research and Practice, 31,* 458–460.

Schwebel, M., & Coster, J. S.(1998). Well-functioning in professional psychologists: As program heads see it. *Professional Psychology: Research and Practice, 29,* 284–292.

Sexton, L. (1999). Vicarious traumatisation of counsellors and effects on their workplace. *British Journal of Guidance and Counselling, 27*(3), 393–403.

Skovholt, T. M., & Ronnestad, M. H. (1992). Themes in therapist and counselor development. *Journal of Counseling and Development, 70,* 505–515.

Smyth, J. M. (1998). Written emotional expression: Effect sizes, outcome types, and moderating variables. *Journal of Consulting and Clinical Psychology, 66,* 174–184.

Watkins, C. E. (1983). Counselor acting out in the counseling situation: An exploratory analysis. *Personnel and Guidance, 61*(7), 417–423.

4
CHAPTER

W. Paul Jones
Robert L. Harbach

A Syllabus for Self-Supervision

Practicing therapists should have established procedures for continuing professional growth and monitoring the quality of services delivered. Said more simply, it is "good" to "stay good " and even better, to "get better." Although divergence of feelings about professional issues in counseling and therapy seems often to be a simple mathematical function (number of opinions equals number of therapists in the room), this appears to be the exception. We've selected a profession in which isolation is often the norm, in which boredom and burnout may be inevitable, and in which the long-range positive outcomes of our work are often inaccessible. Our risks for performance deterioration over time are high, and the continuing education required to maintain our licenses may be insufficient to avoid the risks.

Convergence of opinion about the importance of this issue, of course, is only a beginning. Divergence appears quickly when we attempt to identify tools to implement a process of continuing growth. Is it possible to be both the subject and the object, to be both supervisor and supervisee? Could (and should) licensing requirements be modified to require a self-supervision plan? In even suggesting the need are we adding more burden to an already overburdened professional practice? Building on the self-monitoring information and examples presented in the previous chapter, our goal with this chapter is to suggest a practical model to integrate self-supervision in the context of professional practice.

☐ Scope

Before detailing the "syllabus" implementation model, it is helpful to briefly review the scope of self-supervision, using the time-honored tools of who, what, when, where, why, and how. Who should be engaged in self-supervision? What is self-supervision? When should such supervision begin? Where should the supervision take place? Why is self-supervision important? How can a self-supervision procedure be implemented?

Who

There are actually two questions here: Who should be involved in self-supervision and who is capable of self-supervision? The first has an easy answer. All practicing therapists should be involved in self-supervision to maintain and/or enhance their work.

In reference to the second question, Leith, McNiece, and Fussilier (1989) writing from a cognitive behavioral perspective suggest that there are two critical skills: observation and problem solving. Noted in the first chapter was Morrissette's (1999) position that self-supervision is both rigorous and critically important. Four features were specifically cited from the perspective of family therapists: knowledge about systems theory, insight into the therapeutic process, a self-initiation, and willingness to experience vulnerability. Learning theory suggests that supervision is essentially a learning event. Humanistic theories suggest that self-supervision is to be engaged in a process that is motivated by an internal potential to grow (Hershenson, Power, & Waldo, 1996). The previous chapter in this book identifies three critical skill areas: the ability to identify and attend to cues, the capability of using a variety of strategies including self-talk and journaling, and a commitment to ongoing self-evaluation.

What

A simple definition of self-supervision is that it is a systematic process in which professionals work independently to monitor and direct their own professional development (Donnelly & Glaser, 1992; Morrissette, 1999). The critical elements in this definition are "systematic, independent, and monitor." Effective self-supervision is a planned, organized, and ongoing process, implemented by the practitioner without direct intervention by an external supervisor.

There is some divergence in the literature (Lowe, 2000) about whether self-supervision is best viewed as an intermediate step prior to "person-to-person" supervision or is in fact the long-term objective for all supervision. The former gives self-supervision a very limited scope, the practitioner's tasks in conceptualizing a case prior to discussion with an external supervisor. The latter appears more consistent with contemporary thought and views self-supervision as the universal supervisory goal.

When

Thinking back to your first practicum experience, we all began our clinical experience under a precise microscope. Every word, every gesture, every cognition was analyzed and critiqued by a (hopefully) kind and empathic supervisor. As we successfully progressed through the practicum and internship experiences, the level of supervision gradually decreased until eventually we received that first license for independent practice. No longer were we required to justify our treatment plans and procedures to an experienced therapist. We were free to steer the ship without assistance, guidance, or interference from anyone else.

The journey in the preceding is probably a shared experience for each reader of this material (although for some, a less than empathic managed-care clerk may have now replaced the trained supervisor as the monitor of the treatment plans and procedures). The preceding journey above also identifies the "when" of self-supervision. At whatever point our work is not being directly monitored by an external supervisor, self-supervision of that work becomes crucial. It could in fact be argued (e.g., Keller & Protinsky, 1984; Lowe, 2000; Morrissette, 1999) that initial supervision should include some direct focus on developing the skills to enable a later shift to self-supervision.

Where

Use of the journalistic "where" is a bit of a reach in defining the scope of self-supervision. There is, though, at least one element to be considered. Is your self-supervision conceptualized as just something you "automatically" do while engaged in practice or is it instead a more formal process in which you specifically set aside blocks of time for appraisal and review of the quality of your work?

Our premise is that self-monitoring during therapy sessions is a given, an essential element of professional practice that is not likely to be sufficient alone to ensure continuing growth in the quality of service. The "real-time" monitoring should be supplemented by something equivalent to the typical 1-hour per week supervisory sessions during training.

There is need for specific "set-asides"—that is, time in which there is direct and active reflective critique of each case and each session.

Why

The reasons why self-supervision is crucial are, by far, the easiest to justify. Several chapters in this book speak directly to features in the practice of counseling and therapy that unattended can lead to decrement in the quality of service. Boredom, isolation, even the setting of your practice are among the factors that can contribute to "wearout," if not "burnout."

The fact that most do not really understand what we do can provide a ready rationalization for what should be an unacceptable quality of service. Poor reviews by our clients can be self-explained away as simply artifacts of working with disturbed persons. The fact that most of our work is done in isolation from direct observation by others supports, if not mandates, focused attention on self-monitoring.

How

A story is told that during World War I, a reporter asked Will Rogers, the renowned humorist, if he could suggest a solution to the submarine menace that was threatening American shipping. "Certainly," he is reported to have said, "all you have to do is boil the ocean." When the reporter objected, Rogers responded that all he had been asked for was a solution, not a method.

We are reminded of this in reviewing the literature on self-supervision. All agree that ongoing professional growth and development is a good thing; nearly all appear to agree that self-supervision is a good thing. Typical, though, for important issues in our field is that the devil is in the details.

A practicing therapist makes a conscious decision to embark on a systematic plan for self-supervision. What are the required elements? What are the specific steps? Said most simply, how in the world do we do this?

The specific elements to be included and emphasized in self-supervision are, of course, likely to be heavily influenced by the theoretical orientation of the practitioner. Lowe (2000) provides guidelines for a constructivist perception of self-supervision, and Morrissette (1999) details a model from a family systems perspective.

Self-monitoring is a critical element in all forms of self-supervision, and a study by Matthews and Marshall (1988) suggests that there may be some reciprocal relationship between theoretical orientation and self-monitoring style. Persons identified as high self-monitors were those whose behavior is highly governed by attention to situational cues; low self-monitors were defined as those whose behavior was more likely to be governed by perception of enduring characteristics. High self-monitors were more likely to endorse a variety of therapeutic modalities and approach therapy from an eclectic orientation. Low self-monitors were more likely to emphasize a consistent theoretical framework and a uniform therapeutic approach.

Acknowledging that one's theoretical orientation will certainly determine some desired elements in self-supervision just as it does in therapy, we also believe that there are common elements that cut across the lines of our varied theoretical orientations. One way to approach self-supervision (Haber, 1996), in fact, is for therapists to simply "make believe" that they are supervising self from behind a one-way mirror. Using a template of our universally shared experience, the closely supervised practicum, the remainder of this chapter is a syllabus to implement such supervision.

☐ The Self-Supervision Syllabus

It may be especially important for us to begin this section with a bit of a disclaimer. You are unlikely to find anything truly "new" in the materials that follow. We intentionally include some of the most basic elements of clinical practice, things like microcounseling skills that have long since become automatic. It is that very automaticity that warrants their inclusion. We are creatures of habit, and after finding a style that appears to work well for us, we are likely to re-examine the elements of it only when it does not appear to work with some case. The premise here is that in self-supervision *all* aspects of therapy warrant periodic examination. The fact that some element in the current therapy style appears to be working well does not preclude the possibility that even better results might be obtained with some adjustment in that style.

What is different here, of course, is that you are asked to play two roles: supervisor and supervisee, subject and object. To operationally differentiate those two roles for self-supervision, you may find it helpful to assume that you have been employed (or recently reassigned) to teach a practicum supervision course, and, as luck would have it, you have only one student in your course. How would you (or have you) gone about defining the methods and procedures for such a course? What characteristics do you want to communicate to your supervisee? What are your objectives for this supervisee?

The Simulated Supervisor

Borrowing from typical syllabi used in teaching prospective counselor-educators to be supervisors and from elements in the *Supervisory Working Alliance Inventory* (Efstation, Patton, & Kardash, 1990) some important features in the assignment of "you as the self-supervisor" might include:

- Negotiate a standard time to meet with your "supervisee."
- Include review of audio- and/or videotape of the "supervisory" session.
- Maintain some form of log of the "supervisory" session.

In your "supervisory" session, you might expect to be evaluated by "you as the supervisee" on features, including:

- Focus on the needs of the client with whom the session was conducted.
- Systematically review the session in the context of the complete case.
- Explore alternative ways this session could have been conducted or this case could have been conceptualized.

The Simulated Supervisee

Okay, so now you have gone back in time to when you were a wet be-hind the ears, practicum supervisee; you are being observed through a one-way mirror because no one is yet sure that you won't mess this up on your own. You anticipate being critiqued on every movement you make, every word you speak. On the face of it this is about as appealing to most of us as thoughts of an impending root canal. We've all gone through this, and the operative term for most of us is probably "have gone" already. Why would anyone in their right mind want to go back through those hoops again?

The answer is that we wouldn't, and fortunately the reality is that we won't be doing that exact same thing again. The only social (professional) pressure in self-supervision is that which may be self-imposed.

The mindset of supervisee seeking assistance and/or reassurance, though, remains the desired outcome of the process. In order to gain from self-supervision, there has to be a beginning admission that self-supervision is needed, that the current level of skill application is not the optimal level of skill application. And, there must be a willingness to commit to the requirements of the "course."

Universities now frequently offer in-service training for professors who want to improve the quality of their classroom performance. The audi-ence for such courses is typically composed of two groups: those who are required to come and those whose classes already are delivered with a high level of instructional performance.

A comparable phenomenon seems likely to be evident in self-supervision of counseling and therapy. Some may engage in the process because outside forces require it. Of the remainder, the majority are likely to be those who already are "above the norm" in ongoing reflective thought about the quality of service being delivered.

This is significant because a key feature in the self-supervision process is to dedicate a regular time block for such activity, and this request is being made to those whose practices are more likely to be successful to the extent that finding the time block is difficult. It is for this reason that return to the mindset of supervisee is particularly important.

Few, if any of us, can easily point to an empty block of time in a busy workweek. There just aren't any regular periods of time in which we have nothing else to do. But, if we were "required" to engage in an hour of supervision each week, we would of course be able to find the time. Treating the self-supervision "as if" it were a supervisee's mandate is one way to ensure that the needed time is made available.

A second area in which the supervisee's mindset may be critical is in regard to the audio- and/or videotaping of therapy sessions. How long has it actually been since you taped a session to use for later review of the quality of your work? For most of us, certainly including the authors, such taping stopped when it was no longer required. We might occasionally tape a session for a particularly troublesome case. We might tape a session when we have reason for concern about future legal issues. But, going through the bother of obtaining the client's permission, setting up the equipment, and so forth, for personal quality control just doesn't usually happen.

Self-supervision, of course, does not require every session to be taped or even that every supervisory session include review of a tape. Most of us, though, would agree that reviewing our work in taped sessions was an important part of learning effective clinical skills. It would thus seem reasonable to assume that some return to the process could be equally helpful for maintaining quality control and to enhance clinical skills.

Supervision Content

To illustrate, let's assume that you have decided to use the "as if" model for self-supervision with 1-hour per week scheduled for reflective review and analysis in a simulated supervision session. Among the areas of focus expected in traditional supervision (Getz, 1999) are counseling skills, case conceptualization, and professional role issues, including ethical, legal, and regulatory concerns. Each of these areas can also be incorporated into your self-supervision.

Assume, for the reasons noted in the preceding, that you have decided your self-supervision sessions will include periodic monitoring of basic clinical skills as well as more complex analysis of case conceptualization and session content.

Although dated, a still useful model for the basic skills review is the skills identified by Ivey and associates and typically defined as microcounseling (Ivey, Pedersen, & Ivey, 2001).

You may remember the five behaviors identified with the acronym S-O-L-E-R, the set of physical behaviors that have been shown to aid in communication to the client that you are in fact attending to the information being presented. The five behaviors are: *s*, face the client squarely; *o*, assume an open posture; *l*, lean forward toward the client; *e*, maintain eye contact with the client; and *r*, have a relaxed posture. You may, by the way, remember as a beginning practicum student feeling a bit overwhelmed at being told you should "relax" while following the other instructions; you were multitasking before the word was invented.

Let us quickly acknowledge the obvious that these are very basic skills that have long since become routine and assumed in your practice. Having granted that, be honest now, how long has it been since you monitored yourself to see if in fact your physical behaviors were still consistent with these guidelines?

If feasible, and perhaps as one way to "get in the spirit" of the self as supervisee mindset, we suspect that you might find it interesting to relive the supervisee experience by actually videotaping one of your therapy sessions to be reviewed in one of your supervisory sessions. We recognize, however, that there may be some logistical barriers difficult to surmount. Few, if any, of your current clients would be likely to feel comfortable with an obvious camcorder, and most of us do not practice in settings where unobtrusive video recording is available. Neither of us would probably feel comfortable in explaining to a client that we felt a need to review our basic clinical skills because of the obvious credibility implications.

Depending on the arrangement of your particular office, though, there may be a technological possibility that could simulate the "through the one-way mirror" concept of self-supervision. For reasons detailed in the technoconsultation chapter of this book, you may want to have one of the small, inexpensive video cameras attached to your computer. If the computer is in the same area in which you conduct therapy sessions, it may be possible for the camera to be on and aimed toward you with a small picture on the computer screen out of the line of sight of your client.

You may or may not find it feasible and/or appropriate to go all the way back to analysis of your physical attending behaviors. Regardless of your decision about those primary skills, it is important as a part of the self-supervision process to periodically review other basic microcounseling skills, for example, your responses intended to reflect feeling, content, and summarization. The question is not whether the skills have been learned. Obviously, they have or you would not be where you are now. The question is whether those basic skills, designed to help elicit and clarify the client problem, are still being effectively used.

The logistics for "you as supervisee" to provide "you as supervisor" with the tool to monitor these skills are, of course, not complex. Few clients would question a request to audiotape a session. Many, based on what they have seen in the popular media, probably assume that sessions are already being routinely taped. Your explanation of the safeguards taken for confidentiality of the tapes provides a useful additional opportunity to review all aspects of confidentiality.

For experienced clinicians, this review of basic clinical skills may provide an important safeguard to ensure that we are not inadvertently leading the client to our "problem of choice." In our initial training, the supervisor served as the monitor to ensure that our responses led to the client's understanding of the problem and enabled the client to clarify if not select specific targets for intervention. For the experienced clinician, the skill now evident in using probes and guiding the verbal flow carries with it a risk for leading the client toward the clinician's area of comfort. Listening to yourself through the ears of a supervisor may provide surprising insight into why so many of your clients now seem to be presenting with such similar problems. Have we not all, at some point, wondered why so many of the clients we see on a given day seem to be confronting such similar issues?

Continuing the example of the once per week schedule, we would suggest that the review of basic skills through review of audio tapes should come very early in the sequence of supervision. The literature on observational research (Gay & Airasian, 2000) strongly suggests that observation will be more objective when the observer is focused on only one thing at a time. We believe this concept generalizes to your approach to self-monitoring during self-supervision of your audio material. As a skilled clinician, your work demands that you simultaneously attend to a variety of stimuli. It will be at least tempting for those multiattending skills to be evident when you review your tapes. You may find yourself concurrently thinking about how you have conceptualized the case, what you want to do next with this client, and so forth, while you are trying to be focused on your application of basic clinical skills. It will be much more effective if you make a conscious effort when supervising your performance to separate the different functions the tape review can serve. Listen once, all the way through, only for your application of probes and other responses designed to understand, not lead the client. If you do not already own one, variable speed tape players are available at many of the discount electronic outlets. These inexpensive devices compress speech, increasing the speed of playback while holding voice pitch constant and can significantly reduce the amount of time spent in reviewing a tape.

Still assuming a 1-hour per week self-supervision schedule, a good rule of thumb may be to devote the first session of each month to the basic skills monitoring with, of course, particular attention to review of initial and other early sessions. For all who have had experience working in hospital settings, the importance of documentation needs little emphasis. The rule there often is simple. If it isn't written down, it didn't happen.

If you were teaching a beginning or advanced practicum, maintaining a log of each supervisory session would be required. A comparable log for your self-supervision sessions is certainly of equal if not greater importance. What did you focus on in the self-supervision session and what was the outcome of that focus?

In monitoring basic skills, the focus in self-supervision is on you. What did you do? Why did you choose that response? How appropriate was your delivery?

In the second content area to be considered here, a broad view of case conceptualization, the focus changes from you to the client. This client focus includes how effective you were in examining clients' problems, diagnosis, dynamics, and goals, and in identifying methods that might be most effective for achieving them. The self-supervisor also focuses on his or her knowledge, skills, development, and internal dynamics, which may contribute to or detract from competent counseling (Brammer & Wassmer, 1977).

Case-conceptualization, of course, is at least in part contingent on your theoretical orientation and the setting in which the services are being delivered. There is a common thread, however, a focus that leads to an understanding of the client.

In a rehabilitation mode, for example, let's say, that you are working with an adult woman suffering from schizophrenia. Did you focus on the client's stress level, resources, and reality testing? Did you consider what kinds of social support are available to her now? To what extent are the symptoms of schizophrenia interfering with her ability to function in home and work settings?

In reviewing the tapes of recorded counseling sessions, the self-supervisor might observe, "When the client was confronted about the importance of taking her medication she smiled a little, like she enjoyed hearing that I (self-supervisor) care about her well-being." What does this imply about our working alliance? Is there a possibility that maintaining the symptoms could be achieving some form of secondary gain?

If you are working in the framework of one of the brief therapy models, several questions can be asked regarding your conceptualization of the case. Have you clearly identified the target behaviors? Did you obtain sufficient information about conditions that appear to be serving to maintain the current behaviors? Did you use the "miracle question" to identify the client goal? Did you use the "first sign" as a tool for identification of intermediate behaviors? Are you using some form of rapid assessment scale to identify progress toward goals?

As noted, how you evaluate yourself in your conceptualization of a case depends of course on what you are trying to accomplish. Regardless of the specific elements emphasized in your theory of choice, though, self-supervision should include attention to your identification of the goals, current circumstances, and intervention plans.

The case of the client, Sam, illustrates some components of case conceptualization. Sam is a 16-year-old adolescent who grew up in a small town in central Texas. His father is a prominent cosmetic surgeon. Sam's mother is the principal at Sam's high school. Sam has a younger sister, who, according to Sam, is a disappointment to their parents because she is just an average student and has plans to become a paralegal. Her parents of course want her to become a lawyer and do not understand why she does not shoot for a higher goal.

According to Sam, his father early on "wrote off" his sister and, to a certain extent, his own stagnant career and focused on Sam's success (vicarious syndrome). Sam has worked hard to fill the expectations of his father. He has always earned excellent grades in school and has won full scholarships at prestigious universities that will support his undergraduate education and extend to training in medical school. Sam states that being around his father causes him to fear his own fallibility, and he seeks to avoid anxiety-provoking situations.

Sam is a very intelligent and articulate young man who appears to be much more competent and capable than his self-image implies. Other than his self-concept, there is no evidence of problems with reality contact. He appears willing, even pressured, to discuss his problems, and he seems highly motivated toward reducing them.

His primary problem involves extreme and exaggerated consternation about his own fallibility and his need to perform every activity perfectly, no matter how inconsequential. This overriding fear has impaired his ability to function in work and social settings, as well as his ability to perform even routine tasks. This anxiety is also manifested by a number of physiological symptoms, including constant vigilance, distractibility, and irritability; pervasive muscle tension, expressed by his occasional feelings of panic. Thus, it seems that anxiety is his primary problem.

Sam's symptoms clearly fit the DSM-IV criteria for generalized anxiety disorder. People with this disorder suffer from pervasive, long-standing, and uncontrollable feelings of dread or worry that involve a number of major life activities. The focus of these anxieties is much broader than is the case with more circumscribed anxiety disorders such as panic disorder or simple phobia, and they are not solely associated with any other Axis I diagnosis. People with generalized anxiety disorder display somatic signs of apprehension, including muscle tension, fatigue, and irritability (American Psychiatric Association, 1994).

Sam's therapy can be conceptualized as a process involving four general steps:

1. The therapist's initial aim is to establish rapport with client, by explaining the approach. Explanation may be especially important if a cognitive-behavioral approach is selected because this approach requires much more direct, active participation than initially expected by many clients, especially those like Sam. It is important that the client is made fully aware of what to expect. It is important to establish this basis of hope to foster the client's expectations for change.
2. At the next level it is important that Sam assists in the identification of specific goals for his therapy. Initial goals are often too general, and the therapy process itself can be used to facilitate identification of mutually acceptable and appropriate therapy objectives.
3. In preparing a treatment plan, consideration would appear warranted for some use of relaxation/imagery training. This technique is often suggested for clients who show a great deal of physical tension and seem amenable to this treatment modality.
4. Last, there should be evidence of a review by Sam and the therapist of the issues and goals Sam has targeted. Investing some time in going over both initial complaints and plans, contributes to the development of an effective therapeutic alliance.

The final area of self-supervision content to be explored in this chapter may be the most important in regard to protection of both your clients and yourself. It is generally agreed (Borders et al., 1991; Getz, 1999; Holloway, 1995) that effective clinical supervision includes some attention to professional roles, including ethical, legal, and regulatory factors. Clearly, self-supervision warrants attention to these issues as well.

Your primary resource for self-monitoring in this area will be in the guides and casebooks specific to your specific professional identity, for example AAMFT (2001), ACA (1995), American Psychological Association (1992), NASW (1999). Detailed, if not exhaustive, guides to appropriate actions and cautions are provided, and these may be supplemented with additional guidelines for special areas of practice, for example, CyberCounseling (ACA, 1999). Here, we will just highlight an area where particular concern may be prudent, client confidentiality.

We all understand the basic concept that, with the exception of suspected child abuse and other circumstances when disclosure is essential to prevent clear and imminent danger to the client or others, information is to be to be held in complete confidence. The situation, though, can sometimes become cloudy when working with children or adolescents with conflict between consistency with the rules and perceptions of what appears to be in the best interest of our client.

More problematic in contemporary practice in regard to confidentiality is the extent of stored information. Publicity about cases of stolen identity and subsequent financial ruin have raised our general awareness about safeguarding our own personal information and should be generalized to concern about information from and about our clients.

Attention to privacy and confidentiality is more than just a suggestion. It is a mandate in many therapy settings. Implementation of electronic transaction and security rules in the Health Insurance Portability and Accountability Act (HIPPA) includes specific privacy requirements for any provider who uses electronic transmission in any form, ranging from claim submission to transmission of patient information via fax (APAIT, 2002).

Consider, for example, that when you simply send an e-mail to a client as a reminder of an appointment, you are in fact "telling the world" that this individual is seeking therapy services. Encryption is available, but how many of us would even consider that as a need when sending an appointment reminder?

In this same vein, how many people have some access to the computer on which you probably have stored sensitive if not embarrassing information with specific client names? Before too quickly responding that no one else could use your computer, consider: Do you clean your own office? Probably not. Do you observe the actions of the persons who provide this service? Again, a technological solution is available (password protection), but how many of us use it?

The problem, of course, is not limited to technological storage. Have you ever simply thrown a flawed report into the wastebasket without shredding it? And what steps, if any, do you take to preclude others from being aware that an individual is coming into your office for an appointment?

In addition to self-supervision, it is anticipated that you will have occasional need for interaction with another service provider about a specific therapy case. We all understand the rule that your client's prior written consent is required if the identity of the client is to be revealed. But, even when practicing in an urban setting, many of us have a client pool with somewhat narrow boundaries. How often have you inadvertently revealed the identity of a client, simply in the detail of describing the case?

Breaches of confidentiality may be especially frequent if you make use of appraisal instruments in your practice. You probably do not hand score the tests, relying instead on some form of scoring system or service. Thus, the responses of the client, often identified by name, are available to the person who enters the data, the person responsible for monitoring the data analysis and reports, and so on. The issue is simple. How many people should know that client Mary Smith reports that she frequently considers suicide, that she has participated in extramarital affairs more than twice in the last 5 years, and that she is terrified when going into a crowd? Obviously, the answer is that no one other than the client and yourself should have access to the information. The question, though, is: What steps do we as therapists take to ensure that such responses remain private?

Before leaving the material about confidentiality, one other point warrants attention. Let's assume that you do in fact take extra precautions for confidentiality in your work setting. Computers are controlled with passwords. Documents are filed in locked storage cabinets and are shredded before discarding. Waiting rooms are not easily visible from sidewalks or hallways. That's good, but what about the documents you take home? Lulled into a false sense of security by the sanctity of the home, privileged and sensitive information may be readily available to visitors, both invited and uninvited.

☐ Final Thoughts

We began with a premise that acceptable operational definitions for the scope of self-supervision were both identifiable and reasonable. Borrowing the "six honest servants" from Kipling (1902), this chapter has examined the "who, what, when, where, why, and how" of self-supervision. Can it be done? Without a doubt the answer is an unconditional Yes, it can. A strong argument, in fact, could probably be made that all of us are already involved in self-supervision. The better question is: Are we doing it well?

Working from the familiar to the unfamiliar is usually a good practice in all learning tasks, and we've suggested here that it will be valuable to perceptually return to the time when you were in training for practice. You've been encouraged to select the best of what was provided to you by your external supervisors and apply it to your own work. Toward that end, we've proposed a "syllabus" with defined tasks and suggested content areas for your self-supervision. This material, at best, is intended to serve only as an initial guide. How you actually implement the self-supervision is, and we believe should be, a highly individual matter.

Writing this chapter has served to remind both of us of the need to beware of our automatic responses. It remains important to take time to occasionally "grade self" on the delivery of the most basic of the clinical skills, the ones which have become so ingrained that they receive little conscious consideration. None of us are immune to the risk of getting stuck with the familiar. No therapist has ever "good enough" to preclude further skill enhancement.

☐ References

American Association for Marriage and Family Therapy. (2001). *AAMFT code of ethics*. Washington, DC: Author. Retrieved January 7, 2002, from http://www.aamft.org/resources/lrmplan/ethics/ethicscode2001.htm

American Counseling Association. (1999). *Ethical standards for Internet on-line counseling*. Alexandria, VA: Author. Retrieved January 7, 2002, from http://www.counseling.org/gc/cybertx.htm

American Counseling Association. (1995). *Code of ethics and standards of practice*. Alexandria, VA: Author. Retrieved January 7, 2002, from http://www.counseling.org/resources/codeofethics.htm

American Psychiatric Association. (1994). *Diagnostic and statistical manual of mental disorders* (4th ed.). Washington, DC: Author.

American Psychological Association. (1992). *Ethical principles of psychologists and code of conduct*. Washington, DC: Author. Retrieved January 7, 2002, from http://www.apa.org/ethics/code.html

APAIT. (2002). *Getting ready for HIPPA: A primer for psychologists*. Washington, DC: American Psychological Association Insurance Trust.

Borders, L. D., Bernard, J. M., Dye, H. A., Fong, M. L., Henderson, P., & Nance, D. W. (1991). Curriculum guide for training counseling supervisors: Rationale, development, and implementation. *Counselor Education and Supervision, 31*, 58–82.

Brammer, L. M., & Wassmer, A. C. (1977). *Supervision in counseling and psychotherapy*. Westport, CT: Greenwood.

Donnelly, C., & Glaser, A. (1992). Training in self-supervision skills. *The Clinical Supervisor, 10*, 85–96.

Efstation, J. F., Patton, M. J., & Kardash, C. M. (1990). Measuring the working alliance in counselor supervision. *Journal of Counseling Psychology, 37*, 322–329.

Gay, L.R., & Airasian, P. (2000). *Educational research: Competencies for analysis and application* (6th ed.). Upper Saddle River, NJ: Prentice-Hall.

Getz, H. G. (1999). Assessment of clinical supervisor competencies. *Journal of Counseling and Development, 77*, 491–497.

Haber, R. (1996). *Dimensions of psychotherapy supervision: Maps and means*. New York: Norton.

Hershenson, D., Power, P., & Waldo, M. (1996). *Community counseling: Contemporary theory and practice*. Needham Heights, MA: Allyn & Bacon.

Holloway, E. L. (1995). *Clinical supervision: A systems approach*. Thousand Oaks, CA: Sage.

Ivey, A., Pedersen, P., & Ivey, M. (2001). *Intentional group counseling: A microskills approach.* Pacific Grove, CA: Brooks/Cole.

Keller, J. F., & Protinsky, H. (1984). A self-management model for supervision. *Journal of Marital and Family Therapy, 10,* 281–288.

Kipling, R. (1902). The elephant's child. *Just So Stories.* Retrieved January 7, 2002, from http://www.boop.org/jan/justso/

Leith, W. R., McNiece, E. M., & Fusilier, B. B. (1989). *Handbook of supervision: A cognitive behavioral system.* Boston: College Hill.

Lowe, R. (2000). Supervising self-supervision: constructive inquiry and embedded narratives in case consultation. *Journal of Marital and Family Therapy, 26,* 511–521.

Matthews, C. H., & Marshall, L. L. (1988). Self-monitoring and intake interviewers' theoretical orientation. *Professional Psychology: Research and Practice, 19,* 433–435.

Morrissette, P. J. (1999). Family therapist self-supervision: Toward a preliminary conceptualization. *The Clinical Supervisor, 18,* 165–183.

National Association of Social Workers. (1999). *NASW code of ethics.* Washington, DC: Author. Retrieved January 7, 2002, from http://www.socialworkers.org/pubs/code/code.htm

Dana L. Comstock
Thelma H. Duffey

Confronting Adversity

As life would have it, painful situations, even tragic ones, arise during the education and careers of counselors and therapists. Adversity can be disruptive to the therapist, the client, and the life of the therapeutic relationship. Its effects can be experienced as abrupt, insurmountable, unspeakable, ongoing, and, at times, joyful. Therapists, too, lose children and loved ones. They struggle with chronic, debilitating, and life-threatening illnesses. They experience unrewarding, unfulfilling relationships and undergo separations and divorce. They suffer emotional and physical violations. They are victims of oppression, discrimination, and hate crimes. Therapists grapple with the ghosts of childhood trauma. Sometimes, they spiral out of control. Therapists, too, deal with the joys and stressors of change, friendships, childbirth, adoption, love, parenting, and many other uncertainties and are vulnerable to suffering in all the ways that people suffer.

Our goals in this chapter are multifold. First, we build into the training, supervision, and practice of psychotherapy the very real fact that therapists are vulnerable to adverse life circumstances during the course of their educations and careers. We present both the personal and therapeutic complexities that may arise as a result of these experiences, which include the concomitant shame and guilt that may arise while developing and maintaining a professional identity in the face of adversity. We also provide a means for monitoring professional abilities in times of crises, while providing encouragement and suggestions for self-care. If you are reading this and are currently struggling with adversity, we hope to provide you with some tools for managing your life's course. We also hope to normalize the difficulties and complexities that arise during times of transition, crises and loss.

We address some varying perspectives on the often-controversial topic of "self-disclosure." We also explore some of the complexities involved in assuming a decision *not* to self-disclose. We look at shifts in professional identity and the presence of shame during adversity, and will make recommendations for maximizing personal and professional levels of resiliency during times of adversity. Last, we explore the ways in which we can "do better" at working with others while seeing ourselves through life's many challenges.

☐ Self-Care and Adversity in the Culture of Psychotherapy

It would take our imaginations, a few bad dreams, and a close look at our own lives and the lives of people we have both invited into our lives and stumbled across, to concoct a list of all the adverse situations that one could face in the course of a lifetime. The themes presented here do not have any one particular situation in mind. They are simply considerations synthesized from an assortment of contexts that are presented to provide a means for you to take an honest look at the emotional and therapeutic fallout that an individual who functions as a counselor should consider.

Adversity may come from the fallout of a historical trauma, it may be abrupt, or it may be ongoing, as in the case of a debilitating illness or in the management of the special needs of a loved one(s). One of most common considerations when undergoing adverse times is whether or not to take time off from work or school, and if so, how much (Gerson, 1996; Givelber & Simon, 1981; Morrison, 1997). The reality for many therapists is that they are in practice to sustain an income. Money and insurance are often, and sadly, at the heart of a decision to take time off regardless of how the therapist is holding up.

Another consideration is the issue of *when* to go back to work if, in fact, time off is taken. How do you *know* when you are ready? Some things in life aren't necessarily meant to stop hurting, or to become *less* challenging. Personal therapy is always an option, but sadly, Mahrer (1997) tells us that "Most therapists are not patients in continuous, lifelong therapy, nor do they seem to turn to therapists whenever problems seem hard to handle" (p. 2). If you are dealing with a debilitating illness, it's frightening not to know when another setback may occur, and the stress of going back to work may only exacerbate health concerns. We are not even sure that we can expect to truly know when we are ready, especially in cases where there is an enormity of caregiving demands in the therapist's life.

The experience of being immersed in a life trauma can cloud our judgment, and often, our deserved self-interest can get in the way of therapeutic work. It is necessary to note that some therapists may turn to work as an escape; even though they feel depleted and have nothing to give (Colson, 1995; Dewald, 1990; Figley, 1995; James & Gilliland, 2001; Tinsley, 2000). The therapist's self-care and emotional needs are often negated in an effort to prove one's competence and capabilities. Givelber and Simon (1981), two of the first writers on this issue, refer to this dynamic as the succumbing to "one's professional ego-ideal" (p. 142).

The need to present our expertise and competency in spite of difficult circumstances is in large part caused by our cultural value of "never let them see you sweat." In our culture, we are not generally socialized to freely attend to our own needs. If everything is right in our material world, we aren't supposed to "need." Being "needy" or "vulnerable" is undesirable and frowned on. The thought of a therapist being needy is almost taboo. There are times, however, when we are allowed to care for ourselves in the name of somebody else's well-being. Chasen (1996), after the death of her 12-year-old son Shaun, considered committing suicide. She was concerned with the impact her suicide might have on her clients, particularly on that of a young man she was seeing who had struggled with suicidal fantasies since childhood. She even worried about a failed attempt and confessed to buying a copy of Humphry's (1991) *Final Exit* to make sure she got it right. In the end, she decided against it: "Not a very good role model" (Chasen, 1996, p. 9).

In contrast to the dominant culture, the culture of our profession *does* warrant (and generally expects) that we take care of ourselves and exercise judgment that would be consistent, or ideally better, than what we expect of our clients. Paradoxically, we are seemingly expected to do so with little or no disruption to the therapeutic relationship. Given that, therapists often blindly continue work, having lost sight of their vulnerabilities. In some instances, the therapist may feel "more alone, or so humanly overwhelmed with fear, rage, or self-absorption and withdrawal as not to be able to optimally handle the impact on the self, much less on one's patients" (Morrison, 1997, p. 240). With this in mind, there are some things we'd like you to consider.

1. Your life circumstances, past, present, and future, may collide with those of your clients.
2. Given the severity of the trauma and the extent of the damage, you may need to make serious considerations about the client's course of treatment.

3. Your clients may feel trapped in the therapeutic relationship, unable to leave because they need to take care of you.
4. Your clients may sense you are ill, distracted, hurting, or depressed, even if you have chosen not to disclose your circumstances.
5. Your clients may feel guilty about getting better when they sense you are hurting.
6. You may have mixed feelings about getting better, when you sense *they* are hurting.
7. You may feel concerned that your healing (or lack of healing) is off course and in full view of your clients.
8. If circumstances warrant that you do share information, your clients may feel guilty about the nature of their own issues, given the severity of yours.
9. You may feel moved at the love and concern your clients show you in the face of their own pain.
10. Your clients may not care what happens to you, for the moment, and may ask *not* to be told.

To best gauge your functioning, take stock of how your loved ones and colleagues are experiencing you. Do you seem to be yourself? If not, what are they noticing different about you and how can you best attend to this? These questions can serve to guide the therapist who may be struggling with balancing professional work with personal adversity. Jim's story, as presented in the following paragraphs, illustrates the complexities involved in such a challenge.

Jim is a counselor and the director of clinical services for homeless individuals. This past year he was diagnosed with a rare and potentially fatal blood cancer, a low-grade B-cell malignancy called Waldenström's macroglobulinemia. At the time of our interview, he had two treatments of chemotherapy left to complete. During treatment his physical appearance had dramatically changed because of hair loss and weight gain from steroids he has had to take. Jim is often unaware of the degree to which he has changed (besides the obvious hair loss that, according to him, was thought to be a fashion statement by some of the individuals he serves) and relies on the support and feedback of his colleagues to help him gauge how his appearance may impact his clients. He shared how he and his colleagues have developed a culture of mutual care by stating:

> This is hard work. There is a lot of trauma involved. What we have done to take care of ourselves is to give ourselves permission to say what we are thinking. I discuss my illness in staff meetings and I ask, "Okay, what do you see that clients are going to see?" Of course, the hair was the first thing, and they also shared that I looked a little more stooped. They know

me like a book because we've worked together for a long time. They can tell by looking at me when I'm having a bad day. Certainly this is adversity, but it's an empowering thing to have so many people, even those that work for me, to be so authentic with me.

Jim's adversity is physically evident. As such, the adversity can be handled in various ways. By his account, his condition is freely discussed in staff meetings and with clients as needed. A byproduct of this experience seems to be the authenticity and freedom with which he is able to relate to others. This freedom does not come easily to all helping professionals. Indeed, self-disclosure of adverse situations by therapists is commonly fraught with feelings of shame and fear. Making the choice to self-disclose within a therapeutic context can be intimidating.

☐ The Debates on Boundaries and Self-Disclosure

Exploring issues related to self-disclosure is complex and difficult. These difficulties are confounded in that the issue of therapist self-disclosure historically has been the subject of much debate. Indeed, self-disclosure within a professional context is identified as an ethical issue, and discourse on the ethics of any professional practice can be highly charged. Terms such as ethics, boundaries, competing needs, and self-disclosure are heated in that they are integral to a clear (albeit black and white) understanding of the terms of a therapeutic (ethical) relationship (Colson, 1995; Craig, 1991; Greenspan, 1986, 1995; Lazarus; 2000; Miller, Jordan, Steiver, Walker, Surrey, & Eldridge, 1999; Morrison, 1997). Conservative guidelines suggest that therapist anonymity is best for the client (regardless of the theoretical orientation) and communicates a covert message that should a client ask, or be curious of any personal circumstances of the therapists' life, adverse or otherwise, there is something wrong with the client's understanding of the process.

Our feeling is that many individuals seek therapy to enhance their relational capacities and that by "ignoring the obvious," we are teaching people how to stay out of their emotional lives and how to ignore their needs. In this context, the stance of anonymity, often in the name of "maintaining a boundary," is not only unhelpful; it is also shaming, oppressive, and has the potential to be abusive.

Miller et al. (1999) suggest that we rethink the notion of boundaries so that when redefined, they can be seen as a place of meeting rather than the drawing of a line. Thinking of boundaries as *a place of meeting* serves to diminish the risk that boundaries will be communicated in a condescending context. Boundaries, in this philosophy, communicate an essence of "safety, clarity, and privacy" in a "context that holds some promise of mutuality" (Miller et al., 1999, p. 4). Authenticity and thus, self-disclosure, are useful in allowing both the therapist and client to represent themselves in ways that *keep the process moving* (Miller et al., 1999).

These disclosures are not (as disclosures are often thought to be) reckless. Rather, the process of such disclosures communicate a deep respect for how difficult it is for clients to trust, much less heal, in a relationship where they may feel unsure of the well-being of the person who is meant to help them. We also want to communicate a deep appreciation and respect for the complexities and dilemmas therapists face in making decisions to acknowledge or share some aspect of personal adversity, seen or unseen.

While reviewing the literature for this chapter, we came across a very helpful, yet perplexing book that addresses this issue. Although the content was interesting and on target, the title was *Beyond Transference: When the Therapist's Real Life Intrudes* (Gold & Nemiah, 1993). To intrude, according to Webster's dictionary, means to "to push or force, without invitation or permission" or "to come in inappropriately or rudely" (Mirriam-Webster Online, 2002). Clearly, the inherent message is: Adversity is something that we should consider, but don't forget that the life of the therapist is something very different from the life of the therapy. When things go wrong in your life, things better stay the same in your work. Never mind that the life altering circumstances are experienced, in and of themselves, as "intruding."

In the more humanistic (versus psychoanalytic) literature, the nature of adversity or "temporary emotional imbalance" (Emerson & Markos, 1996, p. 111) is treated more kindly. Involuntary self-disclosure with regard to adversity is addressed with more understanding and tolerance. Yet, with this understanding comes a dangerous message to the therapist that, at some point, they must "get over it." Emerson and Markos (1996) write that "One needs to watch, however, for the temporary impairment that, if not handled through counseling, time off, or other remedies, becomes part of the counselor's habitual behavior" (p. 112). In our view, the nature of adverse circumstances does not warrant a "getting over." Life-altering situations change the life of the therapist, the person of the therapist, and the life of the therapy. Healing, whatever form it takes, is and should be, a habitual behavior.

The ways in which disclosing personal adversity is handled in the therapeutic context depends on many factors. The issues that came up repeatedly in our interviews and in the literature review were the theoretical orientation of the therapist as well as their degree of acceptance of personal vulnerability in the therapist. Both of these factors attributed to the therapist's sense of openness and comfort in making decisions regarding disclosure, as well as the timing of such disclosure.

Miriam Greenspan (1986), one of the pioneer writers on the therapeutic benefits of self-disclosure, describes her experience of losing her infant son while being a therapist. To engage in her work, she needed to engage as a person, complete with vulnerability, tears, and suffering. She noted, "I think that most of my clients were surprised to see that I could cry about my son and then move on with the work of being their therapist; that it was possible to be this vulnerable and this strong at the same time. . . . In most cases, my vulnerability led them to make breakthroughs in exposing their own" (Greenspan, 1986, p. 15).

Carter Heyward (1999) later describes this dynamic of mutual care in *When Boundaries Betray Us* by sharing that:

> If therapy is a process that helps folks learn to be more fully present in the world, more fully ourselves, why would a client not expect her therapist to engage questions drawn from deep within her soul? It was to me spiritually essential that, in therapy, I be part of a mutually transformative process, not plopped on a couch in front of an "automatic teller" that had been programmed in medical school to be kind and empathic. I believed then, and believe even more now, that all psycho spiritual healing—not some, all—is steeped in unpretentious, honest, relational participation in which we share stories and experiences; compare notes and notice differences; disagree, collide, and compromise; seek ways through impasses; and are delighted, sad, sorry, and excited *with* one another. (p. 69)

Greenspan (1986), again, in her earlier writings, set the stage for this discussion. She distinguished between a client's therapeutic experiences with a distant therapist from that of a personal therapist. She observed that a distant therapist could elicit anger from clients by being emotionally withholding, whereas a personal therapist could trigger a client's fear of intimacy by emotionally gratifying some of the client's needs for inclusion into the experience of the therapist. She noted, "Working with a client's responses to my self-disclosures is one of the best ways I know for working through the client's fears of closeness in a relationship" (Greenspan, 1986, p. 16).

We have found that to be the case. Each of us has struggled with issues of adversity and self-disclosure in recent years. We have also had to weigh the consequences of disclosing versus nondisclosing difficult aspects of our lives with our clients and students. In some cases, we handled these situations with congruence and authenticity. In other cases, we felt clumsy, awkward, and even inept. In either case, we had nothing to draw on from our educational experiences to guide us in making these decisions.

☐ Challenges of Therapeutic Self-Disclosure

In a paper on empathy and shame, Jordan (1997) makes a plea for authors writing about therapy "to please say what is happening in the therapy relationship, not what theory prescribes or what sounds smart or clever or theoretically informed" (p. 153). As students make their way into the mental health profession and struggle with developing a sense of competence and identity, they do so with a backdrop of academic training that may not prepare them to speak freely of their uncertainties or mishaps (Kottler & Blau, 1989). This owes, in part, to shame-based supervision, texts that do not and cannot adequately address the elusive relational factors at work in the therapy process, and the simple reluctance of noted professionals to discuss their mistakes in therapy, much less the impact their lives have had on the therapeutic process (Jordan, 1997).

Rigid ideals regarding self-disclosure are typical of most traditional training programs. As such, a discourse on the topic of the "therapist's adversity" as the actual process is neglected and practically taboo because this "impact" is not supposed to exist. If, in fact, it does, it is debatable whether or not you are doing good therapy (Philip, 1993). Many mental health professionals are taught that they can and should "check their lives at the door" so as not to be distracted from their clients' needs. In many ways, the issues of the therapists' self-care and the care of the client are often viewed as separate and mutually exclusive. In fact, Western cultural ideology is reflected in many models of psychotherapy that promote the development of the bounded, separate, autonomous self as a healthy and desired goal of human growth and development. In this model, the meeting of the "different" lives of the therapist and the client is thought of as a reckless collision rather than a complex and fluid asset to mutual growth (Greenspan, 1995; Heyward, 1999; Katzman, 1994; Miller et al., 1999).

Unless the issue of "adversity" informally makes its way into a student's training, there is little or no preparation for dealing with personal life crises in the therapy relationship (Kottler & Hazler, 1996; Morrison, 1997). Instead, a heavy emphasis is placed on nondisclosure, which leaves both students and professionals with no models of how to integrate their personal and professional identities. Therapists experiencing adversity are in conflict with the "mythical supertherapist ideal." For a better exploration of the complexities of adversity, we'd like to invite you to look at your views regarding self-disclosure and vulnerability. For seasoned professionals, it may be helpful to reflect on how your attitudes have changed (if at all) over time. Explore your attitudes using the following questions as a guide.

1. What do you feel is appropriate self-disclosure?
2. How much disclosure is too much?
3. What kind of self-disclosure do you see to be most useful?
4. What did your academic experience teach you about this issue?
5. What does it mean to be a "good enough therapist"?
6. How do "good enough therapists" handle adversity in their lives?
7. What did your respective socialization/culture teach you about how to manage your adversity?
8. What is it like for you to think of a therapist as "vulnerable"?
9. Have you ever experienced having your vulnerabilities exposed?
10. What was that experience like and how did you handle yourself?

Therapist self-disclosure of adverse life circumstances is an important therapeutic issue, which we feel should be addressed in the educational experience. The lack of guidance and practice in exploring issues of adversity could contribute to one of two therapist errors: the creation of a sterile detached environment, or inappropriate or unhelpful therapist disclosure or involvement. Sadly, therapists who do decide to disclose certain aspects of their personal adversity often make these decisions without professional guidance or support. Lazarus (2000) suggests to educators and supervisors that:

> Rather than instilling a fear of lawsuits in our students and terrorizing them about the dangers of running afoul of licensing agencies, let us teach them how to navigate the complex issues of duality, intimacy, boundaries, individual ethics and personal integrity. Out of fear, too many therapists practice in a bizarre and dehumanizing way. Some therapists create such highly sanitized treatment environments that they lose sight of human and humane concern. Instead of producing frightened conformists, our training programs should focus on turning out caring and enterprising helpers who have the confidence to think for themselves. (p. 3)

By exploring issues of self-disclosure, educators and supervisors can engage students in a meaningful discourse about "authentic relating" and how it is an essential part of the therapeutic relationship. It also would be important to include in this discourse discussions about how myths associated with the "therapist image" impact our ability to address the therapist's adversity and vulnerabilities during training.

☐ Professional Identity: Competence, Failure, and Shame

By reviewing the personal reflections of therapists who have dealt with unspeakable adversity, by interviewing professionals in the field, and by revisiting our own experiences, we have identified a critical process of growth inherent in such an experience. In this process, we have an opportunity to redefine who we are, both as human beings and therapists, as we are transformed by life's challenges. As difficult as this process may be, there is a lack of contextual consideration of this issue in most therapist developmental models. In other words, these models do not address the complexities of professional identity in light of life adversity, or in light of the experience of a sudden onslaught of adversity(s).

The covert message to therapists-in-training, and professionals alike, under these circumstances, is profound. Read: *Handle yourself as a professional regardless of what happens to you in your life. If, through bad luck or bad karma, adversity arises in your life, do not allow it to affect your work. If, in fact, it does affect your work, know it's affecting your work and take time off. But take care not to take too much time off. The expectations of you, as a healer, are quite different from those of other human beings. The message is "Just handle it."*

What then, do we do with our professional identity when we have become, through nothing more than our own suffering, agents of both healing *and* pain? Kottler (1991) makes the point that "Most effective therapists present an image of someone who is genuinely likeable, who is safe and secure, and who is attractive and approachable" (p. 73). When this image is suddenly shattered, there is a shift in identity from "strong and healthy to vulnerable and ill; from caregiver to caregetter. For some, there are powerful feelings of shame in this loss and transformation" (Morrison, 1997, p. 238). We feel that these feelings are complicated by unrealistic expectations we have of ourselves as "human therapists" which, often sadly, begin in training experiences.

Many therapists, in spite of personal and professional expertise, often wonder if they're the best person for their clients. Jordan (1992) speaks to this by stating, "Because the work is difficult and often not immediately rewarding, there is much room for self-doubt or possibly shame, a secret belief that someone else would be better at this" (p. 153).

This shame is often exacerbated by social interactions. Miller and Ober (1999), with regard to losing a child, make the point that we often do not have the language to express the experience of this type of grief. There is "no name for the parent who loses a child, nor for the brothers and sisters of a child who dies, nor for the others . . . and no word for the state of having lost a child" (p. 19). In essence, an individual's experience may feel invalidated, minimized, or made invisible when we don't have words to name it. She goes on to suggest that our grief becomes more powerful when it is unspeakable, and that it remains "crouching in the shadows of our lives, unpredictable, a locus of rage, of despair, of fear, looking for an opportunity to be heard" (Miller & Ober, 1999, p. 21). This dilemma is inconsistent with the image most of us have of the "good enough therapist." We aren't routinely taught that good therapists can and do struggle with such painful distractions.

Because pain is a condition highly avoided in our culture, we are conditioned to grieve briefly, lest we make others uncomfortable, or even worse, lest we cease to be fun companions for others. It would make sense, then, that many people undergoing painful circumstances feel alone, isolated, and lost. The internal feelings we experience while in loss are so incongruent with the glitz of shopping malls, restaurants, and material life in general, that many of us feel like fish out of water during these times. And when one is a therapist, we have the added component of exposure and can subsequently feel as if we are in a fishbowl. Oftentimes, we are.

Clients can exhibit a myriad of responses to their therapist's losses. Some reactions, more than others, understandably evoke a heightened sense of shame in the therapist. Chasen (1996) shared that after the accidental death of her 12-year-old son Shaun, a female client who had been having difficulty conceiving abruptly quit therapy and "fled from my terrible situation, as if the death of my child could be 'catching'" (p. 7). Gerson (1996) disclosed that after her late pregnancy loss, some patients expressed "rage, fear, or disdain for me. Sympathy was replaced by pity, and I became a sign of danger to them, a reminder of chaos or a carrier of badness" (p. 61). She suggests that our client's feelings may be exacerbated in that they want therapy to take place "in a make-believe world devoid of birth, death, and tragedy" (Gerson, 1996, p. 60). When the reality of adversity strikes, some common consequences, for therapists and clients alike, are a shaken belief system and a challenge to faith.

☐ Lack of Hope: Loss of Faith

This challenge comes in many forms. For therapists undergoing adversity, acknowledging the degree of distress they face depends on the level of awareness they have and the coping strategies that they may employ. Such acknowledgment could also depend on the circumstances surrounding the adversity, the timing of the impact, and the hope for recovery. We imagine that if you are someone who is now immersed in the deep, lonely pits of adversity, you are well aware of what you are facing, and in fact, may be considering what hope awaits you at the end of this experience, if any.

Seeing light at the end of the tunnel is frustrated when adversity is philosophically approached by well-meaning others. Comments that are intended to be encouraging, such as "God never gives us more than we can handle" or "Time heals all wounds" are, especially soon after a death, usually dismissed as unhelpful, irritating and a sign of not understanding (Frantz, Farrell, & Trolley, 2001, p. 192). Such experiences can exacerbate a sense of disconnection in our personal relationships. These painful disconnections are often accompanied by a loss of faith.

Letty, a graduate counseling student, was dealt a hand of fate during her first internship when her mother was suddenly diagnosed with lung cancer. Three weeks later—in the throes of dealing with the shock of her mother's diagnosis, her health care, the demands of parenting and graduate school—she, herself, was diagnosed with breast cancer. Just 3 months later, her mother died. Now, 5 months after her mother's death, and her own surgery and chemotherapy, she writes:

> I feel so confused, as far as my faith is concerned. I used to believe in God and lately when I've written letters, I can't even write the words "God Bless You," like I used to. I feel like a hypocrite writing that phrase when I can't even go to church (as if going to church gave me the right to write "God Bless You" in the first place). I used to pray with my mom and my son and I don't know how to do that anymore. My core beliefs have taken a tremendous shaking. The very essence of who I am and what I believe has been challenged. I've always agreed with and often preached the saying that "life is change," but I never expected a full restructuring of my core foundation.

Sue Irsfeld (2001), in an article on the loss of faith, shared her feeling on these issues after losing her infant daughter, Rose:

> I wonder if anyone ever deliberately sets out on a journey of faith, or if it is simply a condition of life. Because life is a journey. Those who travel minus faith are frequently stunned by what they judge to be the randomness of events; no armor can protect them, no rainbow can uplift them. I know this is so, because for a time I traveled among them. . . . I lost so much that day. A life. A dream. A prayer. And God. Rather than accept a God who could allow such things to happen, I embraced the Great Nothingness, where nothing is hoped, so nothing can be lost. Where nothing can be expected, so nothing can disappoint. Where there is no one to blame when things go wrong. (p. 85)

For therapists dealing with a loss of faith, one must be cautious with the fallout of this experience. Do we have faith in the love and care of others? Do we have faith that we *will* move through adversity? Faith that we *can* be helped? And faith that we, as therapists, can help others? The light of hope and the restoration of faith do not serve to diminish the devastating and painful aspects of adversity: "Rather, they slowly and usually unexpectedly emerge as the dawn of healing replaces the lonely darkness of grief" (Frantz, Farrell, & Trolley, 2001, p. 192). Irsfeld (2001) closed her article, "Journey of Faith," by writing:

Faith is a mystery; it is a journey without a map. It unfolds like a rose, sometimes tightly budded, sometimes in full bloom. When you think it has withered, it sprouts somewhere else. When you think you've got it figured out, you discover a deeper layer of petals or a path you never knew existed. (p. 88)

A restoration of faith is one way in which people experience some healing following loss or adversity. Frantz, Farrell, and Trolley (2001) were interested in all the ways that people change following the death of a loved one. They interviewed 397 individuals who had been coping with bereavement issues for at least a year. A summary of *all* changes, both positive and negative, include:

1. A greater, and more active appreciation of the preciousness of life and relationships.
2. An increased sense of self-confidence by having demonstrated resilience in the face of such pain.
3. A deeper level of intimacy, connection, and affection in personal relationships.
4. An ongoing sense of depression, helplessness, and loneliness.
5. Coping often involved being able to, at times, be immersed in the grief, while paradoxically making constructive efforts to escape the pain (e.g., work, travel, keeping busy by meeting life's demands).

The majority of therapists who move through adversity in their lives report changes in their therapeutic connections. Such changes include:

1. An overall increased intensity of the therapeutic space
2. A heightened sensitivity to their clients' pain
3. A deeper appreciation for the perseverance their clients' have shown in the face of their own adversity
4. An increased experience of the toxicity in their clients (Gerson, 1996)

Mendelsohn (1996) reported that after the death of his terminally ill 11-month-old daughter, Anna, he "felt a new sense of conviction regarding the resilience and plasticity of the analytic relationship" (p. 26). Jordan (1992) notes that in spite of the growth that pain can bring, few who have been hurt by life's suffering would have chosen such a path. And yet, facing pain can lead one to a deepened sense of awareness of life's sacredness and to our need for others. It can also generate in us a desire to reach out to others and, ultimately, to be transformed by our own compassion.

Gerson (1996) adds that each crisis in our lives provides a backdrop for the experience and development of therapists as human beings. Our integration of these experiences directly impacts the relationship that we have with our clients and our willingness or ability to be with them during adverse times. In addition, our experiences with crises may deepen our perspectives and encounters with such existential issues as "freedom, responsibility, will, courage, choice, or limitation" (Gerson, 1996, p. xv). We are then given the gift of evolving feelings, thoughts, and behaviors that ultimately can be expressed within the therapeutic relationship, generating greater intimacy and growth for both patient and therapist.

☐ Doing Better Through Transformative Journeys

Loss provides an ultimate opportunity for personal transformation. But first, loss brings with it a vulnerability that few of us wish to acknowledge. Still, as we honor its presence and connect with each other through our losses, we have an opportunity to transform our experiences and "do better" with ourselves and each other. But the rulebook on how to be vulnerable while being the responsible party is blank where this is concerned. Or if not, it prescribes sterile, "appropriate" responses that we can only hope to be able to make. There are times when we must work outside the box and let the circumstances of each relationship write the rules. It is up to us to negotiate the complexity of needs and responsibilities that surround us. There are no easy answers. There are serious questions. Doing better means we must each come to terms with our choices and ultimately to find our own way. Some suggestions for therapists undergoing adversity include:

1. Be realistic about self-expectations and take an honest look at how much of this work you feel up to.
2. In light of your level of coping, you may need to take time off, limit your caseload, and/or refer new clients to other therapists.
3. If you continue to work through adverse times, it may be to escape. It may also be motivated by financial interests. It may also be that you are underestimating or denying how truly taxed you feel.
4. Seek reality checks from peers and loved ones. Ask and be open to how they are experiencing you. Much of what they see will be what your clients are seeing.
5. Be aggressive with self-care and don't take any feedback in jest (or even argue about it). Even though we are mental health professionals, we, like other human beings, are sometimes out of touch with what we need, be it time off, medication, hospitalization, therapy, or a long vacation.

6. Let people help you. It may feel awkward that you have elicited the care from others that you have been so accustomed to giving.
7. Never say "no" to friends or colleagues offering to provide child care, prepare meals, run errands, or simply sit with you. If you can't use the help in the moment, suggest a better time.
8. Ideally (although it is not always possible), be proactive. If you know how you'll be "hit" by something, work to get a safety net in place.

Doing better and improving clinical skills, in the context of adversity, means that we are honest with ourselves about our vulnerabilities. It also means that we develop an honest understanding of how our life circumstances and experiences continually shape our fluid identity, both personally and professionally. Doing better means letting go of shame in relation to vulnerabilities. In evaluating our sense of readiness to do the work of therapy—either in the midst of an ongoing crisis or at the tail end of one—Hartling et al. (2000) suggest that we ask ourselves, "What are the places of our own fear of exposure and sense of unworthiness? What do we value? What happens when clients seek to meet us psychologically where we feel most vulnerable?" (p. 11).

In the face of adversity, doing better sometimes means doing something different, something for us, whatever that may mean for each of us, respectively. Frantz et al. (2001) suggest that one way of dealing with grief (and in our opinion this goes for all adversity) is to seek a balance between facing it head-on and turning our backs to it for periods of time. This doesn't mean turning away from others, it means being with others in play, humor, recreation, nature, or meditation. Being with others who are open to a fluidity allows you to turn away from and back into adversity as needed.

Developing the ability to do this takes time and is dependent on where individuals are regarding the seasons of their career. With regard to adversity, Letty shares the wisdom she has gained in graduate school:

> I guess in a weird way, we're lucky, we counselors. We get to analyze ourselves while we're falling apart, and we also get to use the memories of our pain to understand our clients when they come to us in pieces. As for me, I now know what it feels like when someone says, "I felt like my whole world came crashing down." I think about the death of my mother and how it literally kicked me in the ass and hung me out to dry. In this profession, it appears that when adversity strikes, it's somewhat like attending a seminar on how to improve your therapy sessions, without paying hundreds of dollars for it. It's kind of funny or maybe just lucky for us, in a creepy sort of way.

Adversity is a reality of life, and we have many thoughts on the transformative growth process that can result from these experiences. Our sense is that, at every turn, we can "do better." Formal training or years of experience are not enough. It is clear to us that expertise can only come from the transforming experiences, beliefs, and worldviews that result from working through the relatively benign and more significant of life's adversities. We must engage our own lives if we are to be with others in theirs. Living life while being a therapist is paradoxical. It is a challenge. It is a privilege. It also can be a burden. It is ultimately a gift. The richness of our experiences, however light or dark, provides the context for our understanding, compassion, engagement, and commitment. It allows us to love and be loved. In that, there is no better form of self-care.

☐ References

Chasen, B. (1996). Death of a psychoanalyst's child. In B. Gerson (Ed.), *The therapist as a person: Life crises, life choices, life experiences and their effects on treatment* (pp. 3–20). Hillsdale, NJ: Analytic Press.

Colson, D. B. (1995). An analyst's multiple losses: Countertransference and other reactions. *Contemporary Psychoanalysis, 31*(3), 459–478.

Craig, J. D. (1991). Preventing dual relationships in pastoral counseling. *Counseling and Values, 36,* 49–54.

Dewald, P. A. (1990). Serious illness in the analyst: Transference, countertransference, and reality. In H. J. Schwartz & A. S. Silver (Eds.), *Illness in the analyst: Implications for the treatment relationship* (pp. 75–98). New York: International Universities Press.

Emerson, S., & Markos, P. A. (1996). Signs and symptoms of the impaired counselor. *Journal of Humanistic Education and Development, 34,* 108–117.

Figley, C. R. (Ed.). (1995). *Compassion fatigue: Coping with secondary traumatic stress disorder in those who treat the traumatized.* New York: Brunner/Mazel.

Frantz, T. T., Farrell, M. M., & Trolley, B. C. (2001). Positive outcomes of losing a loved one. In R. A. Neimeyer (Ed.), *Meaning reconstruction and the experience of loss* (pp. 191–212). Washington, DC: American Psychological Association.

Gerson, B. (1996). An analyst's pregnancy loss and its effect on treatment: Disruption and growth. In B. Gerson (Ed.), *The therapist as a person: Life crises, life choices, life experiences and their effects on treatment* (pp. 55–69). Hillsdale, NJ: Analytic Press.

Givelber, F., & Simon, B. (1981). A death in the life of a therapist and its impact on the therapy. *Psychiatry, 44,* 141–149.

Gold, J. H., & Nemiah, J. C. (1993). *Beyond transference: When the therapist's real life intrudes.* Washington, DC: American Psychiatric Press.

Greenspan, M. (1986, Summer/Fall). Should therapists be personal? Self-disclosure and therapeutic distance in feminist therapy. *Women and Therapy, 5*(2/3), 5–17.

Greenspan, M. (1995, July/August). Out of bounds. *Common Boundary,* 51–54.

Hartling, L. M., Rosen, W., Walker, M., & Jordan, J. V. (2000). Shame and humiliation: From isolation to relational transformation. *Work in Progress, no. 88.* Wellesley, MA: Stone Center Working Paper Series.

Heyward, C. (1999). *When boundaries betray us.* Cleveland, OH: The Pilgrim Press.

Humphry, D. (1991). *Final exit.* New York: Dell Publishing.

Irsfeld, S. (2001, May). Journey of faith. *O Magazine, 85/88.*

James, R. K., & Gilliland, B. E. (2001). *Crisis intervention strategies* (4th ed.). Pacific Grove, CA: Brooks/Cole.

Jordan, J. V. (1992). Relational resilience. *Work in Progress, no. 57.* Wellesley, MA: Stone Center Working Paper Series.

Jordan, J. V. (1997). Relational development: Therapeutic implications of empathy and shame. In J. V. Jordan (Ed.), *Women's growth in diversity* (pp. 138–161). New York: Guilford Press.

Katzman, M. A. (1994). When reproductive and productive worlds meet: Collision or growth? In P. Fallon, M. A. Katzman, & S. C. Wooley (Eds.), *Feminist perspectives on eating disorders* (pp. 132–151). New York: Guilford Press.

Kottler, J. A. (1991). *The compleat therapist.* San Francisco: Jossey-Bass.

Kottler, J. A., & Blau, D. S. (1989). *The imperfect therapist: Learning from failure in therapeutic practice.* San Francisco: Jossey-Bass.

Kottler, J. A., & Hazler, R. J. (1996). Impaired counselors: The dark side brought into light. *Journal of Humanistic Education and Development, 34,* 98–107.

Lazarus, A. A. (2000, September 15). Not all dual relationships are taboo; some tend to enhance treatment outcomes. The National Psychologist: The Independent Newspaper for Practitioners. Retrieved August 7, 2001, from http://nationalpsychologist.com/articles/art_v9n7_1.htm

Mahrer, M. R. (1997). How may the practice of psychotherapy be advanced by finding out how therapists deal with their own personal problems? *Psychotherapy in Private Practice, 16*(2), 1–10.

Mendelsohn, E. M. (1996). More human than otherwise: Working through a time of preoccupation and mourning. In B. Gerson (Ed.), *The therapist as a person: Life crises, life choices, life experiences and their effects on treatment* (pp. 21–40). Hillsdale, NJ: Analytic Press.

Miller, J. B., Jordan, J., Stiver, I. P., Walker, M., Surrey, J., & Eldridge, N. S. (1999). Therapists' authenticity. *Work in Progress, no. 82.* Wellesley, MA: Stone Center Working Paper Series.

Miller, S., & Ober, D. (1999). *Finding hope when a child dies: What other cultures can teach us.* New York: Simon & Schuster.

Mirriam-Webster Online. Retrieved January 1, 2002, from http://www.m-w.com/dictionary

Morrison, A. L. (1997). Ten years of doing psychotherapy while living with a life-threatening illness: Self-disclosure and other ramifications. *Psychoanalytic Dialogues, 7*(2), 225–241.

Philip, C. E. (1993). Dilemmas of disclosure to patients and colleagues when a therapist faces a life-threatening illness. *Health and Social Work, 18*(1), 13–19.

Tinsley, J. A. (2000). Pregnancy of the early-career psychiatrist. *Psychiatric Services, 51*(1), 105–110.

6
CHAPTER

Sherrill Wiseman
Carol Scott

Hasta La Vista, Baby—I'm Outta Here: Dealing with Boredom in Therapy

As mental health professionals, most counselors and therapists, along with their respective professional associations, claim the right to a fair degree of self-regulation. If we wish to practice as self-regulating and ethical counseling professionals, then it behooves us to accept both the responsibility and the challenge of ensuring that we are constantly monitoring and enhancing our competency to the very best of our ability. Active awareness, self-supervision, and continuing to learn new ways of being more effective at every level are all facets of "doing better" as counseling professionals.

One of the challenges we face as counselors is that of battling boredom, staying energized and engaged with clients for the duration of every therapy hour. There are few careers or professions that demand such unwavering stints of attention for such sustained periods of time. Most jobs or occupations allow for a multitude of infinitesimal breaks, a quick trip to the water cooler or washroom, a cup of coffee, a brief non–work-related phone call, a stretch, or a refreshing few-second stare out the window. But counseling requires a more or less continuous and disciplined focus, an unremitting attendance to someone else's problems, concerns, thoughts, and emotions for the entire time the client is with you. This attention is required client after client, session after session, week after week, and if you are fortunate and skilled enough to be successful, year after year.

It should come as no surprise that providing counseling or therapy may become overwhelming, repetitive, monotonous, and even boring at some point. Most counselors and therapists have had some experience with this burden of boredom, whether it's caused by their own physiological state, a mind overwhelmed by the concerns of so many, or a particular client's style of relating (Geller, 1994; Hamburg & Herzog, 1990; Kottler, 1993; Morrant, 1984). As counselors, we are expected to recognize and see to our own boredom and burnout. Corey suggests that our ultimate success in dealing any potentially ethical and/or competency-based issue will benefit from developing a problem-solving process. As part of that process and this discussion, we necessarily need to: (a) define the problematic issue of boredom from different perspectives; (b) recognize the "face" of boredom; (c) identify possible root causes of boredom; and (d) collect and evaluate solutions to boredom based on moral, ethical, and professional imperatives (Corey, Corey, & Callanan, 1998). In so doing, we can detail a series of steps to be taken on our way to becoming the best we possibly can be professionally.

☐ The Meaning of Boredom

Boredom has been defined as a form of aversion that arises from our dislike of some aspect of our experience (Goldstein & Kornfield, 1987). To reduce that aversion, we may separate or withdraw from any particular moment in time. Such a separation can create a void, an experience empty of interest, empathy, or stimulation. This void can be destructive if we experience the "nothingness" as aversive, and seek to fill it with distractions. In this way boredom can become a chronic way of negatively viewing and experiencing our world, or in a therapy session, our client. In the worst-case scenario, boredom may open the door to unprofessional or unethical behavior. This very "nothingness," however, can be both motivating and rewarding when we experience a moment of discovery within it. If in this separation or void we can begin to explore both the antecedents and the antidote to boredom, it may become a time when we are able do our best work (Kottler, 1993).

A therapist may experience and define boredom as an absence of personally relevant meaning, either in how she expresses herself through her work or in the goals she sets for herself professionally. Most of us can have no way of knowing what it is that we hope to contribute or achieve without developing a personal mission statement that identifies our own values and principles (Covey, 1990). The way we practice therapy needs to be congruent with who we are as individuals and who we have aspired to become professionally. Failing to take our authentic selves into the therapeutic process will likely distance us from both our clients and ourselves; therefore, it may result in a loss of interest in what we are doing, precipitating a state of boredom. Struggling chronically with boredom may well limit our future as therapists.

As well as having an existential reference and meaning, boredom also may be defined by delineating the very things that are not happening on an experiential level. One therapist, a seasoned veteran of thousands of sessions, said, "I'm not often bored, and if I am, I assume what that means is . . . nothing is happening." That's a fairly succinct cut to the chase. "Nothing happening," meaning nothing happening on an emotional or cognitive level: no tinder flash of empathetic understanding or rapport; no gut level revelation of emotion; no epiphanies for either client or therapist; no intensity, no tension of any kind (unless it's being able to steal a glance at the clock without the client seeing); no evocation of concern beyond the given on the therapist's part; no peaking of curiosity, sharpening of determination, or shared sense of satisfaction at solving a puzzle or having the pieces fall into place; nothing new to discuss; no increased clarity; no deeper understandings; no feeling of closeness or progress; nothing happening in the behavioral department; no different answers or maybe no answers at all to the questions, " If you don't want to be doing this, what do you want to be doing? With whom do you want to do it? Where do you want to do it? When and for how long do you want to do it? In what way do you want to do it?" Just a "we've been here, done this, got the T-shirt" kind of feeling. Now that's boring! "Nothing happening," just may say it all.

☐ Awareness: How Do I Know It's Boredom?

It may be easier to recognize the presence of the more intense and therefore interesting emotional states; for example, surprise, awe, enthrallment, concern (and also distain, anger, revulsion, attraction, or fear), than it is to recognize the state of boredom, which is essentially a state of losing interest, noxious though it may feel (Geller, 1994). Because of this, we need to be on the lookout for boredom as counselors and therapists. We need to be aware of how boredom manifests to each of us personally. It appears, according to the following testimonies, that the experience of boredom is a very individual thing.

One psychiatrist, dividing his time between the demands of hospital "inpatients" in the morning and a busy private practice in the afternoons, said, "I know I've reached the bored stiff point when I don't care what people are saying, it doesn't matter how much pain they are in. The patient might say to me, 'My whole family has just been wiped out.' And I would be saying something flippant inside my own head like, 'look on the bright side, your grocery bills will go down.' I just really don't care!"

One therapist comes to her awareness around boredom when she finds she has stopped listening to what the client is saying and has started talking to him or her in her own head, things she would never say out loud. "Do you know how boring you are? Say something! Do something! For god's sake!" Another therapist clued in to her own ennui when she felt herself "slipping away" during a session. She knew she was bored, she said, when she mentally started conjuring up a grocery list.

It's possible to recognize boredom in our behavior. One counselor felt it was a "time and clock thing." "I know I'm bored when I find myself looking at the clock every two minutes and each of those two minutes begins to seem like an hour."

Boredom may manifest physiologically and can be experienced as sleepiness or a profound fatigue, which may magically vanish with the next patient or client (or for bored clients, with the next therapist!) (McHolland, 1989). There probably isn't a man, woman, or child who hasn't experienced this symptom of boredom at some time in their life, described by yet another practitioner as "chicken head": " I must be falling asleep because my head starts to slowly fall to my chest and I find myself jerking it back up like a chicken pecking for feed."

We are no different than our clients inasmuch as we are our own best experts as to what we may be experiencing on an affective level. It requires that we first pay attention to the emotional state we happen to be in at any given time, and second that we explore the meaning we are giving those specific feelings. Coming to the awareness that we are bored may not be enough in and of itself, but it's an obvious and necessary preliminary before the cause and solution to boredom can be explored.

☐ Root Causes of Boredom: What It May All Be (or Not Be) About

A variety of causal agents are reputed to result in boredom for the therapist: a particular therapist's personality profile, which may require more stimulation than the average client can provide (De Chenne, 1988); the personality profile of the client who doesn't speak the therapist's language, preferring instead a diminished, tedious, or concrete style of relating and/or metaphorically impoverished speech (Geller, 1994; Kottler, 1993; Taylor, 1984); the presence of countertransference issues for the counselor or therapist, necessitating the emergence of denial-enhancing boredom (Altshul, 1984; Flannery, 1996; Kottler, 1993); the stultifying impact the environment itself can have, illustrated by one counselor's account, when it is so restrictive it leads ultimately to boredom from a dearth of creative opportunities; and finally, boredom as a result of the therapist's own physiological state of being stressed, fatigued, or over-whelmed by his or her own personal problems (Morrant, 1984).

☐ Boredom: As a Personality Profile for Both Therapist and Client

Many exit the psychotherapy profession as a result of the boredom that arises from failing to take themselves authentically into their work. Per-haps that is a risk for certain personality types. Conceivably, those thera-pists in need of high stimulation and excitement and their antithesis, those therapists in need of the safety of sameness and repetition, may be in greater danger of becoming bored.

Timothy De Chenne, in writing about boredom as a clinical issue for therapists, talks about the personality profiles of individuals who find cer-tain kinds of tasks boring. His theory seems to suggest that certain per-sonality traits, when found in constellation, predispose an individual to boredom when his or her job possesses monotonous aspects. The traits he refers to are: (a) an ongoing high need for action and stimulation; (b) an extroverted as opposed to introverted orientation; (c) a lack of opportu-nity to get needs met outside the job; and (d) the lack of ability needed to create or imbue those same tasks or jobs with the necessary stimulation (De Chenne, 1988). Although De Chenne doesn't specifically target the average therapist as one who would necessarily fit into a "low skill level" category, it's certainly possible to extrapolate.

Practicing the "art of understanding" often requires infinite patience and the ability to hear the same or similar stories over and over. The inevitability of accepting that what seems immediately obvious to you the therapist may in fact take the client a long time and many repetitions to truly grasp, internalize, and use. It makes sense that the less skilled, less creative, and/or more constrained by inexperience a therapist is, the greater the possibility that change may take longer. This could certainly be frustrating and boring to someone who has a customary, ongoing high need for action in every part of his or her life (or his or her client's life!).

De Chenne goes on to suggest a tentative link between the individual with an external orientation (in which he feels social extraversion plays a significant part) and susceptibility to boredom. Although he stops well short of saying "extraverted therapists beware," he does leave the reader with the cautious impression that the externally oriented personality may, under certain circumstances and when coupled with a "high degree of intrinsic activation," face greater challenges in staying energized and armed against ennui.

In addition, he purports that the therapist who struggles with unmet or frustrated needs both in and out of the therapy room will similarly require more in the way of rewarding stimulation than most clients can provide. It's a generally accepted theory that counselors whose lives are restricted and impoverished outside their role as therapist are less able to cope with clients who don't intrinsically generate interest with either their stories or their style. Conversely, it's thought that counselors whose lives are full and in balance and whose own issues are examined and dealt with, are less dependent on their clients to fulfill them, theoretically at least, should be more able to tolerate boredom in the therapy room (Altshul, 1984; Corey, Corey, & Callanan, 1998; Kottler, 1993).

People who consistently report strong feelings of boredom do not score well on tests designed to measure their creative ability at problem solving. Traits inconsistent with creativity include anxiety, rigidity, and low ego strength, lack of spontaneity, dependency, and overreliance on conventional attitudes. These same traits are also predictors of boredom (Schubert, 1978). Perhaps, when these traits are brought into the therapy room either by client or therapist, boredom for both ensues?

The therapist with a high need for safety and low stimulation may create boredom as she avoids change and growth by repeating the same therapeutic interventions over and over. This "one size fits all" school of therapy, which may also prevent her clients from being authentic and unique, may allow her to see them as boring. Her days as a therapist are routine and predictable. She relies solely on the techniques she learned as a student, especially those that are well represented by research. She rarely brings her intuitive creative self into a spontaneous intervention. Spontaneous and creative does not mean unethical or beyond professional standards, it just means thinking outside the box.

Some clients also leave their authentic selves at the door in an attempt to avoid risk. These clients may use a boring demeanor to keep their therapists at arm's length: the client who sits curled up passively in the same seat, in the same position every session, without much movement, with little affect; the client who speaks in a barely audible voice with little or no inflection and no excursions into passion for any reason; the client who repeats the same grievances over and over and remains closed to any apparent insight into his or her own role in relationship; the client who remains at a purely concrete or content level, "How do I feel?" (He or she responds to the question with confusion.) "With my fingers, of course!"

"Clients who appear chronically boring believe they are essentially unlovable and have discovered a very effective way to keep others at a distance" (Kottler, 1993, p. 153). Unconsciously or consciously using such a demeanor as an alienation technique prevents the very connection that the client believes on some level will inevitably be followed by rejection or abandonment.

To prevent boredom, a match between therapist needs and client needs for increased or decreased stimulation and for creative, spontaneous approaches or repetitive, constrained approaches may be necessary.

☐ Boredom: As a Form of Countertransference

Countertransference may be thought of as projection, feelings engendered in the therapist by some aspect of the client's style or mode of relating that may get in the way of practicing ethical and effective therapy. Corey feels countertransference becomes destructive when the therapist's own unresolved conflicts or unmet needs get tangled in the therapeutic relationship, thereby preventing objectivity (Corey, Corey, & Callahan, 1998). Boredom has a long and venerable history of being considered a defense mechanism conjured up by the therapist him- or herself to obscure issues that are cloaked in this form of countertransference because they are not consciously palatable (Altshul, 1984; Finnell, 1985; Kulic, 1985).

In exploring root causes of boredom, Kottler (1992, p. 129) concludes that there is merit in acknowledging, "We do tend to withdraw from those clients who do not meet our expectations. And we do have varying propensities for becoming bored, depending on whatever is going on (or not going on) outside the office." Boredom arising from issues that are largely "countertransferencial" and therefore therapist-generated may be the most difficult to diagnose, particularly in the moment:

> (*Carol*) My client was a woman in her late thirties, not well educated but very street smart. A compulsive talker who complained incessantly about how unappreciated she was by her husband, her teenage children, her family of origin and her friends. She droned on and on with no expression of affect other than her indignant rage. Rage centered on how much she did for them but how they all disappeared when she needed someone to talk to. Whenever I tried to interject, she would quickly say, "I'm not finished with this story yet!" and she never did finish! As this client talked (and talked and talked) she stimulated unconscious memories within me . . . myself as a teenage girl, sitting at the kitchen table, listening to my mother go on and on about how stupid and lazy everyone in her life was. Her attacks stopped only long enough to take another drag on her cigarette. If I tried to leave, "Mum, please, I have homework!" I would be ordered to sit down and "Just you listen! Someday you'll know what I'm talking about!" . . . In retrospect, I always found myself responding to this particular client with stifled yawns and a terrible sleepiness (of which she seemed to be completely unaware).

Amazingly, I wasn't sleepy at all in my next therapy hour with another client. If I had been able to uncover the meaning of my sleepiness at the time, I may well have dealt with it differently. Instead, I only pretended to listen. I lost all my empathy for this client just as I had ultimately lost all empathy for my mother. I was relieved when a few sessions later she pronounced herself "cured" and left therapy.

☐ Boredom: Countertransference as a Way to Avoid Cognitive Dissonance

Many of us have watched colleagues who have seemed to go from enjoying their work to gradual disinterest. Often we can observe this phenomenon accompanying a deteriorating intimate relationship outside the therapy room. It's hard to continue to enjoy your work when increasingly home life has become unsatisfactory, or worse, intolerable. Rather than face this discrepancy many will distance from their work as well, saying that now "work also feels boring."

Boredom as an escape from an unbearable discrepancy between what we feel and what we think we should be feeling is a theory supported by the literature on job burnout and boredom (Pines, 1996). A good relationship seems to be able to prevent job burnout. Perhaps this is because it allows us to feel congruent and contented at the office when we bring our real and authentically happy self to our therapy work. There may be guilt for the therapist who realizes she feels like a fraud in the therapy room because of the healing that has not taken place in her own personal life. Boredom may be a welcome escape from this dissonance.

☐ Boredom: As This Particular Form of Countertransference? NOT!

The literature abounds with psychoanalytically flavored notions that boredom is usually a result of countertransference issues in the therapist (Finnell, 1985; Flannery, 1996; Hamburg & Herzog, 1990). Boredom arises, it is theorized, to defend against unacceptable or threatening impulses and anxieties. Sexual feelings or material containing sexual themes are commonly implicated (Strean, 1993).

> (*Sherrill*) Possibly this is true for some. It's the antithesis of my own personal experience. Any time a frank or core discussion of sexuality or sensuality triggers a hint or whiff of sexual feelings in me it's as though every neuron in my brain snaps to attention. It's a package that's labeled "Fragile . . . Handle with Care!" Furthermore, having once been vaguely

propositioned by a client that, admittedly, I found attractive, boring is not exactly the term I'd use to describe the experience. Tiptoeing through a minefield, afraid at any moment it might go boom, is probably a more accurate description. The tension inevitably created, if my own experience was anything to go by, was hopefully and intentionally directed towards more deftly handling the situation by: normalizing any attraction in the light of the therapeutic relationship; complimenting the client on taking the risk to "put it on the table"; reiterating boundaries; and sensitizing myself to the possibility that this may have meant someone had messed with this client's boundaries somewhere, sometime before. I didn't do a lot of yawning, struggling to keep my eyelids open, clock watching or any other expression of boredom with which I'm familiar!

☐ Boredom: The Result of a Restrictive Environment

Sometimes jobs, even counseling jobs, may become boring not because of any intrinsic qualities of either counselor or client or even necessarily the dynamics between them but because the environment or the job itself may have a finite scope and possibility. Such a situation restricts the opportunity to stretch yourself or learn anything new to the point where boredom becomes almost inevitable.

One career counselor writes from this very circumstance, a small Northern Quebec reserve:

Career counseling is only part of my job and I'm totally bored with it—not just the career counseling but my whole job. There are a lot of routine tasks, paperwork and so on, that I have to do daily, and there is absolutely no creative outlet in this work, and that is what I crave. I had lots of it as a teacher, but very little as a counselor. Some people enjoy reliable routines, but I do not. For the first couple of years, as I was learning the job and its varied requirements, I found it satisfactorily challenging, and as it gradually became routine, I kept adding new tasks to my job to keep it demanding and interesting, but there is a saturation point where restrictions of time and energy prevent any additional duties being introduced and there are none that I can now eliminate or replace.

You must understand that career counseling is only a part of my work, and, here, it is extremely restricted because of living in such a remote area. There are a very limited number of jobs available to the people. The four main local employers are the band office, the school board, the health board and the construction company. A few people have started their own small businesses: car repair, video rentals, a hardware shop, and a little cafe, but they mostly employ family members. There is no industry or big business of any kind, and apart from going out on the land to continue the traditional pursuits of individual hunting, trapping and fishing, very few people have any interest in leaving the community to seek work elsewhere, so that leaves them little to choose from in the way of careers. Consequently, I am repetitively advising my clients on how to obtain training to operate heavy equipment (snow plows, backhoes, etc.), to become nurses, childcare workers and secretaries, or to start up small businesses.

I find it frustrating and boring, but until this region becomes more developed or more people are prepared to leave their homes, families, culture and language behind in this village to seek their fortunes in a city, there will be few changes in the opportunities available to the local people.

☐ And If You Hear Hoofbeats . . .

Morrant acknowledges the possibility that feeling bored and sleepy may be a result of a protective countertransference, but in addition he states

> Boredom and drowsiness can also be physiological; that late night; the madness of a martini at lunch time; a flattering attack of fashionable hypoglycemia. It can be due to one's mind being weighed down by personal problems that dwarf anything a patient can produce. Of course, if one heeds some of the charges leveled against one by one's spouse and offspring, one must admit one can be extremely boring one's self. (Morrant, 1984, p. 431)

☐ How "Real People" Supervise Themselves and Deal with Boredom

A truism derived from cognitive therapy states: "There is no event that has any meaning other than that which we give it." The meaning we give boredom, in all likelihood, determines the strategies we develop in order to deal with it and will probably change as we grow professionally in experience and confidence. Initially for many of us, being boring or being bored can carry a stigma not terribly dissimilar to masturbation. It's not something we want to be caught "doing" . . .

☐ Boredom: An Anathema for Both Client and Therapist

(*Sherrill*) It wasn't that I'd never expected to see him yawn. After all, I'd been a client of his, engaged in quasi-psychoanalytic therapy once a week for three years. Some small sign of inattention or faltering interest was only to be expected after that amount of discourse, especially since the bulk of the discourse was usually mine.

Given that he seemed determined to limit himself to the occasional thought-ful comment or question, it was perhaps inevitable that he would periodi-cally tire of the process before I did. And besides, being a fledgling therapist myself, I already knew how to defend against letting his human frailty get me where I lived. Without even thinking about it, I could say to myself, "His yawning says so much more about him than it says about you! After all, you don't know what's been going on in his personal life. Maybe his kids get him up at all hours. Maybe he was on call last night and had to go into the hospital, repeatedly. You don't have to take this personally! Just because he sat in front of you, yawning without shame or apology, doesn't necessarily mean he finds you uninteresting, dull, repetitive, and/or lack-ing the ability to intrigue or engage him."

However, all this insight, all this professional knowledge and objectivity couldn't stop me from instantly arching my eyebrow and inquiring, in a voice designed to freeze out all but the most exceptionally obtuse, "Do let me know if I'm boring you!" Fortunately we had very good rapport, so when he grinned back at me and replied "Don't worry, I will," I believed him . . . more or less. Unfortunately, owing to my therapeutic inexperi-ence and naivety, it crystallized in me a determination never to expose a client of my own to any similar moment of excoriating self-doubt. In short, I wasn't going to be caught dead yawning, not in a therapy session, not in front of a client! That's when I began perfecting the "Jaws of Steel."

In truth, there is no shortage of authors in the realm of psychotherapy promoting the idea that boredom is an anathema in the therapy room. One such author writes: "It wounds to be considered dull, that one acts like chloroform upon one's therapist" (Morrant, 1984, p. 431). If it's gen-erally considered socially unacceptable to communicate boredom and ennui, how much more profoundly damning is it be to communicate that professionally?

(Sherrill) My social self would certainly like to be unfailingly courteous and attentive at all times to all people. The reality is, apparently I'm not. Apparently I have an unparalleled ability to "check out" if a conversation turns to certain topics: the stock market, mutual funds, cars, underground sprinkler systems, the latest in computer technology . . . you get the pic-ture. I'm told my eyes glaze over and it's obvious I'm off somewhere in my own head. "Hasta la vista, baby! I'm outta here!" as my husband puts it. But if I was, and continue to be, embarrassed to be caught "checking out" socially, my neophyte therapist self was absolutely mortified to think, god forbid, I might ever let on to a client that I found their communication boring. Probably because I have always presumed most clients come with the unspoken expectation that they can count on their therapist, who is after all being paid for his or her attention, to be always empathetically interested in what they have to say.

In my earlier years of practice this appeared to be a huge dilemma. If the reality was that any therapist who stated he or she was never bored with any of his or her patients was either in denial or inexperienced (Flannery, 1996), while the expectation was that a therapist shouldn't show boredom "when we are bored or angry with a patient we usually castigate ourselves severely for such feelings and failings" (Morrant, 1984, p. 432), then obviously there was a resulting dilemma that dictated I had better find a way to ensure that I could professionally mask what I was personally feeling. Hence, the "Jaws of Steel!"

Desperate to be seen as a compassionate and interested therapist, and to avoid looking bored at all cost, I found that it was physically possible, if I slid my lower jaw forward while pulling my tongue up to the back of my throat and simultaneously clenching my lower and upper jaws really hard about an inch apart, to stop a yawn in its tracks. At the same time, this meant that the cords stood out on my neck like granny veins and my nostrils flared like a bull in heat, but . . . at least I wasn't yawning! So intent was I not to manifest boredom, that it never occurred to me my "Jaws of Steel" might not be so discrete and might in actual fact be far more alarming for my client to witness. That is, until one day a client actually leaned forward and, with a quizzical look, enquired, "Are you in pain?"

It was to be several years down the road, a fair bit of experience and a lot of really excellent supervision later, before I could straighten out the confusion between what was appropriate socially when it came to being bored, and what was legitimate, useful and possibly even ethically mandatory in therapy.

☐ Boredom: What Constitutes an Appropriate Approach?

Most of us, while doing our obligatory stint in graduate school, didn't receive any direct or deliberate instruction on how to deal effectively with our own boredom. Consequently, when feeling bored we may assume the appropriate strategy is to politely ignore it, deny it, hide it, or try to get rid of it by getting rid of the client! It's not surprising that rather than proactively approaching boredom with specific strategies, many of us just react. Outright denial may or may not do the defensive trick for some.

When a client expresses negative feelings toward her or his therapist, the therapist can draw on a rich repertoire of strategies to deflect or discredit the client's feelings. For example, when one client confronted his psychoanalyst for falling asleep in one session too many, the clinician broke his usual pattern of evasiveness with a blunt denial. "What were you doing then?" his client asked. "Because you were making this snoring noise and, look, there's a spot of drool on your necktie." (Russell, 2001, p. 3)

One clinician felt as long as he adhered to a 90-day rule he could stave off mind-numbing boredom. This meant that every 90 days he had to take a week off. He related that if he goes past the 90-day mark he finds himself thinking aggressively. "I can handle coming out of a session and fantasizing about yelling at a patient," he said, "but when I come out of a session fantasizing about physically assaulting them, I know I've gone over the 90-day mark. I walk over to my secretary and tell her to book me off for a week."

Another common defense against the client felt to be unalterably and chronically boring is the therapeutic equivalent of the "Golden Hand-shake." It may be done with the absolute best of intentions. It may be done when session after session is experienced as boring and distancing. It may be done bearing in mind the fiduciary nature of the counseling contract. But when nothing productive is happening and no apparent progress is being made, many therapists, in reacting either to sheer frustration or to ethical concerns, do what they can to move the client out or on to another therapy arena. And this may happen in spite of the fact that the client appears to be willing to go on paying for sessions ad infinitum.

Most counselors committed to the idea of being change agents are loath to act merely as paid babysitters. "For example, therapist Kathleen White declared that when she doesn't 'feel connected' with a client after two years, 'I try to get them out. I can't bear it.' How does she do this? 'I don't pick up on their signals,' she explains, 'I don't say, "Oh, you poor baby,"' when they want me to. . . . And then they leave'" (Russell, 2001, p. 3).

> (*Sherrill*) One of my earlier solutions with a client, who came month after month with the same non-varying litany of complaints and no apparent interest in changing either his cognitive framework or his behavior, was to move him on to group therapy. Often group is a very reasonable and logical progression for clients. But if I'm going to be scrupulously honest, with this particular person, I know I was hoping that "the group" would confront him, as well-run groups are wont to do, with the absolute boring tedium of his solidly "help-rejecting" process. At the time I was apparently unable, for whatever reason, to do so myself.

Diana Russell in "Intimacy for Sale" puts forward the idea that most therapists are "consummate actors," obliged to "feign interest" and "stifle our yawns" even when we are really bored silly (Russell, 2001). But what if we are not really obliged? What if feigning interest and stifling yawns isn't really in the best interest of either therapist or client? What if this often socially acceptable manner of dealing with grinding boredom isn't particularly useful, or even if scrutinized carefully, particularly ethical when applied to the counseling process? If one believes, in the best of worlds, that the therapist-to-client relationship strives to model authenticity and congruency, doesn't feigning interest just perpetuate a false and inauthentic status quo?

> (*Sherrill*) I think it's possible (and even possibly probable) that for all the years when I "put up with" what felt like very boring sessions I was really protecting myself. I think the thought of naming boredom as boredom was frightening because I was sure it would result in hurting the client's feelings. Not only did I pride myself on having the rep of being "A Very Nice Person Who Doesn't Go Around Hurting Other People's Feelings," but hurt people can and often do lash out. The last thing I wanted was to be the target of some client's angry fallout.
>
> I had to be challenged directly in supervision and a significant part of my helping paradigm examined and retooled before I could see my way clear to a different approach. I had to be guided to a place of realizing, that giving the client honest, congruent and relevant feedback on his or her behavior was probably in the client's best interest. If you believe, and I do, that a client's behavior is always purposeful, whether conscious or unconscious, and that the behavior, over time, mirrors their style of being with others, actually naming the "B-word" opens up the possibility of exploring how being boring serves the client. Additionally, it gives the client important information on how his or her behavior may be impacting others. To withhold this information may deprive the client of the very information he or she may need in order to have the leverage and motivation to change.
>
> Undoubtedly, good timing and creating safety within the therapeutic relationship so that your client can trust that your feedback is given only with the intention of being helpful is critically important. It took a certain amount of fortitude but the first time I actually told a client that I was experiencing the time we spent together as boring, she merely smiled wryly and said, "I know, I've heard that before." It wasn't nearly the conflagration I'd been bracing for and not long after, as we began to explore what being boring did for her (and it was doing a lot!), I found myself being altogether fascinated!

If it's the situation, rather than personal or interpersonal dynamics that is being experienced as boring, some solutions might be (again, from the hinterlands of Quebec):

> What do I do to combat the boredom now that I've found there are no new challenges to add? I try to concentrate on enjoying the people that I work and deal with, I take care of the routine tasks with the minimum of fuss, and I indulge my creativity as much as possible in my free time. I plan to do this for another year and a half (seeing light at the end of the tunnel is an enormous help) then take early retirement and concentrate on writing. If I can't make any sort of living at that, then I'll look for another job, perhaps part-time teaching in continuing education.
>
> Another thing that has helped me is twice taking a whole year off. We have a deferred salary program where we can work for three years at 3/4

salary and then take a year off at the same rate of pay. It's wonderful!! For 3 years, it gives you something to look forward to, and the year off is extremely refreshing. The first time I did it, I dreaded coming back to work, but except for the few days it took to readjust to a nine-to-five routine, I found that all those minor irritations that were driving me to distraction before the sabbatical suddenly seemed negligible. It's the perfect way to avoid boredom and burnout.

In a lighter vein, the following suggestions come from therapists who have confronted tedium and monotony head on and have come up with some creative and useful ways to up the ante in the fight against boredom.

One therapist uses puppets in what is essentially a Punch and Judy type of puppet show, for couples who tend to repeat the same arguments over and over without much understanding of how they sound. Taping a boring session is also a possibility, having the client listen to herself and come to her own awareness probably has more impact and is possibly more palatable than doing the confronting yourself.

Another therapist takes her clients for "walk and talk" therapy when she knows she has a predictably boring session coming up. "That way" she says, "I know we'll end up with circulating endorphins and if nothing else is accomplished we'll both end up feeling better!"

Still another therapist switches to different learning modes. "I do psychoeducational teaching about say, the physiological effects of anxiety or depression, rather than just continuing to conduct the usual therapy routine. I may use diagrams, flow charts, pictures or cartoons to illustrate what I'm talking about."

One counselor advocates giving written homework, or quizzes and questionnaires to clients to promote at least some activity and provide more structure and stimulus for thought and discussion.

In an entirely different approach, one counselor looks to making her environment more stimulating. She makes sure her session room contains meaningful pictures and personal tokens. Although these tokens may be meaningful only to her, they provide a temporary visual focus and a momentary respite from a boring session.

One suggestion to ameliorate a state of chronic boredom on the therapist's part was to take on a student for supervision. "It pushes you to become more knowledgeable and it's hard to be bored when you are learning something new."

In the same vein, another proposal was to go to workshops, read books, or learn some new form of therapy; body work, art therapy, music therapy . . . it was felt that even if you didn't want to become a specialist in that particular area, it would be rejuvenating to learn about some new therapeutic form and it would be useful even if you just took away one or two new ideas.

In the specific instance where a client has become stuck on some circular argument and it's going round and round ad infinitum, one therapist, a firm believer in the mind–body connection, stops the process by administering an "allergy test."

> For example, if I have client that has been vacillating for a long, long time whether or not to leave an unsupportive relationship, and it's getting tedious, I have the client write down three competing beliefs on separate pieces of paper. The first belief might be "I am a complete and healthy, happy and whole person on my own" the second something neutral, "I need to go shopping"; and the third "I need this relationship in order to be complete and happy." Then I have the client hold each piece of paper in turn, in an outstretched hand and think about it while I press down on her arm. It's usually visibly evident when the statement that is an accurate reflection of her own inner truth is held, because then her arm will have the strength to resist my downward push. When she's holding the neutral statement it will dip a little and when she holds the unhealthy or untrue statement her arm will have no strength and will dip right down. Seeing a visible demonstration of this is pretty mind-blowing for most clients and more interesting than just continuing to discuss the usual pros and cons.

One counselor believes that altering her own schedule; coming into work later in the day, taking longer for lunch, going home sooner, or taking long weekends is her best answer to what might be an otherwise boring schedule.

One suggestion that comes up over and over again is,

> If you want to liven things up, get things going in another direction, then get the client to speak in a different voice, either literally or metaphorically. If he normally whispers make him shout. If he is boring as a client make him switch "chairs" with you. Let him be the "therapist." You be the "client." Let him see what it's like to struggle with boredom!

☐ Solutions to Boredom: What the Experts Suggest

Solutions to boredom have been researched since the inception of the profession. Much of what has been written is still cogent and relevant. The following excerpts contain a representation of the most "tried and true" remedies to boredom from the therapist's perspective.

Altshul (1984) suggests some timeless solutions to combat boredom. He recommends therapy for the therapist in order that he or she might get a handle on dealing with unmet needs outside of the therapy session. He promotes the idea of the therapist working to bring balance to his or her own life so that whatever needs arise will be met in an appropriate way and place. Additionally, he suggests a cognitive reframe whereby, as therapists, we remind ourselves that we are doing the most interesting work known to "reflective man" and that we are undoubtedly meeting many of our own unconscious needs by choosing to do this kind of work in the first place.

De Chenne has similar views to Altshul. "Certainly when therapists experience widespread boredom in both their professional and personal lives, the operation of defense seems strongly implicated. In this case clinicians would be well advised to seek out personal therapy in an effort to explore the origin of their ennui." He also recommends supervision and consultation. "A third party can be enormously helpful in disentangling the web of contributing factors" (De Chenne,1988, p. 80).

Morrant also prescribes being in balance and "on one's game." "It is appropriate to buoy up one one's physical health with proper holidays, exercise, food and sleep. It is also appropriate to ensure one's personal life is as emotionally, socially and sexually enriching as possible—I dare say, a tall order. It helps to have some 'physical' hobbies from skiing to sculpture, and preferably with a group of people who have nothing to do with psychiatry." And last but not least, coffee and jokes! "When free coffee was supplied to mental health clinics in Czechoslovakia therapists were artificially enlivened and sessions with clients were more stimulating." And where appropriate . . . "Can one step gently down from an unwanted pedestal by using kindly humor with the sense of proportion and creativity that it brings?" (Morrant, 1984, p. 433).

Basch advocates battling boredom actively: "Don't permit yourself to sink into sullen passivity. Become active with the patient. Search for what might be going on, if you don't know already. Don't hesitate to hypothesize out loud about what might account for the patient's silence, his aimless drifting or his recital of seemingly insignificant details" (Basch, 1980, p. 102).

Kottler recommends focusing on the reality that every client is a unique individual and processes even seemingly common problems in his or her own unique way; that whether or not it appears blatantly obvious at first, each client encounter holds the potential for us to learn something new about our own personal growth. He recommends taking on challenging cases and working with skilled supervisors so that we are continually challenged and refreshed by new learning and different perspectives; and finally, he offers the reassuring belief that it is eminently possible to keep boredom "at bay" if we are prepared to work consciously and creatively (Kottler, 1993).

☐ Conclusion

It is largely up to the therapist how the boredom that is (likely) experienced by both therapist and client will be addressed. Boredom can be a reason to jettison either the client or the field of psychotherapy altogether. Boredom can be a symptom, red-flagging the state of the therapeutic union. Boredom can be a diagnostic tool, allowing a differential diagnosis to take place: Is the boredom acute? Just today? Just with this client? Or is it chronic, a state of the therapist's mind or world over the long haul?

Boredom can be the thin edge of the wedge into the client's experience, providing clues to both therapist and client as to why the client may be having the very difficulties he or she is having. Boredom can be the instrument through which the therapist is able to reach and impact the client in such a way that awareness and connection take place and change is effectively facilitated. Finally, boredom can be an opportunity, the means by which client and therapist together can stretch their awareness, understanding, creativity, skill, ability, and compassion.

☐ References

Altshul, V. A. (1984). The so-called boring patient. *American Journal of Psychotherapy, 31,* 535–545.

Basch, M. F. (1980). *Doing psychotherapy.* New York: HarperCollins.

Corey, G., Corey, M. S., & Callanan, P. (1998). *Issues and ethics in the helping professions.* Pacific Grove, CA: Brooks/Cole.

Covey, S. R. (1990). *The 7 habits of highly effective people.* New York: Simon & Schuster.

De Chenne, T. K. (1988). Boredom as a clinical issue. *Psychotherapy, 25,* 71–81.

Finnell, J. S. (2001). Author's forum http://www.ippnj.org/finell.htm The Institute for Psychoanalysts and Psychotherapy of New Jersey. (Reprinted from: Finnell, J. S. (1985). Narcissistic problems in analysts. *International Journal of Psychoanalysis, 66,* 4330.)

Flannery, J. (1996). Boredom in the therapist: Countertranference issues. *British Journal of Psychotherapy, 11,* 536–544.

Geller, J. D. (1994). The psychotherapist's experience of interest and boredom. *Psychotherapy, 31,* 3–16.

Goldstein, J., & Kornfield, J. (1987). *Seeking the heart of wisdom.* Boston: Shambhala.

Hamburg, P., & Herzog, D. (1990). Supervising the therapy of patients with eating disorders. *American Journal of Psychotherapy, 44,* 369–380.

Kottler, J. A. (1992). *Compassionate therapy: Working with difficult clients.* San Francisco: Jossey-Bass.

Kottler, J. A. (1993). *On being a therapist.* San Francisco: Jossey-Bass.

Kulick, E. M. (1985). On countertransference boredom. *Bulletin of the Menniger Clinic, 49,* 95–112.

McHolland, J. D. (1989). Client-therapist boredom: What does it mean and what do we do? *Psychotherapy Patient, 3,* 87–96.

Morrant, J. C. (1984). Boredom in psychiatric practice. *Canadian Journal of Psychiatry, 29,* 431–434.

Pines, A. M. (1996). *Couple burnout* . New York: Brunner-Routledge.

Russell, D. E. H. (2001) Intimacy for sale. FEAR US/Psycho Oppression, from http://www.fearus.org/psycho.htm

Schubert, D. S. (1978). Creativity and coping with boredom. *Psychiatric Annals, 8,* 74–82.

Strean, H. S. (1993). *Resolving counterresistances in psychotherapy*. New York: Brunner/Mazell.

Taylor, G. M. (1984). Psychotherapy with the boring patient. *Canadian Journal of Psychiatry, 29,* 217–222.

7
CHAPTER

Jesse Brinson
Joseph M. Cervantes

Recognizing Ethnic/Racial Biases and Discriminatory Practices Through Self-Supervision

How does one recognize one's own biases and racism? This dilemma is one that any sensitive and introspective individual would want to entertain, particularly if that person practices as a professional helper. The following set of assumptions suggests particular values that apply to most mental health practitioners: born and raised in the United States; growing up in predominantly homogenous or multicultural neighborhoods, familial and community socialization that supports varying levels of racial identity, understanding, and integration (i.e., being educated and socialized with people from either similar or dissimilar racial and cultural backgrounds). The following example by the second author (JMC) provides a perspective into the often hidden dynamic that is prevalent when one is caught off guard to either spoken or unspoken biases in one's professional work.

> John and Mary Anderson are a Euro-American couple who, along with their two adolescent children, James and Perry, were seen for family counseling as the result of the boys' recent experimentation with drugs and alcohol. At the start of the first counseling session, the parents were overtly surprised that they had been referred to a professional who was not Euro-American and who they suspected may not be as competent to help their family situation. These remarks were implied by the parents, who stated directly to the provider (JMC) in this case several initial questions regarding

competency that included schools graduated from, level of training, and experience with adolescents. These comments were made following their brief disclosure that their housekeeper who happened to be a woman of Spanish-speaking background and who spoke little English, seemed to have minimal awareness of their family needs and appeared to not understand instructions in their day-to-day interactions. It became obvious during the first session that those feelings were being transferred over to the family therapist, and could prove to be a major issue in the development of therapeutic trust. It was important to recognize the series of feelings that were accumulating for this writer in the introduction of this family to the counseling process. Feelings of discrimination, cultural entitlement, and ethnic and cultural bias were interwoven narratives in my personal reactions to this family. The first session ended professionally with a resolve to look at specific areas of concern for their two disruptive adolescent boys.

Following some personal reflection and consultation in light of the feelings that had been engendered with the first counseling session, a second session followed primarily with parents to gather background history and information. This second session proved to be a major turning point and learning for myself, who realized that several inaccurate assumptions had been made about this family's behavior. The father was an immigrant from Poland who had arrived in the United States as a teenager and learned to struggle with ethnic and cultural bias in part by perfecting his English so there would be no hint of his immigrant status. His wife was from Germany and the only child of parents who had endured the chaos and atrocities of World War II. She reported that she survived ethnic and racial strife and the politics of human catastrophe through the sheer determination of her father, who was a humanist and committed to the welfare of all people. This unexpected and unique revelation opened the doors to a more intimate understanding of their personal and family lives, and the turmoil that they were both suffering from the as-yet-unexplained and inappropriate behavior of their children.

The opportunity to be aware of one's own inherent biases and yet not allow these reactions to interfere in the counseling process provided a unique perspective toward both self-awareness for the second author as well as an entry into the lives of two resilient individuals who were struggling to understand the dynamics in their own particular family. Failure either to be aware of these emerging feelings or reconcile them in some way would have severely impacted any professional assistance that might have been provided in the care of this family.

Recognizing the impact of racial biases and prejudices in one's professional work is an expectation that is required of all professional counselors (American Psychological Association, 1993; Arredondo et al., 1996; Brinson, 1996; Brinson & Morris, 2002; Sue, Arredondo, & McDavis, 1992; Sue & Sue, 2003). Understanding how these issues impact one's ability to work as a counseling professional, specifically as a supervisor/educator with students in training, is critically important. Moreover, the extent to which supervisors can recognize their own racial biases and prejudices becomes useful as a system of knowledge and meaning for personal discovery and organization of their reality. Unfortunately, racial biases and prejudices are not coded structures with formal patterns and identifiable components. In essence, without a well-defined framework, biases and prejudices may go undetected by the average person. In fact, racial biases can range from those that are imperceptible to those that are transparent.

Brislin (1996) provides several expressions of racial bias thinking, all ranging from low detectability to the most blatant. Given that racial biases and prejudices can vary along a continuum, it is very likely that many people are unaware that they maintain varying degrees of racial bias. In fact, in the case of a helping professional, the individual may choose to take a politically correct stance and offer several reasons why he or she could not manifest any level of racial bias. This perspective is taken often because to admit personal bias means that the helping professional is unfair, negative, and intolerant toward another group of people. Clearly, this worldview is antithetical to the profession of counseling. On the other hand, and perhaps more importantly, to admit racial bias could mean social reprisals, such as negative evaluation within his or her work environment, or legal action initiated by a client.

On the basis of our collective experience, we have come to learn that many helping professionals manifest varying degrees of racial biases. We have also come to understand that many helping professionals often are not aware of their racial biases. As human beings, however, our verbal expressions often communicate our thoughts and feelings regarding issues pertaining to our own biases and prejudices. The literature supports the notion that language usage can frequently indicate the extent to which a person may manifest varying degrees of racial bias (Hidalgo, 1986). Although this is not an inclusive list, it does provide examples of statements that individuals in the counseling profession have used to communicate their lack of racial bias. To the trained listener, or a person with extensive experience dealing with racial bias, it will be clear that many of these individual comments reflect varying degrees of discriminatory attitudes ranging from the imperceptible to the obvious. Consider some of the following examples.

"My parents didn't raise me to be racist; they raised me to evaluate people on the basis of their intelligence, not their skin color."
"I have a best friend outside of my ethnic/racial group, so I cannot be racist."

"I frequently date outside of my race, so I can't be prejudiced or racist."

"I allow those people to enter my home and eat dinner at my table, so I couldn't be racist."

"I listen to their music all the time, so I'm not racist."

"I allow my children to play with their children, so I could not be racist."

"We have people in my family from all different backgrounds, except African American, so I can't be racist."

"My mother is white my father is black, so I cannot be a racist."

"When I see you I don't see a color, I just see a person."

"When I was younger my parents had one as my babysitter, so I don't have prejudices against those people."

"Some minority groups are more sexually promiscuous than others; that is why some groups have more children out of wedlock."

"When they move into your neighborhood, the first thing they do is have a block party."

"The reason why the Asian groups do so well is because they have such great family values."

"Those people are always coming over the border looking to steal jobs from Americans."

"They discard their Middle-Eastern clothes, marry our women, then they blow up our buildings."

Many of these responses represent often-cited statements from individuals that directly or indirectly communicate some degree of racial prejudice. Language is a means by which practitioners can recognize their racial prejudices.

Practice with clients and their families who are racially are cultural/ethnically different requires distinct awareness of the therapeutic relationship, goals, and prescribed interventions (American Psychological Association, 1993; Sue, Arredondo, & McDavis, 1992; Sue & Sue, 2003). Failure to implement a self-evaluative process in one's work will likely lead to a failed counselor–client relationship, over- or underevaluation of problems, impaired judgment, and ultimately counseling failure. In addition, poor treatment outcome as a result of either conscious or unconscious discriminatory practice can easily lead to legal liability and malpractice (Grosso, 2002). In brief, the expectation to incorporate a self-supervision process in one's role as a professional counselor is a critical principle toward ethical and effective practice.

The principal thrust of this chapter is to encourage increased self-awareness and self-supervision of one's biases, prejudices, and possible racist attitudes and behaviors. It is also the intent of this writing to elaborate on the self-monitoring of ethnically and culturally biased thinking and behavior, and provide a contextual and developmental understanding to these unhelpful attitudes. Recommendations for increased awareness of one's unexamined and prejudiced reactions toward ethnic and cultural differences also are given. Case illustrations and discussion are offered in order to augment learning about increasing the counselor's development of an unprejudiced/nonracist personal and professional identity. In addition, personal stories from each of the authors are shared to provide a greater appreciation of the concepts presented herein. Minimal distinction is made between the language of biases, prejudices, and racists attitudes, given that all three represent negative thoughts, feelings, and behaviors that are inconsistent with professional standards of growth.

☐ Self-Supervision

The concept of self-supervision, although only recently being recognized as an accepted professional modality in the literature (Morrissette, 2001), actually has a several decade history of description. It is not the intent of the current chapter to review the writing about self-supervision, and the interested reader is referred to Meyer (1978) for a historical overview of this concept. This chapter incorporates the definition by Steiden (1993) on the monitoring of one's professional actions and activities.

> Self-supervision is deliberate thinking about one's actions, independent of others. This evaluative or reflective activity is performed to better understand how we operate as therapist and/or supervisors and to offer opportunities to take a different view or position in the clinical context. (p. 2)

Why the focus on self-supervision regarding the context of whether one is racist or not? The U.S. Bureau of the Census (1995) reports that communities across the country have become increasingly more complex with regard to the presence of diverse racial and cultural groups. Tatum (1997) argues in her discourse on conversations about race that most individuals, inclusive of professional counselors, know very little about racial identity development. In her understanding, this limited awareness about how culturally diverse people incorporate mainstream culture often leads to ethnic bias and the development of racist attitudes. Thus, mental health educators and supervisors are not immune to the development of such attitudes, especially if unmonitored in practice and ultimately unexamined. As noted by Jones (1996), the understanding of race as it impacts attitudes, motives, interpersonal behaviors, policy, and law is a complex issue. Thus, race, ethnicity, and cultural awareness cannot be underestimated as a core issue that affects counselor education activities, inclusive of supervision. The need for a self-supervision function becomes a salient, developmental resource within this context.

Self-supervision characteristically begins with self-examination that expectedly leads to self-awareness (Langs, 1979). The supervisor must understand how his or her racial, cultural, and ethnic background impacts his or her work with a supervisee and what role these factors might play in making clinical and professional decisions (Jordan, Brinson, & Peterson, 2002). For example, consider the following observations of supervision as they possibly result in unintentional stereotyping on behalf of the supervisor when working with the counselor trainee:

1. The supervisor might assume that a female trainee requires more support and guidance as compared with a male trainee.
2. The supervisor might assume that a male trainee is able to lead and take charge of more difficult case situations than a female trainee.
3. The supervisor might lower expectations for an ethically/culturally diverse trainee, and in fact, may find it surprising when this trainee possesses well-developed clinical and communication skills.
4. The supervisor might expect that a trainee who is a person of color would find him- or herself feeling most comfortable in clinical and professional experiences involving similar client populations and concerns.
5. The supervisor might solicit and expect more qualitatively distinct opinions and ideas from Euro-American trainees as compared with trainees who are people of color.
6. The supervisor might become defensive if questioned ostensibly by an ethnically/culturally diverse trainee; yet consider the same behavior demonstrated by a Euro-American trainee as a sign of intellectual curiosity.
7. The supervisor might assume that all people from a particular ethnic/cultural group manifest varying degrees of racism, and cannot evaluate the trainee as an individual, separate from his or her racial or cultural group.
8. The supervisor could contend that any professional or personal disagreements between supervisor and supervisee ultimately involve issues pertaining to race, culture, or ethnicity.

Indeed, becoming aware of our racial beliefs and perceptions about people who are culturally and racially different becomes a rich source of meaning, experience, and knowledge in the move toward self-supervision of a nonracist identity. The following case example helps to illustrate this.

Mary is a 30-year-old woman, divorced, with a strong religious orientation, and a student in her beginning practicum. Mary's client, a 40-year-
old white female, married, works as a blackjack dealer in one of the local
hotels. The client is always personable, well-groomed, and similar to Mary,
expresses a deeply religious orientation. The client is seeking counseling
because she is thinking of divorcing her husband of 10 years. The client is
having an affair with a married man. During the third session with the
client Mary asks the client to describe personal qualities of the husband,
then compare those against the boyfriend's personal qualities. She describes
the husband as cold, aloof, and very condescending. She says the husband
never passes an opportunity to demean her. He constantly criticizes her
weight. She says that he is a good father but a lousy husband. The daughter
really adores him. On the other hand, the boyfriend is warm, respectful,
and a really nice person. He buys her flowers without her asking for them.
At this point, given that the client describes the husband as a good father,
Mary decides to give the client a reframe so she might think differently
about her marriage. Mary states, "Although your husband is not a warm
person, and the other man seems to be a caring person, I'd like you to
think about this scenario. Think how worse it would be if you were married to an African-American man and you had to cook collard greens and
chitterlings every day. You could also be beaten up if you didn't cook his
food just right." The client, in a state of bewilderment, responds, "My boyfriend is black and he does not eat collard greens." Mary immediately turns
three shades of red. She apologizes to the client and says perhaps she used
a bad example. The next week, the client did not show for counseling.

Although Mary may have been well-intentioned, the client could not
understandably see the meaning that this practicum student was wanting
to convey. What the client saw was a person who was quite possibly naïve,
or a case of racism in practice. During supervision Mary acknowledged
that the statement was made in poor taste, and said she meant absolutely
nothing by it. Interestingly enough, Mary was taking a multicultural class
concurrent with her beginning practice course. The previous week the
instructor had given a lecture on the inappropriateness of culturally biased language in therapy. Mary had reported that this was a most infor-
mative lecture.

This incident had a major impact on the first author (JB) as a supervisor. The self-monitoring narrative developed as follows. On one level, as
a supervisor who happens to be African American, and the fact that Mary
was taking the multicultural course with the first author (JB), the incident did prompt some internal anger and hostility. Although Mary is a
beginning trainee and could be subject to verbal slips based on her anxiety or nervousness, I found myself retreating into the all-too-familiar "all
whites are racist" thinking, a comment that I have conditioned myself
not to make in an academic setting. I immediately associated Mary's com-

ment as a pure indication of her racist ideology. I rationalized that she probably had contempt for me as her supervisor. Then, almost as quickly as I began to consciously castigate Mary, I immediately refocused on myself. How dare I make the assumption that one comment can define who and what a person stands for? Could not Mary refer to me as a racist for having this assumption about her? Furthermore, this was not Mary's first experience with culturally diverse issues in counseling because another client, a Vietnamese American, in her practicum had developed a strong therapeutic relationship with her. I quickly realized how convenient it is to explain behavior in terms of a person's race, rather than looking for more plausible explanations of behavior. I also realized that Mary had done some good work in my multicultural class. It was obvious that she was in a positive transition stage of her identity development. Thus, it would be erroneous of me to think of her as a racist. This internalized monitoring prompted the initiation of self-supervision. As described here, my own process of self-reflection resulted in a supervision session, and a recognition that I had biases that were operating against the counselor trainee.

☐ Contextual and Developmental Overview

Prejudice toward others different from one's reference group is an inherent part of living in the community (Takaki, 1993). A lack of prejudice signals a lack of interest in one's self. Thus, paradoxically, prejudice helps to facilitate a healthy discrimination between one's family and reference group, and those who do not necessarily belong. However, a prolonged and unexamined prejudice can initiate the development of a racist mindset, namely, an irrational belief that unfairly prejudges the individual based on physical, social, and historical characteristics (Jones, 2002). This prejudging can have significant negative consequences as witnessed in current social and political upheaval in the world community. At the micro level, the educator/supervisor with these unexamined reactions can have a salient impact on the education of students. It is helpful to briefly review some of the primary influences that promote the development of racist attitudes in individuals. These influences broadly tend to include: personal/family background history, values assimilated through the educational process, and ethnic/cultural/racial learning.

Background History

Family socialization and influence provide the foundation for the psychological and emotional lenses one employs to navigate through life.

Unexamined, parental views lead to the development of prejudice and racist postures toward others who are ethnically, culturally, and linguistically different (Sue & Sue, 1999). Some examples of what may appear to be innocent remarks can have a profound effect on identity formation as it relates to biased attitudes toward others. These examples are noted in the following narrative comments.

> My father was a businessman who ran a very successful neighborhood market. He would rise at 5:00 A.M. every morning, eat breakfast, then he would be off to work no later than 6:00 A.M. When I reached the age of eight, my father decided to instill his work ethic into me. Now I had to rise and shine at 6 A.M. Needless to say, that 1-hour difference was extremely difficult for me. I would occasionally get a little prodding with my father's belt. The prodding was sometime accompanied with a comment such as: "Boy, while you are in the bed sleeping, the man is trying to figure out a way to get your money." As I reflect on this today, I guess this was his way of saying the early bird catches the worm. On the other hand, someone else might say my dad was a racist and that statement indicates such. Nonetheless, I still get up at 5 A.M. every morning, and my bank account doesn't seem to be tied into the time of starting my day.

Other counselors have shared similar stories about innocent remarks and the impact on one's behavior. One counselor trainee shared how her father would get her up early, every morning, sit her at the breakfast table, get a glass of white milk and pour into it one drop of chocolate syrup. He would then stir it up rather vigorously and while staring intently at her he would say "You see there, honey, one drop will turn everything chocolate." Obviously, several explanations can be interpreted from this example; the student has since come to understand that her father was trying to discourage her from contemplating a future relationship with a man of color. I commonly refer to this as the "little dab will do you" technique. To this day, the supervisee experiences uneasiness when in a clinical stetting or social setting with a man of color. As we discussed how this might play out in our supervisory relationship, she indicated that I (JB) am different from most African-American men because of my educational background. Early family socialization can play an important role in how we perceive ourselves as culturally different individuals and groups.

Given that families influence how we perceive and interact with other people, exploring family of origin issues can be a very useful process for self-supervision of counselors in training. In this exercise we particularly look for unconscious messages that counselors received from their parents regarding culturally different groups. We start out with a narrative story.

> Picture yourself at 10 years of age sitting around the Thanksgiving table with all of your immediate and extended family members. Create the scene as elaborate as you like. Make sure you create a very festive occasion. Now

that you have the scene, I am going to change one thing in the scene; I am going to change you. You are now a 10-year-old child of an ethnically/culturally different background. Now notice how your family members treat you. What is different? How are they experiencing you? What are your parents saying to you? Are they happy to have this Latino/African-American/Vietnamese, etc., child at the table? (*Reader: Fill in your own prejudice.*) Think about what you have heard your parents say about ethnically/culturally different people. Now they are saying this about you. How does that make you feel? Change the scene. A knock on the door and additional family members join you for dinner. What is their reaction to your presence? Now think about the messages you learned from your parents about ethnically/culturally different people. Does it account for why you have more or less contact with these populations? (Adapted from Axelson, 2000)

Obviously, most parents are well-meaning and want the best for their children. However, many parents either consciously or unconsciously create environments where their children adopt negative stereotypes and beliefs about culturally different groups. Whether one was raised in a mainstream family or an ethnic minority family, one can identify the various messages or scripts that have come to influence one's thinking and behaving toward people with different values, beliefs, and cultures. These scripts continue to influence one's thinking and behaving with people encountered at work, schools, social settings, and even in clinical counseling and supervision. In particular, views on interracial dating, marriage, and messages regarding racial groups are absolutely communicated to children during their formative years. Marrying someone who is not a member of your religious faith can be taboo in some culturally diverse families. The messages that certain groups are lazy, criminally minded, and prefer living in squalor exists in the upbringing of many children. Children are taught that some groups are biologically predisposed to superior or inferior intellectual functioning. If raising a racist child were considered a crime, a significant number of parents could be charged with child abuse. It is important to examine what role one's family plays in the development of attitudes toward culturally different people.

Learning about various racial and cultural messages we received during various aspects of the developmental life cycle is an appropriate task for counseling professionals. Knowing the link between the family and the choices we make enables us to examine the psychic structures that inform our thinking and behaving toward culturally different groups. Several noted scholars suggest what you think, how you act, even your language, are all created through the family (McGoldrick, 1989; Samovar & Porter, 1995).

Assimilation Through the Values and Educational Process

Schools play an important role in transmitting the cultural values of the wider society. This is because schools serve as socially sanctioned learning systems that teach our children the values and beliefs that are oftentimes communicated at home and within society. By the time children attend elementary school and certainly by middle school, many have already been exposed to their families' views and this society's views about racial, ethnic, and linguistic issues. Thus, most have learned who and what are valued and important in this society. Children have already learned how they are supposed to interact with members of their own group, and have learned what is culturally appropriate to say and do when interacting with members of a different cultural group. Schools, often represented administratively by white, middle-class individuals, unfortunately, reinforce the cultural stereotyping that is oftentimes learned at home and presented in the wider society. For example, in the United States many parents instill in their children the notion that people of color are inferior to white children.

In many American schools, the contributions of people of color to the U.S. society are relegated to a special time of the year. Schools may celebrate African-American heritage during the month of February and/or Latino/Chicano heritage during the month of May, but place limited emphasis on African-American or Latino history during the remainder of the school year. Clearly the "1-month" approach sends the message to our children that the contributions made by African Americans in building U.S. society were not nearly as significant as the contributions of Europeans. Indeed, African Americans as a racial group are considered less capable and deserving and valuable than whites. Similarly, in our society children learn that people of color excel at certain tasks, whereas the dominant white society are better at other tasks. In many instances, schools have adopted this societal notion as their reality. For example, the athletes on many sports teams—particularly the big money sports such as football, baseball, and basketball—are now overrepresented by people of color, whereas the owners, managers, and coaches remain largely white. Many coaches start at the elementary level identifying African-American and Latino players who one day may somehow make them a good coach. On the other hand, if schools were searching for the students for the gifted and talented programs, a peek into the classrooms would reveal that schools think of Asian and white students in that regard.

A salient part of learning during one's formative (school) years about culturally diverse groups continues to influence one's thinking and behavior during our adult years. In other words, earlier learning inappropriately informs us that "I know what whites, blacks, and Asians are good at." These internalized views can make it difficult, therefore, for a white counseling supervisor to view a person of color from a perspective other than the stereotype. A similar observation is analogous to the culturally diverse supervisor working with a Euro-American counselor trainee. The self-examination of these stereotypes can reveal prelearned messages about how to perceive one's professional work with others. Examples of this stereotype in action are:

- As an ethnically diverse counselor trainee working with a white supervisor, the trainee might expect the supervisor to be highly skilled in communication, and more effective at offering advice on interpersonal skill building.
- As a white student or an African-American student working with an Asian supervisor, a trainee might expect that the supervisor may have a problem teaching about building relationships with clients, but he or she would do extremely well with counseling theories and providing research-based strategies for treatment.

As we have implied, an additional way in which ethnic bias is communicated in the schools is in the teaching of history. The historical contribution of people of color to the building of America is rarely discussed in schools. History is told primarily from a Western European perspective. Given that Europeans are presented as the group that developed Western civilization, such a stance reinforces the self-esteem of some children while devaluing the contributions that other ethnic and racial groups have made to the United States. Thus, children of color receive inconsistent and mixed messages about the contributions of their particular ancestors. Perhaps the practice of diversifying history would impact upon the attitudes of children, leaving an impression that the rest of the world has made important contributions to the development of humankind.

It is important to reflect about one's earlier schooling and whether historical information provided was helpful in appreciating other cultures. The following child therapy case, treated by one of the authors (JMC), helps to illustrate this.

> Jenny Runningbear was a 10-year-old female child of mixed Piutet and Cheyenne Indian background. Jenny was a foster child who was referred as part of a referral network established by the Bureau of Indian Affairs through their local community for counseling. Jenny had been removed from her home at the age of five as a result of a history of domestic violence and substance abuse. Since that period, she had lived in three foster homes and was currently residing temporarily with her maternal grandparents. The problem behaviors noted at that time were significant opposi-

tional defiance and poor school performance. In spite of the academic failure that appeared to signal Jenny's rite of passage into middle school, Jenny presented with significant emotional resilience and intelligence. Initially she was found to be very distrusting, uncooperative, and desiring help from no one. By the fourth visit, the therapeutic relationship appeared to be failing until she asked a startling question of the therapist. The question had to do with whether the therapist had ever been oppressed or discriminated against by the "white man." Struggling with an appropriate answer to that question found me as a therapist experiencing significant difficulty responding to a 10-year-old with a level of wisdom that belied her chronological age. This question opened up a therapeutic relationship that began the dialogue of exploration regarding feelings of resentment and anger that Jenny had levied at the "white establishment." Just as important, this question and the pursuing dialog in counseling with this 10 year old also made me question my own perceptions of history with majority culture and its impact on my educational experiences and identification with my ethnic and cultural group.

Jenny was seen for several more visits after the question that opened up several opportunities to the therapeutic relationship. The last session was spent in dialog about the deficits in being labeled American Indian and the impact that it might have on her in her high school education.

Jenny Runningbear was an unusual child who challenged the basic foundation of how I as a treating therapist for this child had to learn to grow up handling strong feelings of negativity and prejudice regarding my upbringing. Mexican and indigenous people were viewed as irrelevant to the historical backdrop of our classroom instruction, with significant devaluing of any contributions my ancestors might have made. Jenny's own struggle with discrimination and the strong anger toward "the white man" revealed a pervasive fear of what it would be like to grow up being American Indian in her community. Jenny's challenge to me as a therapist about my own perceptions of majority culture forced me to review personal history and feelings that have been instrumental in my own learning. This challenge has increased my own self-awareness regarding the impact that ethnicity and culture has had on my relationships with fellow colleagues, clients, and their families.

Ethnic, Cultural, and Racial Learning

Examining one's perspective to race is critically important in view of the fact that "race" is one of the most compelling social constructs developed by society. Race forms the basis for expectation regarding social roles, performance levels, values, and norms and mores for group and nongroup members (Jones, 1996; Tatum, 1997). Omi and Winant (1986) observed that race as a sociohistorial concept defines the features associated with group membership and determines the roles that people are expected to play.

Unfortunately, one of the ways the present society deals with race is not to talk about it in any meaningful way. The engagement of any meaningful dialog about race characteristically occurs when there is potential for racial conflict between groups, most notably whites and people of color. Given this country's history with race, talking about this issue is extremely difficult for many individuals, including mental health educators (Tatum, 1992). However, one should be clear that being a member of particular ethnic/culturally diverse group creates feelings about how one perceives oneself and influences the extent to which one views other groups as equal or not. In brief, racism has no boundaries, thus inferior and superior attitudes abound both within and between ethnic and majority groups across the country. Thus, a more sophisticated and introspective set of questions to ask are: Whom are we prejudiced toward? How have these beliefs impacted our relationships with colleagues, students, our community? How are we committed to new learning about ourselves?

Many groups hold negative perceptions of each other, yet at the same time many groups will do whatever is necessary to protect a nonbiased group image. Studies have shown that some groups embrace humanitarian and egalitarian values, but maintain negative attitudes against some groups in society (Katz & Hass, 1988). Kottler (1994) acknowledges that many counselor educators and supervisors are able to dilute or disguise their prejudices quite cleverly. Given this as a social and political reality, counselor educators and supervisors are reluctant to address their prejudices or biases, and may rigidly guard entrenched views of manifesting a racist ideology.

The following case discussion assists in an understanding of the struggle to be more self-aware of one's biases while furthering one's self-monitoring and improving one's counseling/supervision effectiveness.

> Jose is a 47-year-old Mexican American man who has worked as a crisis counselor in a state-run hospital for the past 15 years. He has the longest tenure of any member of his unit, which includes three white women and six white men. He has a master's degree in counseling, and has completed a number of professional development courses. He is articulate, knowledgeable, and presents himself in a professional manner. Although he has good rapport with his colleagues, he keeps to himself most of the time. According to Jose, most of his colleagues refer to him as a consummate professional. Approximately 2 years ago, Jose applied for the head position of another unit. The position called for a person with a master's degree and a minimum of 7 years of continuous employment with the state. He would

be responsible for supervising nine paraprofessionals, six white men and three white women. However, he would report to the Ph.D.-level psychologist, who happens to be a white man. Jose reported that, on meeting with the psychologist to discuss any specific job duties and responsibilities, he was informed that he might have some difficulty supervising nine people given his lack of experience as a supervisor. The psychologist further advised that Jose "be strong and don't let them run over you." Jose found this to be an insulting comment. He said the supervisor must be racist because he is already questioning his ability to supervise.

This case was supervised by one of the authors (Jesse), who asked Jose if the supervisor could be making some helpful comments. Jose denied the usefulness of these remarks. It was then suggested to him that the supervisor seemed to recognize the fact that some people may have problems with people of color, and the supervisor was likely giving Jose a helpful warning and a supportive gesture. It was Jose's own prejudices that would not let him see that the white male psychologist was really guiding him professionally and attempting to orient Jose to the realities of being a manager. Jose was informed that this is what often happens when one prejudges people from the mainstream society. Our own cultural stereotypes may cause us to miss out on helpful relationships that may prove valuable in the future.

Such supervisees often have had a history of conflictual and negative experiences when relating with men from the mainstream culture. They have usually had a supervisor during some previous job or career that they trusted who they eventually discovered was culturally insensitive. This can cause the development of emotional scars, which prevent the person of color who is a supervisee from relating in a trusting manner with a white man in a supervisory role. In terms of self-awareness, the individual in this case had to learn that not all white men are intent on disempowering or oppressing nonwhite professionals. Professional development among fellow colleagues and supervisors demands that each of us become accountable to our own ethnic and cultural biases, sharpen our awareness, and take responsibility for our reactions and subsequent behavior. Self-reflection is crucial to this end.

An additional case supervised by the second author (JMC) lends additional insight about the role of race in one's professional development.

Tuan Lay is a 34-year-old graduate student who was starting her first semester of practicum. Tuan is Vietnamese by background and has been in the country since the age of 16. Tuan has difficulty with English, although her expressive abilities are generally clear and what is lacking is her self-confidence in the English language. Tuan reported during the initial supervision sessions with me that she had been experiencing significant difficulty with her supervisor who is an African-American woman. Apparently, conflict arose in the initial cases that Tuan was seeing because she was having difficulty understanding her client's life circumstances. The supervisor chastised Tuan, stating that her cultural background might be getting in the way of this as well as the fact that English was not her first language. The supervisor also intimated that perhaps Tuan might be better suited to dealing with clients who were primarily from her own ethnic and cultural background. Tuan reported to me as the faculty member that she was insulted by these comments and felt that the agency supervisor did not understand her circumstances or appreciate her background history, which was distinctly different from her own. Intervention with the agency supervisor found that the supervisor displayed prejudicial comments about Tuan that highlighted this student's hesitancy about being supervised by this African-American supervisor. Resolution to the issue was handled by having Tuan see a supervisor who was a white woman who was more supportive of Tuan's personal and professional development during her first practicum phase.

This case is an interesting example of what appeared to be a prejudicial response on the part of the African-American supervisor toward another person of color as a result of differences in ethnic and cultural background, and language. Further, the fact that Tuan's new supervisor was a white woman who was a better match for Tuan also was an interesting paradox to this scenario. This case reminded me of a long-learned life lesson that no one ethnic and cultural group is immune from prejudice and discrimination. Self-reflection and openness about this issue further made me aware that each of us is liable to our own particular ethnic biases and that it is a continuous monitoring process. Multicultural competency and awareness begin with one's self-awareness and willingness to examine old stereotypes and reactions.

☐ Personal Reflections

Learning to recognize and understand one's prejudicial attitudes and reactions are necessary conditions for being a professional educator in the healing arts. Commitment toward the welfare of the client and subsequently the students in training cannot be underscored sufficiently (California Association of Marriage and Family Therapists, 2002). Nevertheless, personal/professional biases persist, and need continuous monitoring and reflection. The following experiences are offered as examples from each of the authors about how easily biased unchecked reactions and attitudes can develop in the absence of a presumed offending conspiracy.

> (*Jesse*) When I started my new job as an assistant professor, the very first course I taught was beginning practicum. I had six white female students.

I was responsible for meeting with each student 1 hour per week for individual supervision. We met for individual supervision in my office. Although we were watching tapes of client sessions, I was conscious to have my office door open so my colleagues could be aware of my actions. In other words, I had heard stories about how African-American professors had been "set up" by having young white woman claim inappropriate behavior on their part. So I did not give each student the benefit of the doubt. I did not allow myself to establish meaningful relationships, which could help me as well as the students grow personally and professionally. I was being prejudiced against white women, assuming they were weak enough to be manipulated as pawns in a scheme to get the black man. I guess the conspiracy theory perpetrated by many African Americans truly lived in my heart. On reflection, I was being sexist against white women, while also being racist against white people. I have since come to learn that not everyone is out to get me, that there are good people who are white, but I still approach each social encounter with a white person with a certain degree of caution. I guess that is life in America as a black man.

(*Joseph*) In many years of practice as a child and family psychologist, I (JMC) have frequently encountered couples and families from the majority culture who express significant prejudice and disregard for the many Latino individuals they encounter in their daily, personal, and business lives. These comments are typically made during the counseling process and often take the form of the following narratives: "Why are Mexicans so lazy . . . they have been in this country already a long time and they don't seem to learn English. . . . My gardener is a Spanish-speaking man but I am real careful when he is around my children. I just don't trust him. . . . My partner knows some nice Spanish people who are educated and seem to be different from the others that you see looking for work on the street corner." These comments appear to be made without an obvious awareness that the treating provider is Latino/Chicano. During my early professional development, I would take these comments politely and quietly, and not address them directly as part of the treatment issues. This approach caused a significant level of anger and frustration over my own nonreactions and began to affect the professional relationship that would develop in future sessions. These feelings also would at times cause me to generalize about the larger majority population and confirm old reactions and stereotypes that I had developed in my childhood background. As I have become wiser and allowed a self-monitoring process to impact my awareness and development, I now address these issues in the counseling process. These issues have direct impact in the counseling that could be very therapeutic for the respective client–client system to understand about living in a culturally diverse society and dialoguing about any related therapeutic issues that might be occurring between the client and myself. This awareness has caused a significant leap in my ability to be effective in work with Euro-American clientele, and has assisted in the integration of a culturally diverse perspective that serves as a useful teacher both for the families that I serve as well as myself.

☐ Self-Supervision Recommendations

This chapter has attempted to outline those factors that address how racism is endemic in society, and how as professional educators, supervisors, and counselors, no one is immune. The need to develop continuous self-monitoring and awareness is critical in the professional helping of clients and their families. Especially salient is the need to incorporate the self-supervision function in the training of students who themselves are learning through their supervisors about what is taught directly and indirectly. The following recommendations are offered in becoming more self-aware in one's commitment to the healing process with clients and students.

1. Become aware of the self-monitoring one does about one's professional work. As Donnelly and Glacer (1992) point out, there are numerous advantages to self-supervision, such as increased quality assurance of the therapeutic work and the development of an internal, observing supervisor that can provide meta-feedback. Failure to develop an increasingly refined perspective on one's professional work will likely have negative consequences on one's performance as an educator, supervisor, or counselor.

2. Be alert to the blind spots that either have been self-identified or pointed out by other colleagues and students. These blind spots likely may be tied to assumptions about people and groups that could have direct reference to a previously closeted prejudicial belief system. Life provides many opportunities to learn valuable lessons about oneself and others. The counselor educator's job is to listen, pay attention, and learn the meaning of the lesson.

3. Take notice of any related differences in the counseling relationship and interventions that occur with culturally diverse people. Leong (1994) and Sue and Sue (1999) report that prejudicial and racist attitudes can exist at deep areas of unawareness, thus prompting professional attitudes and behavior that are both inconsistent and inappropriate with select client populations. This awareness can help assess any salient differences that may be occurring when one's professional role encompasses a broad ethnic and culturally diverse client population. This awareness also has direct application in any educational capacity that is being filled (i.e., supervision, in-class instruction).

4. Allow regular and consistent time for personal reflection, meditation, and/or prayer if that is within one's internal belief system. It is important to listen to the internal dialog as well as to learn how to quiet the dialog. The more emotionally draining the client population one is treating, the more it is important to take time to reflect and avoid

vicarious traumatization (Pearlman & Saakvitne, 1995). In brief, reflection allows for the transformation of doubt, conflict, and insecurity to become clear, coherent, and harmonious.

5. Be aware that spirituality is the language of many culturally diverse people. Experiences with migration, racism, oppression, acculturative stress, for example, are often emotionally housed in the hearts of these families (Falicov, 1998; Parham, White, & Ajamu, 1999). These experiences are often understood as "the will of God," which then become psychological barriers to positive treatment outcome. Prejudicial attitudes toward ethnically/culturally diverse people could also be reflected in the professional's religious/spiritual stance. This dimension is frequently overlooked in counseling activity.

6. The outline of a personal genogram and listing those family members who contributed to both healthy and unhealthy attitudes toward others are very useful tools. Highlighting the emotional distance, alliances, and personal/historical relationships among and between generations of family increases self-awareness and the understanding of blind spots that would interfere in professional work.

7. The act of keeping a weekly journal of one's inner thoughts, insecurities, observations, and personal development continues to be standard in the profession (Morrissette, 2001). Reflection and self-supervision are a natural outcome when time and investment are made in one's professional commitment to be ethical, competent, and professionally secure.

8. Develop the skill to recognize your culturally biased language. Although it may not be used intentionally to harm others, it often indicates a distortion in our judgment and/or awareness (Axelson, 2000).

9. Practice prompt personal inquiry regarding your community of friendships: Is there related ethnic/cultural diversity among your associates and friends? Has this been an issue for you? How does it impact your professional work as a counselor? Reflection can assist in the creation of a meaningful dialog and increased personal awareness.

☐ References

American Psychological Association. (1993). Guidelines for providers of psychological services to ethnic linguistic and culturally diverse populations. *American Psychologist, 48,* 45–48.

Arredondo, R., Toporek, R., Brown, S. P., Jones, J., Locke, D. C., Sanchez, J., & Stadler, H. (1996). Operationalization of the multicultural counseling competencies. *Journal of Multicultural Counseling and Development, 24,* 42–78.

Axelson, J. (2000). Counseling and development in a multicultural society. CA: Brooks/ Cole.

Brinson, J. A. (1996). Cultural sensitivity for counselors: Our challenge for the twenty first century. *Journal of Humanistic Education and Development, 34,* 195–201.

Brinson, J. A., & Morris, J. (2002). Blacks' and Whites' perceptions of real-life scenarios: A preliminary investigation. *Journal of Humanistic Education and Development, 40,* 132–139.

Brislin, R. W. (1996). Prejudice in intercultural communication. In L. Samovaar & R. Porter (Eds.). *Intercultural communication: A reader* (pp. 366–70). Belmont, CA: Wadsworth.

California Association of Marriage and Family Therapists. (2002). *Ethical standards for marriage and family therapists.* San Diego: Author.

Donnelly, C., & Glacer, A. (1992). Training in self-supervision skills. *The Clinical Supervisor, 10,* 85–96.

Falicov, C. J. (1998). *Latino families in therapy: A guide to multicultural practice.* New York: Guilford Press.

Grosso, F. C. (2002). *Complete applications of law and ethics: A workbook for California marriage and family therapists.* (Academic Edition 2000). Santa Barbara: Federico C. Grosso Publications.

Hidalgo, M. (1986). Language contact, language loyalty, and language prejudice on the Mexican border, *Language in Society, 15,* 193–200.

Jones, J. (1996). Psychological models of race: What have they been and what should they be? In J. D. Goodchilds (Ed.), *Psychological perspectives on human diversity in America* (pp. 3–46). Washington, DC: American Psychological Association.

Jones, M. (2002). *Social psychology of prejudice.* Upper Saddle River, NJ: Prentice-Hall.

Jordan, K., Brinson, J., & Petersen, C. (2002). Multicultural supervision. In J. Trusty (Ed.), *Cross-cultural helping.* New York: Taylor & Francis.

Katz, I., & Hass, R. G. (1988). Racial ambivalence and American value conflict: Correlational and priming studies of dual cognitive structures. *Journal of Personality and Social Psychology, 55,* 893–905.

Kottler, J. (1994). Systemic dysfunction among counselors. *Counseling Today, 37*(5).

Langs, R. (1979). *The supervisory experience.* Northvale, NJ: Jason Aronson.

Leong, F. T. (1994). Emergence of the cultural dimension: The roles and impact of culture on counseling supervision. *Counselor Education and Supervision, 34,* 115–116.

McGoldrick, M. (1989). Ethnicity and the family life cycle. In B. Carter & M. McGoldrick (Eds.), *The changing family life cycle: A framework for family therapy.* Boston: Allyn & Bacon.

Meyer, R. (1978). Using self-supervision to maintain counseling skills: A review. *Personal and Guidance Journal, 57,* 95–98.

Morrissette, P. J. (2001). *Self-supervision: A primer for counselors and the helping professionals.* Washington, DC: National Academy Press.

Omi, M., & Winant, H. (1986). *Racial formation in the United States: From the 1960's to the 1980's.* New York: Bantam Books.

Parham, T. A., White, J. L., & Ajamu, A. (1999). *The psychology of blacks: An African centered perspective* (3rd ed.). Englewood Clifts, NJ: Prentice-Hall.

Pearlman, L. & Saakvitne, K. (1995). *Trauma and the therapist: Countertransference and vicarious treatment in psychotherapy with incest survivors.* New York: Norton.

Samovar, L. A., & Porter, R. E. (1995). *Communication between cultures.* Belmont, CA: Wadsworth.

Steiden, D. (1993). Self-supervision using discourse analysis. *Supervision Bulletin, VI,* 2.

Sue, D. W., Arredondo, P., & McDavis, R. J. (1992). Multicultural competencies/standards: A call of the profession. *Journal of Counseling and Development, 70,* 477–486.

Sue, D. R., & Sue, D. (1999). *Counseling the culturally different: Theory and practice* (3rd ed.). New York: Wiley.

Sue, D. R., & Sue, D. (2003). *Counseling the culturally different: Theory and practice* (4th ed.). New York: Wiley.

Takaki, R. (1993). *A different minor: A history of multicultural America*. Boston: Little, Brown.

Tatum, B. D. (1992). Talking about race, learning about racism: An application of racial identity development theory in the classroom. *Harvard Education Review, 62*, 1–24.

Tatum, B. D. (1997). *Why are all the Black kids sitting together in the cafeteria?* New York: Basic Books.

U.S. Bureau of the Census. (1995). *Statistical abstract of the United States, 1995* (115th ed.). Washington, DC: U.S. Government Printing Office.

CHAPTER 8   David Leary

Self-Supervision in Youth Counseling

It's the screams I can't handle in my counseling practice—the screams and the blood. Murderous rage is something I can deal with in theory or on the silver screen as I guess all of us can but when it stands outside your window and is covered in blood, that puts a whole new light on the notion of murderous rage. When the cause of that blood is an attack from a woman, that's difficult to think about. It flies in the face of convention. I usually associate violence with men. But it's hard to ignore reality when there's a bloodied and bruised face staring at me from outside my office. No words, simply screaming. Blood, bruising, a cowering shell of a man, more attacks and then tears. This is confronting and it's really confusing stuff as well.

What's this got to do with counseling and doing better you may well ask? In reality, self-supervision is about the practice of listening carefully to intrapsychic movements, the noises and voices that emanate from within each of us because of the work we do. Sometimes they're about the other, the person I'm attempting to assist. At other times, they're simply about me. However, that theoretical division between *them* and *me* is never so clear. When the calamitous voices from outside me hit the noisy emotion arising within me, it can readily become a jumbled mess. Understanding is never a commodity that's easily found in such a quagmire.

Dealing with the blood and guts of life doesn't rule out the possibility of a thoughtful counseling practice, underpinned as it must be by each counselor's work of *radical reflexivity* in the form of self-supervision. This

127

form of reflection is a whole-of-life process that arises from within and is nurtured by me, as a person and a counselor, so that the voices and noise I deal with each day get a good hearing. I love my work as a counselor but I know that making sense of the cacophonous mess of my work is critical to my survival and the survival of those with whom I practice the art of counseling.

☐ The Rough Guide

This piece of writing is a radical exploration of one approach to self-supervision. Recognising that counseling occurs in the strangest of places and circumstances—even the hurly burly of an innercity youth center—this chapter is about helping counselors deal with their complex and demanding experiences. It is based on the premise that counselors learn best through open and honest reflection on their own experience and that of their mentors.

The chapter begins with an examination of some of the literature that speaks of self-supervision but the core of the chapter is contained in two key therapeutic experiences. The first involves a conversation that occurs within a therapist. This internalized dialog is focused on a new client who is soon to arrive, and it continues with an excerpt from the first therapy session. The second key therapeutic experience involves an explosive event for a group of counselors at an innercity youth center, where stability and order is challenged and they are asked to deal with their own pain and confusion as well as that of their clients.

The literature around self-supervision is technical and dry. Of course, that flies in the face of every counselor's experience of their own practice, where counseling and supervision are dynamic with constant challenges to theory. This chapter examines the art of self-supervision through a transparent exploration of the emotional and therapeutic experiences of one counselor and his team. The candor may shock and even grate, but a posture of honest transparency holds the promise of growth and better clinical practice. It is the journey we must all make!

☐ Mindfulness of Our Practice

Counseling and supervision are quite distinct endeavors, and yet there is a connection between the two. The awareness and insight invariably sought in psychotherapy are also central components in the practice of supervision. Insight and awareness are everything; but there is nothing new in this reality.

As early as 1910, Freud (1900, 1914) was encouraging his colleagues to engage in self-analysis as an integral part of their trade (Blum, 1996; Lane, 1990). Despite that early and clear direction in thinking, the ideas of self-analysis and self-supervision have received remarkably little systematic attention. More than occasionally they are greeted with derision. Although the most comprehensive tome on supervision to appear in recent years (Watkins, 1997b) gives some attention to the significance of self-awareness and self-supervision (Holloway, 1997; Yontef, 1997), there is little thorough exploration of the centrality of self-supervision in many recent works.

Self-supervision has been defined by a number of authors as a systematic process where counselors work independently to oversee their own professional development (Donnelly & Glaser, 1992; Morrissette, 1999; Todd, 1997). Morrisette (1999) and others indicate a number of positive elements to the process of self-supervision. First, it stimulates a *mindfulness* in life on our weaknesses, strengths, relational dynamics, and the development of the therapeutic process. It helps the counselor structure the development of a broad perspective on past and present clinical work. It is a key component in ethical behavior and the maintenance of healthy therapeutic boundaries (Shillito Clarke, 1996). Thus, it is an avenue for proactive change (Lowe, 2000). Finally, it is seen as enhancing professional development and competence (Morrissette, 1999).

However, as Lowe (2000) indicates, self-supervisory processes are "typically viewed as a useful form of preparation for the 'real' supervision rather than as an alternative that can be used in its own right" (p. 511). Bramley (1996) views the process of self-supervision as a private exercise that is preliminary to the crucial process of individual clinical supervision.

Lowe (2000) indicates that there are a number of potential flaws in such a process. In the case of counselors who may not be sufficiently in touch with their own internal material, the absence of an alternative clinical view, provided via some form of supervision, can stifle both personal and clinical progress (Watkins, 1997a). However, self-supervision should be a universal goal within each counselor's practice, and although it should not be undertaken at the cost of more collaborative processes, counselors should have the goal of becoming "self-sustaining" (Todd, 1997, p. 512).

Although monitoring a counselor's practice may have begun as a shared experience with a supervisor during and after initial training, Mollon (1997) indicates that the ultimate aim must be for clinical supervision to be internalized. In such a process where routine is a key element (Lewis, 1991), the counselor gradually becomes his or her own supervisor or self-consultant (Williams, 1995). And yet reflection, a key component of this process is defined as, "the effort to *break the closure* in which we are . . . necessarily caught up as subjects, whether such closure comes from our personal history or from the sociohistorical institution which has formed, i.e., humanised, us" (Castoriadis, 1995, p. 34).

So, it is by definition, an individual *and* collaborative experience. Both aspects are valued and necessary. One cannot exist without the other. Together, they provide a reflexive approach to my inner world and life experience (Protinsky & Coward, 2001). The whole process is an amalgam of thoughtful processes located in a reflexive sequence: self-supervision → therapy session → self-supervision → case consultation → self-supervision → next therapy session (Lowe, 2000). For the counselor, to enter into the emotional world of another is a precious and privileged experience. To do justice to such a task, entering honestly and openly into my own experience is an essential quality of my clinical practice.

☐ Hearing My Thoughts

It's Monday. I'm never all that alert on Mondays, but today is different. I had 3 days off last week and I'm seeing a new client this afternoon. It's somewhat exciting as the discovery of a person's story always is to me. But that excitement is tempered by troubling thoughts of what I'm likely to find in his story and what it may mean for my life, perhaps in the next few years.

The first pieces of the story came last week in a phone call from "Goran." He's 21 years old; he has a strong accent but is competent and comfortable with English. A few pieces of the puzzle emerged in that brief telephone encounter. Another therapist who's assisting his housemate referred him to me. He's originally from Bosnia but fled with members of his family into Serbia when he was 13 years of age. He's a refugee and he's gay. Intriguing but troubling already for me. I said Yes to the referral because I couldn't think of a reason to say No. Come to think of it, I always seem to say Yes when I feel touched by exigent pain. Connection with that pain happens fairly readily for me. I'm touched by the person, but it's also something in me that's touched. Perhaps I sense the connection to my own isolation and pain. Resonance!

☐ Noting Thoughts and Feelings

I always carry a notebook with me. It's a, sort of, portable diary of emotions and thoughts. Top pocket and pen at the ready. These days, there's a quiet inner voice that urges me on to write those thoughts and feelings, my internal dialogs, particularly if they sound trivial, bizarre, mundane, or dangerous. I keep notes, I write anything that arises, and nothing is seen as rubbish; everything is grist to the mill. I make a point of never ripping pages out. Nothing is discarded.

It's a comforting mantra that I learned sometime during my twenties. Originally, it was a way that I could connect with images, thoughts, and feelings that I found to be unpalatable during my early adult years. In the midst of a time where confidence wasn't my big shot, it was sometimes all I had. It was the comfort and discomfort of my own words: words, jottings, and poems in my journals, and my little pocket notebooks. They are my story, one way I hold onto history: windows to the soul of me. Most important, this process of self-analysis was my way of trying to remain open when all my instincts led toward closure. And the practice continues. In fact it is core to my professional life. It is the structured, and routine practice of listening intently to my inner world—voices, elation, attraction, anguish, and fear—that forms the basis of my self-supervision.

> (*David*) Make a note of that, David; monitor the "Yes" within me. I can't seem to get away from the "Yes." What's the imperative there? It's deep within me but I'm not completely sure from where it arises. That desire to please people. That's partly it but it's more than that. It's personalized. I need to be connected. It's tempting to say it's Dad but he didn't always say, "Yes," and I didn't do that with him either. Exactly the opposite sometimes! His connection with me was strange—distant but caring. But I did want to please. Perhaps that's what I sensed in the phone call: a need to be connected, the sense of isolation, stories linking at yet unknown points. No, it's more. I want to please. There's the "Yes," I know its origin: compensating, say Yes, hope he says Yes!

As the day goes on, one word Goran didn't mention keeps resonating in my head. War.

> (*David*) I hate that word. I can't do this any more. There's only so much war I can handle. Don't say that, that's not okay. Innercity Sydney isn't Bosnia. Feels that way sometimes. Be open and available when he comes. Stop that! I am who I am. Available, yes, stupid and ignorant of my own needs, no! If I get the sense that it's beyond me, I'll speak with him and we'll see if I can find another person to help him. What am I saying, he hasn't even mentioned war yet. I haven't even seen him. Calm down, David, stop for a while and wait. Write it. Let it flow. Accept the noisy thoughts. Let the calm arrive in its own good time.

I make some time for reflective writing in the afternoon before Goran is to arrive at 3 P.M. Reflection time? Probably more about clearing my head of other voices and stories, not to mention my own complex desires and fears.

☐ Memories That Trigger!

At 3:10 P.M., I find myself unable to sit comfortably. Goran is late and I begin to pace the floor. Let's get this started, I keep thinking to myself. I hear the phone and my secretary is giving street directions. Okay, that's a relief, he's lost, and a little bit of calm returns.

> (*David*) Wait; don't lose that too quickly, that's anxiety. Write it down. Anxiety about what? A 21 year old I haven't met before? I don't think so. I'm not usually this anxious. What's the story here? Anxiety, fear, the unknown. There's something more and I can't even put it into words, let alone sentences. It's even pre-staccato.

I continue to wait and finally the buzzer rings. He heads for the toilet and I wait patiently. It remains difficult to clear my head.

> (*David*) It's the accent. It's the middle European accent that's ticked off something in me. Ramasan, that's it! Fifteen year ago. I remember; that hurts. Father dead, Ramasan a murderer, 14 years of age. Referred after his release at 16 years, became psychotic after prison. Didn't realize what that was going to be like. God, I've thought about him many times. Never again! Madness, me as target, shadows in him, him in the shadows. My heart still beats fast when I think of him. Sadness, guilt, anger, rage. Slowly, wait. Ramasan's dead now, slowly, that hurts. Memories don't die. I tried . . . and I feel I failed and got hurt in the process. Didn't realize that was still so alive in me. It's the accent. That's the trigger. Note that for later. I've talked and talked of that experience and still it lingers. Gosh, wish it would die. It doesn't, damn it!

Goran arrives. It's a hot blistery day in Sydney. We've had bush fires for weeks and the sky suspends an eerie yellow tinge. He arrives soaked from the humidity, already tired and nervous. Thirsty, he consumes glass after glass of water before we begin.

☐ An Ancient and Haunting Story

After the necessary drowning in water, and a few moments to settle, we begin. He's unsure how to start, but he captures his breath and the story gradually unfolds:

> G: I'm not sure why I'm here. My housemate is seeing a therapist for depression. I asked her to get a name and phone number for me. I wanted to see someone, too.
>
> DL: Why is that?
>
> G: I've been on Zoloft for about 9 months and at first I felt really good.

Even my work mates noticed a difference. But it isn't the same now. I don't feel good anymore. I walk through the city and look up at the buildings and wonder how I could get up there and jump.

DL: When did this begin?

G: A long time ago.

DL: Is there a story?

G: I guess so. I don't know.

DL: (Silence)

G: I was born in Bosnia and my mother and sister fled to Serbia when I was 13 because of the war. All I can remember about that time is waking up each day wondering when the bombs would start again. It was awful but I don't think about it these days. I don't think about much at all really, except how unhappy I am. I hate my life. I don't feel connected with my home, my family, or anyone. I just feel really alone.

DL: (I remain pensive and silent)

G: My father and uncle stayed behind in Bosnia because we all thought the war would end soon. But it didn't. We stayed in Serbia and they stayed in Bosnia. I had a really sheltered life in Bosnia until the war. It's just been really bad since I was 13. When we fled to Serbia, we had nothing. We were refugees.

DL: And you came to Australia.

G: Not till I was 19. Things began to settle down in Serbia and I went back to school and then all of a sudden our application for refugee status came through and we left for Australia. My mother and sister came as well. My uncle was already living here and so was my grandmother.

DL: And your father?

G: He was blown up by a grenade when I was 13.

We wait for several moments in silence. There is nothing I can say and I want to allow him the time to say whatever it is that is good for him.

G: I don't feel much about that. I guess I should but I don't. It's been a long time now and I didn't get the chance to know him as a man. I couldn't even go back to Bosnia for his funeral. It was too dangerous for a male to go back there. My uncle made a video of the funeral but I've never seen it. I don't know why. I just haven't. Perhaps I will some day.

So we came to Australia and I went to university. But it's never OK. I feel guilty all the time: anxious and guilty. That's why I left home. I couldn't handle feeling guilty and anxious all the time at home. They care about me so much and I don't deserve it. I'm gay and they don't know it.

DL: How would they feel about that?

G: Disappointed. My uncle would be angry. He's nice to me but I don't really know them. They would be disappointed for my father.

DL: So you left home.

G: I shared a room with my sister and I felt like the world was smothering me. I couldn't cope being there. I needed to escape. I needed to be in the inner city. I needed to explore what my sexuality meant for me but that hasn't worked either. I'm still unhappy. I still feel guilty and anxious.

I have lots of sex and I feel guilty all the time. I met this one guy in the toilet at university. He was so nice and we met again at the toilet a week later and then again a few days later. It was great. He was so beautiful and I wanted to make something happen with us but he just kept saying that he liked the sex but he didn't like me. Then he wanted to be friends but I wanted more. So eventually I stopped seeing him because I couldn't handle it.

Now I just do the saunas. Sometimes I just sit there on my own. Somtimes I just go into the cubicle and stay there alone, no sex. It feels safe being there. People there are like me.

Sometimes I think what I'm looking for is a relationship in these places. I know that sounds stupid but that's what I'm looking for. I hope that some-one will want to see more than my cock. You know. My eyes! Inside of me! Be with me! It doesn't work that way. So I go home and be alone.

We are there. War, isolation, fear, guilt, and masses of anxiety all around him, around us, and although I don't want to be too close as he unpacks the story that is him, I can't say, No! He's traveled so far and told no one of his story. Saying, No!—here and now—is not within my repertoire, although perhaps I wish it were.

☐ Grounded and Connected

As the next few sessions progress, the story becomes more complicated and intense. He is a young man who can't remember sensing happiness, forever riddled with anxiety and guilt. He always feels alone, targeted by other young people as a "poofter" he gradually isolates himself from friends and even his family. It's too corny to suggest that "survivor guilt" is core to his struggle, although that seems to be there. It's also too complex a story to reduce his terrifying experience of isolation to the loss of a father, the wasting of innocence through war, and the entombment of a life be-cause of burgeoning sexuality. These observations are probably at least partly relevant, but speaking of such things at this stage is what's clearly irrelevant.

People miss the point with him. There's disconnection, silence, and isolation and he must have a fear that here may well be the same. There's a story to be told. Most probably it will be long, terrifying, tragic, and scary, perhaps for both of us. He probably knows that his story is dangerous. His history and his experience cause people to disappear. He will need plenty of time to be convinced that his story won't have a similar effect on me or us. No interpretation is required or useful at this stage in our relationship. This is not the place to begin. But the question is relevant. Where do I begin, given that he keeps coming back and the story keeps unfolding?

There's a groundedness about this story. That's what makes it so riddled with fear for a counselor at the waiting. When I was a younger man, hearing a person's story seemed less complicated. The thoughts associated with becoming involved in the struggles of another person were less tempered by the reality of what that actually means—for them and for me. When I was younger, I was in there, boots and all.

My experience of facing new people within the context of counseling could not be more different today. The question of where to begin is riddled with my own feelings and agenda, a strong sense of the past, and hopefully, humility. It seems the first question for me now is whether I can handle new stories. Sometimes I feel ashamed about this reticence but it is my reality, and this is the only place to begin. If I am to be a good counselor, able to comprehend the pain of others, imbued with a desire for conversation and awareness, I must first be grounded within myself, in my reality and in humility. Connection follows.

☐ Thoughts Require Attention

After the first few sessions with Goran, I note a developing sense of attachment in me toward him: a desire to care for and protect this young man. The evocation is strong and accompanied by sadness and what feels like genuine pity and compassion. Amid the many feelings that I note during our first few contacts is the acute desire to quell the anxious noise that clouds his head—to fix his sense of never being happy. I want him to be happy. Perhaps I need him to be happy. This is really where it gets complex for me. It is the meeting of desires and passionate feelings that arise within both of us, somehow joining within the room in which we meet each week.

I know only too well in theory that to be in touch with one's own noisy mess is to be in touch with shadows and light, vulnerability and resilience: the real me. This is a good and essential practice for any counselor. But to actually live that out on a daily basis is the difficult task that must be undertaken.

To impress on me the significance of transparency and awareness, I engage in clinical supervision, I remember my own personal therapy experience and the practice the strides I once found so painful and difficult.

In the midst of this struggle, as perhaps my most important task, I give practical effect to the significance of mindfulness—transparency and awareness of vulnerability and resilience—by making a mark in my day, each day. I take notes; I listen, I write, I try to stay with my thoughts as I remain with their struggling voices. I supervise myself.

☐ Thoughts Require Conversation

There are moments in each of our lives that push us to the limits of our capacity, and then call for more. In those moments, when facing death or the impact of prolonged illness, life irrevocably changes. It is the magnitude of the moment and the fact that these life-changing experiences are immovable objects that make them such ground-shifting experiences.

Long before any of my family knew that Alzheimer's disease was active in my father, he sent me a card at a rather stormy time in our relationship. The card contained a yellow note stuck to the inside cover. On it he had inscribed the Latin phrase, *non sum qualis eram*, which loosely translated means, I am not the person I used to be. I'm not sure if he quite knew the import of his note but it stuck with me through his years of illness, death, and beyond and has become a mantra for understanding life. *Non sum qualis eram*. I am always changing!

In my early twenties, I entered my own therapeutic process: a critical part of change in my life. I have vivid memories of the time I spent ploughing through silence and resistance toward some exploration. I found it difficult tolerating the experience of aloneness and sense of abandonment. Forming words around this without exploding was near impossible. But when it ended, I had this quite extraordinary experience that it had only just begun, that the formal time together had no more than kick-started the more important therapeutic stuff in my life: an ongoing conversation within me and with others where I grow and change.

What I learned through my father's illness and in therapy is that radical reflexivity—the critical examination of my thoughts and feelings—is a process to be owned over a lifetime. It is generated and inculturated by experiences of conversation that only serve to begin and extend, not complete the task. If I am to grow as a person and a counselor, these conversations, with others and within me—the tolerating of sometimes painful experiences and the forming of words—must issue from the very sinews of my being, infiltrating all parts of me. This process is the very heartbeat of my existence and it is both a private and public affair.

However, finding the space and time for self-supervision is not always easy within the hurly burly of a counseling practice, particularly if marginalized young people are the core of that practice.

☐   Engulfing Noise and Emotion

It's a little after 10 A.M. and I'm wandering around our counseling center. It's a messy place to be. It's an ugly building set in the middle of a ritzy part of town. There's the noise of traffic, guys and girls playing pool, food being prepared, new people arriving, the normal yelling and screaming that young people use to call each other to attention. It's the general humdrum that makes this place a youth center and most of the time; I hardly notice the noise or the voices.

But today is different. All I can hear are the shouts and screams emanating from the parking lot near my office. I've experienced murderous rage before and the memory sticks like glue. The screams I'm hearing sound incredibly familiar. I can already feel anxiety deep within me. The screams continue and as I look out of my office window, I catch a glimpse of a young man with blood pouring from his face. He's been hit in the temple and he's staggering around slightly dazed from the strike.

I get this sinking feeling and the adrenalin begins to take effect within me. Rushing is all I can think to do at this stage. I've seen those movies where the doctors leap like gazelles from ER into the freezing cold to attend a fracas or an arriving ambulance. That's what it feels like: chaos, trauma, screams without faces, blood, and the possibility of uncontainable drama in the middle of a busy innercity suburb.

Ours is a strange place for this area of town. All hours during the day, young people drop in for food, a shower, a place to sleep, or to talk to someone who won't beat or abuse them. It's a shelter for homeless young people, sex workers, or any other marginalized youth of the inner city.

It's all so familiar and hardly an unusual event, but today's chaos is somehow different. First, the voices are unusually loud and violent. Second, the argument goes on and on, moving from one end of the grounds to the other. To make matters worse, all of this occurs within earshot of a police station, a primary school, a church complex, several other kids in trouble, and a visiting professor who just happens to be on my doctoral committee.

Something happens inside of me as all this begins to unfold. Something changes the very moment I hear the intensity of aggression, the loudness, and shrieking voices. A familiar process begins within me. I become aware that other members of the team are having the same experience. That brings about a strange sense of relief in the midst of screams, shocking violence, and the sense that all of this is out of control. I quickly make a check to see that my supervisor is in my office and then head out to the place from which all the screaming emanates. He's quite safe but I'm embarrassed at the scene. It's a momentary thought but it annoys me.

Girl Meets Boy?

Verbal abuse turns to violence. The girl involved in the fight seizes a back-pack from her combatant, a guy I now recognize as her boyfriend. She slashes him repeatedly across the face until blood starts to run again in streamlets. Rather than fighting back, he just stands there mute, cowering from her rage. It goes on and on with little sense of relief. She gets the sense she has the upper hand. This seems to provoke her even further. There seems no end to the violence. I'm not sure what's she's thinking but she appears to be enjoying this opportunity for rage and aggression. All the rest of us are slightly paralyzed.

What we can't seem to discover is an opportunity to physically intervene in a manner that won't inflame the situation further. I have no desire to see her turn on one of my staff. I also don't want the police to be involved if I can possibly avoid it. So we give it time. Interestingly, if the aggressor had been a man and the victim a woman, we would have intervened much earlier. But this time, we waited.

Eventually the steam runs out of the argument for a moment and the guy retreats and runs away, muttering that he is going to kill himself. I dispatch a counselor to his aid and help him to move away and find shelter in another part of the complex. Bruised within and without, he appears shocked and confused. Another member of the team approaches the girl and tries to move her toward the front gate of the Center. She's still screaming but eventually we're able to calm her down.

Just when we feel the situation is calm, Samantha gets wind that he's upset and receiving attention. This stirs her back into action. She breaches the containment line we've tried to establish and heads toward him again, ready for another fight. She's all steamed up and looking just as aggressive as she had not 10 minutes ago. But he's done. There's nothing left in him. He simply stands there and screams a plaintive cry and weeps. With any other person, this may have quelled the rage and finally quietened the day.

Samantha has finally found what seems to us like the moment she longed for. This is fuel to the fire. She is angry and now is even more furious because he is seen as the victim. Her outrage appears to know no bounds. She goes for him again, but this time we are actively involved and able to contain the situation. Separated from each other, we move Danny quietly from the precinct and to an area where there is no possibility of him being seen. Samantha remains at the gate, occasionally glancing with fury to see if he has returned.

Thirty minutes pass and both parties appear calm and exhausted. We all continue to function but feel stunned and wounded. There has been a breach of the safety, a direct attack on one person and a scatter-gun attack on the whole center—young people, staff—and the local community. I know some serious repair work will be needed at some stage but I'm not sure when or how this will occur.

While we all go about our business, there is a strong sense that we are all fretting as a result of the rageful incursion into the center. A number of us tried to intervene, stop the fracas, keep the peace, protect other young people, and separate the warring parties. It was crisis mode and all we could do was restore order and prevent the resurgence of further violence.

Forty minutes pass and Danny returns to the scene to pick up what is left of his shirt, ripped from his back during the early part of the fight. And then the final chapter occurrs both swiftly and blatantly in front of a stunned team and mostly nonchalant young people. Samantha approaches him; the rage all but extinguished. She hugs him, they kiss and hold hands, then disappear up the back lane, aligned again, and oblivious to any impact on the world they have just left.

☐ The Urge to Shut Down

For some young people, this is too normal. One of the them sitting quietly by the front door exclaims, "When's lunch on?" Business resumes. Other young people return to the Center to deal with their own crises. Some are HIV positive, some are addicted to a variety of substances. The majority earn a living on the streets selling their bodies or ripping off the unsuspecting customer by selling aspirin instead of heroin.

Life goes on and although this has shaken the adults, the young people appear almost unaffected by the whole disgusting event. Could that be true? Have they become so numb and blasé to the negativity in the lifestyle they lead? Or is their apparent ease really a shutdown of emotions, a denial, just another way of dealing with the noise and violent voices to which they are constantly exposed? Whatever their reality, I'm far from okay myself, and neither are the other counselors.

We have a scheduled meeting of the team that afternoon and the events of the morning dominate the discussion. There is no bypassing the reality that such events produce doubt and struggle in each of us at the Center. But how do we deal with this stuff? How do I deal with the violence, the pressure to protect, the desire to resolve conflict and keep a team together?

At the end of this particular event, I am more than anxious. Although the crisis has ended, the noise continues and my thoughts kept saying that somehow I've failed in my duty. I can't pin it down and it really makes no sense but that is what I feel. Strange noises, crippling thoughts.

I simply want to disappear. I long to forget the whole thing, including my responsibilities. I want and need to regain some measure of peace.

☐ Not Avoiding Conversation

As a group of youth workers and counselors, violence and suicide are core experiences, almost a daily part of our lives. These experiences need to be managed or survival will not occur.

There is a salutary reminder in the faces of young people who attend the center. It often seems they have this acute awareness and fear that the project they hold—their life—may well be beyond their capacity to manage. I think if I were in their shoes, I'd probably also want to shut down and ignore the noise and penetrating thoughts. That's the very reason we cannot ignore such events, let alone the feelings such happenings evoke in each of us.

During the afternoon team meeting, the chaos of that single hour fills our collective minds and spirits. It isn't our usual Friday meeting. We have a new-found friend with us that day, a visiting professor who observed the devastating events from my office. He already viewed us in our rawest state. He is now with us as we attempt to make sense of this turmoil.

We begin the meeting, each of us speaking of our experience. The focus is very much on what we saw and then, and in great depth, on what our concerns are for each of the combatants and more importantly, those who were unwitting participants in this raucous drama.

Jeffrey sits quietly throughout the discussion, waiting for a moment to comment. There is a lull and then he simply says to all of us, *Yes, but what are each of you feeling?* There is stunned silence. We had been talking for some 30 minutes and none of us had thought to raise the central issue of how we are feeling. It seemed so obvious a point of departure and yet we had left from another place, heading in a very safe direction; talking of them, not us.

☐ Openness in the Midst of Pain

There is reluctance. Initially there are only stammering sounds and furtive glances. Gradually the noises and the voices begin to emerge from the silence that held the raw experience. Words emerge reluctantly from the pain everyone wants to forget. Is it just the pain, or is it also our vulnerability and the failed attempt to keep everyone in our care safe and peaceful? It is all these things and more.

We spend the next hour or so concentrating on nothing else but what we are feeling. Several times, the conversation drifts back toward the young people, only to be prodded back toward our collective center by Jeffrey. It is hard tolerating our experiences and then allowing thoughts to grow around them. In some respects, self-supervision is a private affair but on this occasion, it really needs to be a public account because all of us need to speak, listen, and ponder our individual and collective experience.

It's hard to describe what we feel at this moment. Yes, there are common themes, and some of the noises and voices sound similar but they are also very different. For me, it is the inner noise that said I should not speak, that I should not express my fragility in front of a traumatized group of adults for whom I am ultimately responsible. Thankfully, these sentiments are muttered and challenged and accepted and embellished upon throughout the time we spend together.

It is clear that each of us has had similar thoughts of reluctance: thoughts that the raw stuff that inhabits our individual psyche is not the stuff of which our group conversation is made. Fear, loathing, anger, frustration, a desire to walk away, shattered expectations, loyalty to one or other of the combatants crushed or at the very least bruised. The debriefing in which we engage, our communal supervision, produces a myriad of thoughts and feelings that are sometimes shocking but always real and salient. There is an economy of words but a richness of expression.

☐ Moving Forward

Although demanding and initially quite scary for some, the experience produces a first-phase resolution of the drama of the day. It also leads to clarity of thought at a later meeting dedicated solely to the issues of resolution. In other words, by spending time together, by framing in words our own quite unique perspective on this event, by focusing on us as individuals and as group, by gathering our private and raw thoughts and not bypassing our feelings, a more challenging task becomes possible at another time. Because we spent time on this most necessary conversation, awareness increased, insight was possible, perspective was gained, and we were later able to consider management issues more fruitfully in all their complexity.

At the end of our meeting, all of us were left with a question, a thoughtful thread that reverberates still within the team. What does this experience have do to me and us? Can I forget about the clients long enough to remain with the experience—my experience—and think through the consequences of exposure to such violence? Can I dare to be the person within the counselor? Can I dare to remain with the loss of control? Can I dare to see and experience the very human mess within me that is triggered by the public chaos of others? Can I dare to admit my own humanity and stay with the fact that such experiences strip away the role, any power and position, leaving only the person and his very human experience? Can I listen to these noisy thoughts? Can I do this on my own? Can we do this together?

☐ The Constitutive Role of Conversation

I will remember that team meeting for some time to come. It was feisty and challenging but mostly a moment where, as individuals and as a group, we were called to account, to face the reality of our own humanity and to explore the feelings that generate fear and passion. What has stayed with me from that experience? That it is easier to focus on the other, the clients, than on our own experience as individuals and as a group. It is too easy to hold the myth that I can hear the noises and voice of the other person while not listening to my own thoughts. This dramatic event and the communal experience of listening to the noise within each of us challenged that myth.

Finally, I have learned that individual self-supervision is crucial but there is a point and there are situations where that must be shared. Self-supervision is internalized conversation aimed at change and development but conversation that is truly formative results from the sharing of our common experience. After all, human beings are constituted in conversation (Taylor, 1991).

☐ Learning Self-Supervision

For some within the team, their own capacity to engage in self-supervision predated this extraordinary meeting. Like me, they sit and ponder; although they may be fearful of what they discover within, they nonetheless continue their radically reflexive practice of listening to and noting the movements within.

For other members of the team, sharing the dramatic experience of that day generates a sense of surprise and relief. They have not heard others speak of fear and hate, disgust and disappointment in relation to clients. It is out of this sense of relief that they gain the confidence to think on their own. In other words, their reluctance to think in solitude has its origin in an overwhelming fear of thinking terrible thoughts. Their capacity for creative and transparent thinking, therefore, is stymied by fear. They hold strongly to the belief that their thoughts are theirs alone and that no one else has thought such horrid things. For some, this day is the beginning of developing capacity for self-supervision.

The growing of self-supervision is a complex phenomenon. The individual experience and the shared experience of exploring our internal dialogs complement and feed each other. For some, it begins in solitude. For others, there is a need to hear from colleagues before they can feel free to articulate what they often judge to be abhorrent.

What I have learned as a counselor and director in a busy innercity youth center is that time is of the essence. I know that change cannot be hurried. Externals can, but inner change can never be rushed. What I struggle to hold onto with alacrity is that counselors need time to explore these individual and shared processes, even though such a commodity is always in scarce supply. They also need to experience openness and transparency from their leaders and mentors. This is how they learn the art of self-supervision.

☐ References

Blum, H. (1996). The Irma dream, self-analysis, and self-supervision. *Journal of the American Psychoanalytic Association, 44*(2), 511–532.

Bramley, W. (1996). *The supervisory couple in broad spectrum psychotherapy*. London: Free Association Books.

Castoriadis, C. (1995). Logic, imagination, reflection. In A. Elliott & S. Frosh (Eds.), *Psychoanalysis in contexts: Paths between theory and modern culture* (pp. 15–35). London: Routledge.

Donnelly, C., & Glaser, A. (1992). Training in self-supervision skills. *The Clinical Supervisor, 10*, 85–96.

Freud, S. (1900). *The standard edition of the complete psychological works of Sigmund Freud: The interpretation of dreams* (Vol. 4–5). London: Hogarth.

Freud, S. (1914). *The standard edition of the complete psychological works of Sigmund Freud: On the history of the psycho-analytic movement* (Vol. 14). London: Hogarth.

Holloway, E. L. (1997). Structures for the analysis and teaching of supervision. In C. E. Watkins (Ed.), *Handbook of psychotherapy supervision* (pp. 249–276). New York: Wiley.

Lane, R. (Ed.). (1990). *Psychodynamic approaches to supervision*. New York: Brunner-Mazel.

Lewis, J. (1991). *Swimming upstream: Teaching and learning psychotherapy in a biological era*. New York: Brunner-Mazel.

Lowe, R. (2000). Supervising self-supervision: Constructive inquiry and embedded narratives in case consultation. *Journal of Marital and Family Therapy, 26*(4), 511–521.

Mollon, P. (1997). Supervision as a space for thinking. In G. Shipton (Ed.), *Supervision of psychotherapy and counselling: Making a place to think* (pp. 24–34). Buckingham: Open University Press.

Morrissette, P. J. (1999). Family therapist self-supervision: Toward a preliminary conceptualization. *The Clinical Supervisor, 18*(2), 165–183.

Protinsky, H., & Coward, L. (2001). Developmental lessons of seasoned marital and family therapists: a qualitative investigation. *Journal of Marital and Family Therapy, 27*(3), 375–384.

Shillito Clarke, C. (1996). Ethical issues in counselling psychology. In R. Woolfe & W. Dryden (Eds.), *Handbook of counselling psychology* (pp. 555–580). Thousand Oaks, CA: Sage.

Taylor, C. (1991). The dialogical self. In D. R. Hiley, J. F. Bohman, & R. Shusterman (Eds.), *The interpretive turn: Philosophy, science, culture* (pp. 304–314). Ithaca: Cornell University Press.

Todd, T. (1997). Self-supervision as a universal supervisory goal. In T. Todd & C. Storm (Eds.), *The complete systematic supervisor: Content, philosophy and pragmatics*. Boston: Allyn & Bacon.

Watkins, C. E. (1997a). Defining psychotherapy supervision and understanding supervisor functioning. In C. E. Watkins (Ed.), *Handbook of psychotherapy supervision* (pp. 3–10). New York: Wiley.

Watkins, C. E. (Ed.). (1997b). *Handbook of psychotherapy supervision*. New York: Wiley.

Williams, A. (1995). *Visual and active supervision: Role focus technique*. New York: Norton.

Yontef, G. (1997). Supervision from a Gestalt Therapy perspective. In C. E. Watkins (Ed.), *Handbook of psychotherapy supervision* (pp. 147–163). New York: Wiley.

9
CHAPTER

John A. Casey
W. Paul Jones

Technoconsultation: Getting Help in Far-Flung Places

Maria S. is a full-time school counselor and part-time marriage and family therapist (MFT) practicing in a small town in rural Nevada. She is the only counselor in the school district and the only MFT in a radius of 200 miles. In the school she is a strong and effective advocate for her students. She is also an exceptionally talented therapist, and slowly she has been successful in overcoming the reluctance of many community members to acknowledge the importance of family therapy and seek help. In this setting, Maria is constantly challenged with issues related to professional boundaries. While helping a student make decisions about university admission applications, she, for example, may be dealing with highly relevant information, unknown to the student, that one of the parents has decided to seek a divorce with significant impact on family financial resources. To further complicate the matter, the other spouse manages the only well-stocked grocery store within miles, so regular contact cannot be avoided.

John A. is a licensed marriage and family therapist with an upscale practice on the north side of Chicago. He shares office space with another MFT and a psychologist in a high-rise professional building. There are three other MFT practices in the building along with assorted health care and other professionals. Starting with referrals from an attorney in the same building, John has built a highly successful practice. A significant portion of his work is involved with child custody evaluations, and he has also attained a reputation for expertise in treatment of the effects of sexual abuse. A typical work day, thus, is divided between appointments in his office, required court appearances, and consultation with attorneys. John would like to reduce the extent that his practice is dependent on legal issues but struggles to find time to grow another area of specialty. He lives with his family in a western suburb and spends 3 hours each day commuting by train and bus to his office.

The preceding scenarios, although hypothetical, have a reality base in an amalgamation of real-life experiences of the authors. At first glance, other than some comparable training experiences, the practices of these two therapists would appear to have little in common. With a closer look, however, both share a common problem, isolation from developmental interaction with colleagues.

Maria's geographical isolation from other counselors is obvious. She is "the" counselor in her community. When, for example, she needs to discuss her conflicts with the multiple roles she must play in her work, whom does she ask? Textbooks and perhaps even her university trainers may not be in a position to provide useful guidance. The books have a simple prescription for dealing with multiple relationships: Don't. But perhaps only someone in a comparable setting might really be in a position to understand the implications of "just saying No." Maintaining multiple relationships may well be walking the boundary of ethical practice, but failure to make needed service available certainly seems the greater sin.

Professional isolation in a practice in rural areas like Nevada is, of course, not surprising. We often fail to recognize, though, that practice in a busy urban setting can have just as many features of isolation from meaningful interaction with colleagues.

Consider our example, John A. We can assume that he and the colleagues with whom he shares the office will exchange greetings. It also seems reasonable to assume that when issues arise about the office lease, the copier, paper supplies, and so forth, they find a moment or so to exchange opinions. We could even go so far as to assume that any one of them probably has the skills to serve as a valued consultant to another. But when? We suspect that most all who have worked in a comparable setting would attest to the extremely limited amount of discretionary time actually available. The 10 minutes between scheduled appointments is not conducive to a meaningful dialog. An "appointment" with a colleague could be scheduled, but that's probably money "out of pocket" for both practitioners, particularly when trying to keep up with a successful practice.

This material in this chapter rests on the following four beliefs:

- Professional isolation is a risk in all practice settings.
- Isolation contributes to a lack of continuing professional growth and development.

- Isolation increases risks for impaired performance and burnout.
- Technological resources can be used to both reduce isolation and enhance professional development through self-supervision.

In this chapter we will both identify and describe a sampling of current and potential applications of tools for technoconsultation, ranging from enhanced use of POTS (plain old telephone service) to computer-mediated communication with video cues. Each of these tools is now available for use in self-supervision, but these represent only the tip of the iceberg. The pace of technological innovation moves far more quickly than the preparation and publication of this chapter, so our goal is both to offer suggestions for specific consultation tools that can enhance your self-supervision and to encourage your own creativity in adapting new tools as they become available.

☐ Just Give Me a Call

What about just using the telephone? Consider the following event that occurred in the mid-1980s. I (Paul) from the study in my home in Las Vegas am learning the wonders of modem-based communication from an AT&T technical expert (who happens to be my son-in-law) then in Boulder, Colorado. After several false starts, suddenly our computers are linked. I am impressed. I am thrilled. I am, in fact, so excited that I call out to my wife to hurry in to see what we have done. When she appears, her affect clearly portrays her general disdain for my technical gadgets, but she is a tolerant soul (career social worker), and she asks what's going on. I point to the computer screen, and she watches while I type, "Hi Bruce, how are you?" Then, one letter at a time, at the breakneck speed of 300 baud, scrolling across the screen she sees, "Hi dad, I'm fine, and you?" She asks how we are doing this, and I can hardly contain my excitement in telling her that we are communicating with the computers over the phone line. Anticipating that she will be impressed by this high-tech communication mode and that I will be praised for my cutting-edge mentality, she instead offers something that in retrospect should be a rubric for evaluating all technological applications. Her words are: "Why don't you just pick up the phone and talk to him?"

With the increasing availability of pagers, instant messaging services, real-time chat, and so forth, it's easy to overlook the most universally accessible and familiar of our communication tools, plain old telephone service. It's available 24/7. No special training is required. Reliability continues to exceed most, if not all, of our other resources.

Certainly we now do much better than 300 baud, and there are needs for which other tools are far better suited. However, the message in the illustration remains valid. The desired outcome should drive the selection of tools. And there are some, perhaps still many, instances in which the optimal alternative to face-to-face communication for consultation is the telephone. The use of "appropriate" technology should be our goal.

The efficacy of delivering therapy services via the telephone is well supported in the literature. Examples include its value in reducing feelings of isolation (Shepard, 1987), direct treatment of obsessive-compulsive disorder (Lovell, Fullalove, Garvey, & Brooker, 2000), and family therapy application (Springer & Stahmann, 1998). The telephone has long been used to assist in counseling supervision (Casey, Bloom, & Moan, 1994), particularly when the supervisee is in a distant location (Wetchler, Trepper, McCollum, & Nelson, 1993).

In reference to our focus in this chapter, technoconsultation to reduce isolation and enhance ongoing professional growth and development, the primary concern when the consultation is to come from another provider is finding the time when a connection can be made. I (Paul) have, at last count, four unique phone numbers, all of which are connected to answering devices, none of which (according to my friends) are ever likely to be directly answered. If you are seeking consultation from another provider, the "when to call" question is a critical one. The 10 or 15 minutes between appointments is not sufficient time for reflective thought essential for such consultation, and we are often hesitant to make the evening or weekend calls because we don't want to feel like telemarketers.

Our advice here is probably obvious and straightforward. If your question is more complex than a simple request for a DSM-IV code or referral source, treat your request for phone consultation as if you were requesting a therapy appointment. Set a specific time and time limit for the phone conversation and find some mutually acceptable form of compensation. We recognize that the latter is often awkward, particularly if the other person is a colleague or friend. In those instances, however, it is perhaps even more important to recognize that, as therapists, our time is the primary commodity we have to sell.

Telephone-based therapy or supervision would, of course, have been out of the question when phone lines were shared, the old "party lines." Confidential/privacy issues would have been rampant. Anyone along the line could pick up their phone and hear everything being said. Although in almost all locations, that type of phone service is in the distant past, some elements of that same concern must be considered in contemporary applications as well. If the consultation is through an office phone, how many others in the office have access to that line with a push of a button? And, if the call is to the consultant's home, how many other phones in the home use the same line?

With the wide use of call forwarding, the privacy issue can become even more complex. Many of us, for example, occasionally forward our phone numbers to a mobile phone. Thus, a call made to a land line may actually be answered in an automobile or other offsite location. Some crossed communications are not unusual outcomes when using our cellular phones, and there is always some risk of overhearing all or at least part of another conversation.

Caution, not paranoia, is our suggestion. Insisting on a scrambled, CIA-type telephone link is obviously absurd and misses the point of easier access through use of the phone. Given, though, the wide variety of phone applications in contemporary society, it would not be inappropriate to always ask about privacy before you begin talking about a client. It's probably a safe rule of thumb that any provider who would be offended by your question is a provider from whom supervisory consultation would be of questionable value.

☐ Look at Me While I'm Talking to You

A primary limitation of telephone-based consultation is, of course, the lack of video cues. Later in this chapter we examine some of the special opportunities now available through use of computer-mediated video conferencing. It is also possible, however, to add video cues while maintaining the advantages of telephone-based consultation.

The videophone, first introduced by AT&T at the World's Fair in New York in 1964, was not widely embraced by consumers. For a variety of reasons, such devices remain mostly curiosities, interesting to try but seldom used. More recent development, of course, has focused on harnessing the Internet/WWW in applications of video conferencing. We should also note that choosing telephone or computer is actually not a true dichotomy. A form of telephone communication is also available through the so-called net phones.

In preparing this chapter, we are especially cognizant of the fact that we are describing technological alternatives through a view of what is available at the time of this writing. Internet-based phones and/or video conferencing with audio included may at some point in the near future be viable alternatives for technoconsultation applications. At this point in time, however, the quality of the communication precludes dependence on the audio. Earphones can solve the lack of privacy with audio from the sound card in the computer. But nuances in the voice, often crucial in effective communication, are lost in the audio transmission.

There is, though, a simple and quite inexpensive way to combine your phone and your computer to add visual cues to phone-based communication. To use this combination you need only:

1. A line for standard phone use near your computer
2. An Internet connection that does not use this phone line (e.g., cable-modem, DSL connection, another phone line)
3. A camera attached to your computer
4. Webcam software

It would be rare not to be able to meet the first of these criteria, and many of us have already taken steps for the second. Cameras as attachments to computers are widely available and inexpensive. Webcam software is easily obtained, often free, and detailed instructions for integrating a Webcam in a therapy environment are available in Jones, Coker, Harbach, and Staples (2002).

In actual practice the person on the other end of the conversation can go to an Internet address you provide and watch a near real-time video while talking with you on the phone. Although not as sophisticated as some of the alternatives to be described later in this chapter, the simplicity of this approach is compelling. There is, of course, no privacy of the video transmission; anyone who might stumble onto the address can see the image. That, however, is not especially likely, and, in any case, the quality of the transmission essentially precludes a loss of confidentiality through lip reading.

☐ Send Me an E-Mail

After telephone consultation, electronic mail is easily the next most widely adopted form of technoconsultation in current use. It is a readily available and easy form of communication between therapists in adjacent offices and on different continents. It is available for both one-to-one and group interactions.

As university professors, we have found e-mail communication useful with practitioners and graduate students. The examples that follow, taken from standard supervision practices with preservice graduate students, are easily generalized to consultations between and among practicing therapists as a part of self-supervision.

Obviously, safeguards to maximize confidentiality must be taken, such as withholding of client names (or even initials), locking the hard drive with password protection when not in use, using encryption when available, and deleting files in a timely manner. References to a Website for more resources can be easily included with an e-mail. Particularly sensitive information can be sent in an e-mail with the heading "Do not forward without permission of the sender."

Group e-mail is another alternative. As university supervisors of interns, we have used group e-mail as both a daily "check-in" tool between weekly in-person meetings and as a way of allowing interns placed in farflung locations to converse with the other interns in the metropolitan area. Consider the reinforcement, support, and professional growth that would become available if a group of like-minded therapists made it a practice to "check-in" with each other on a regular basis.

A recent example with counseling interns illustrates the concept. I (John) encouraged the use of "daily check-in" e-mails among eight school counseling interns at the University of Nevada, Reno. Although the group met in a live seminar one night each week for 90 minutes, it was hypothesized that many issues were not brought forth during the group meeting because of time and memory constraints. Each student and the faculty member agreed to allow their e-mail address to be shared with all of the others in the group. In the first week, e-mail sharing was sparse, as incorrect addresses were noted as "undeliverable mail." After corrections were made, however, the eight group members and one faculty member generated a mean of 22.4 e-mail messages per week over the following 13 weeks. The most active participant sent out 39 e-mail messages, whereas the least active participant sent nine messages. The content was analyzed and tabulated under the following categories: (a) request for assistance for new topics; (b) response to request for assistance in (a); (c) expression of feelings; and (d) other. (Note: an e-mail may contain more than one of the categories; thus the percentage total may exceed 100%.) The post-semester content analysis of all e-mails revealed that 53% of the e-mail communication included a request for assistance; 61% of the e-mail communication included a response; 84% included an expression of feelings; and 16% included other topics (most frequently a follow-up of topics discussed in the weekly live seminar, followed by questions about course assignments to the instructor and, finally, announcements about upcoming events). An end-of-semester course evaluation indicated that the students unanimously and enthusiastically endorsed the inclusion of e-mail communication as a supplement to weekly live seminars, with comments that included: "Writing to the group about a problem just before bedtime helped me sleep better . . . " and "The time in seminar is so short that we don't always have time for my needs; e-mail gave me a second option."

Although in self-supervision applications the content emphasis probably varies from that of the preservice therapists, the underlying value seems to remain constant. Just substitute "didn't have time to finish this conversation when we visited in the office" for "didn't get to this in seminar," and add the opportunity for input of several therapists, not just ones with whom daily or weekly contact is likely.

You Don't Have to Be Nearby

A major advantage of the electronic modalities is the opportunity to communicate over long distances. Continuing the idea of generalizing from standard to self-supervision consultation, I (John) have often been responsible for supervising interns placed in rural communities such as Ely and Jackpot, Nevada. Both Ely and Jackpot are over 8 hours from a university and have no commercial airline service. You really have to "want to get there" in order to get there.

Adapting our standard supervision techniques was a state mandate. Schools in rural Nevada, like many rural areas of the United States, frequently cannot recruit credentialed counselors to fill vacant positions. Thus, the state allows "provisional credentials" to be issued to teachers in rural schools with expectation that distance learning and summer enrollment in the "big city" could be combined to complete the counseling training. Our dilemma was in how to deliver ongoing supervision.

A solution to this dilemma in a recent semester allowed the one intern who was in a rural setting to receive the group supervision required by accreditation exclusively through group e-mails with the students enrolled on the campus. End of semester feedback was enthusiastically positive by all students, reporting that all learned from each other via the e-mail communication across rural and urban settings.

Particularly relevant for consideration as a self-supervision modality is whether e-mail supervision interactions approximate the quality of face-to-face communication. State licensing and national accreditation groups are still struggling with this question. A literal interpretation of the standards for the accreditation group most closely associated with the preceding scenario, for example, says that the student in the rural area did not receive sufficient supervision. Credibility for the approach, however, is evident in that a ranking official of that accreditation group in fact pioneered a comparable application for remote locations in another state.

Join the Group

An increasingly popular tool for reducing isolation and enhancing professional growth has been the proliferation of counseling and therapy-related listservs. When people join a listserv, they submit their e-mail address, which subsequently enables them to receive posted e-mail messages from anyone else who has also joined. When a listserv becomes large, the subscriber may find entering the command for a "digest" condenses all of the dialing mailings into one "super" mailing, with a list of topics of the day heading up the single e-mail message.

Perhaps the largest and most popular listserv for counselors since the 1990s has been the International Counselor Network (ICN), founded by Ellen Rust, an elementary school counselor in Tennessee. Now housed through the University of Tennessee at Knoxville, there are typically about 1,000 persons around the globe subscribing to the ICN on a given day. In addition to the current message, thousands of postings since 1995 have been archived at the ICN website that are searchable by a variety of parameters, including topic or author, on virtually any topic in the field. Although no guarantee can be made about who actually posted the message, the site nonetheless offers a bountiful assortment of valuable information for the practitioner. The URL for the ICN is http://listserv.utk.edu/archives/icn.html

☐ Computer Conferencing: More Than Just E-Mail

Internet-based conferencing provides a variety of opportunities for a therapist to avoid feelings of isolation. Its most basic application, the text-chat, requires only a browser and an Internet connection and opens the doors for communication across wide geographic boundaries. Sussman (2000) identified text-chat as one of the primary alternatives available for exchange of information in therapy environments, and Delmonico, Daninhirsch, Page, Walsh, L'Amoreaux, and Thompson (2000) describe use of this modality to provide a virtual support group for doctoral students in counselor education, an application quite comparable to its potential use for practicing therapists.

Let's Chat

A basic text-chat application involves simply logging in to a chat room and communicating through typed messages. Chatrooms are, of course, ubiquitous in the Web environment. For use in technoconsultation, though, privacy and confidentiality may be significant concerns.

Open chat rooms typically offer virtual "private rooms" through which your communications are not open to others logged into the chat area. Although this provides some measure of security, we would encourage caution, particularly with sites that are offered free of charge. Remember that somewhere there is a Web master responsible for oversight of the chat area, and that person has direct access to all of the communications.

If text-chat is being planned for use in an ongoing consultation relationship, it may be worthwhile for either you or your consultant to consider implementing a personal chat system. The essential software is available at little or no cost. The only other requirement is a Website to which files can be uploaded. The specific location for uploading, and permission to execute the software on the Web server is obtained from the Web master. Installation is necessary at only one site. For example, if you install the software, your consultant needs only the address and a Web browser to access the chat. Detailed instructions for implementing your own text-chat system in a therapist's environment are available (Jones, Coker, Harbach, & Staples, 2002). Free and/or inexpensive software can be easily located in a Web search with key words text chat software.

Using your own text-chat software does not, of course, completely remove concerns about privacy and confidentiality. Unless you are also running your own Web server, there is still somewhere a Web master with access to the communications. And, as with all forms of computer messaging, packets of information with potentially sensitive information are making their way across the Internet.

Effective communication via a text-chat program presumes that the users are fluent in written communication and are reasonably competent and comfortable in use of a computer. The former is certainly a reasonable assumption for therapists and their consultants, but the latter may or may not be evident. Hackerman and Greer (2000) provide a useful overview of special features to consider in computer-mediated communication, including suggestions for how to add perceptions of warmth to what can appear to be a cold, if not harsh modality.

The cautions and concerns are not intended to discourage use of this modality. Text-chat programs enable distant communications with no charge other the standard cost for your Internet access. This modality can be used to exchange documents, for example, test results or case notes that can enhance the value of the consultation. A feature of online interactions that can be especially useful in consultation and/or supervision applications is that the communication typically is saved in a log file for a lasting record of the exchange of ideas.

Privacy and confidentiality issues must be considered, and if you make extensive use of this modality, consideration of some form of encryption is warranted. Certainly, referring to clients by initials or aliases and eliminating other identity cues not needed for the consultation seems to be the best practice. In fairness, though, we emphasize that such issues do not disappear when using standard face-to-face interactions. One could, in fact, argue that the use of online modalities has brought much needed attention to the extent to which we actually do protect information about our clients.

One feature of typical text-chat applications that can become problematic, particularly if the conference involves more than two participants, is a slow exchange of message. The actual speed of communications is dependent on several factors, including the quality and type of your Internet access. This can be especially troublesome when your message is a question. You send the question. Nothing comes back in response, and you are left wondering whether the message was received or whether instead your technoconsultant is pondering a response.

The various instant messaging applications offer a partial answer to this dilemma. These programs, offered by most major Internet software providers, typically work by establishing direct "socket" connections between computers and deliver essentially real-time speed in exchange of messages. Some also include cues that the person on the other end of the line is in the process of preparing a response, especially helpful information in situations where some reflection is often desirable before a response is made.

With some computer programming expertise it is possible to obtain both the speed and the cues that message is in preparation with software designed specifically for use in a therapist's environment (Jones, Coker, Harbach, & Staples, 2002). As a general rule of thumb with the standard messaging services, though, we believe that the increased speed and the cues that messages are in preparation would come at a high cost in compromised confidentiality. Their best use is probably implicit in the name, instant messaging. They provide a great tool to send short messages but are generally not well suited for the sometimes lengthy exchange of ideas necessary for enhancing clinical skills and performance.

Let's Add Some Pictures

Of the computer-based communications for supervision and/or service delivery, video conferencing is one of the more frequently mentioned modalities (Manhal-Baugus, 2001; McFadden, 2000). This modality has been suggested and/or demonstrated as a viable tool for a number of applications. Hart (2000) describes its potential for enabling enhanced faculty–student interactions. Masi and Freedman (2001) include video conferencing in their review of the literature regarding employee assistance services delivered through technology. The results of a trial with video conferencing to deliver psychiatric services (Mannion, Fahy, Duffy, Broderick, & Gethins, 1998) were described as sufficient to warrant further trial. Video conferencing has been used for both general (Ball, Scott, McLaren, & Watson, 1993) and neuropsychological (Troester, Paolo, Glatt, Hubble, & Koller, 1995) assessment applications.

In considering the use of video conferencing as a technoconsultation tool, there are some important cautions. In most, if not all, instances the sophisticated hardware and software technologies associated with telehealth applications are unlikely to be feasible tools for regular thera-pist–consultant interactions. Unless provided by your employer, the cost is prohibitive, and even if the resources are available in your employ-ment site, the logistics of scheduling usually preclude effective use for this purpose. Thus, for our application, video conferencing is defined as the use of one of the free or relatively inexpensive software programs with a small camera connected to your computer.

The smaller scale video conferencing software typically allows for com-munication either through an embedded text-chat or the sound card on your computer. Our experience suggests that the latter is unlikely to be satisfactory. The quality of the transmitted sound is often marginal, and the lack of match between video and audio is disconcerting. Privacy is also problematic with the aural transmission.

In reference to establishing a trusting relationship when using this modality, Muehlfeler, Klein, Simon, and Luczak (1999) found no differ-ence in the mean ratings of trust among persons meeting for the first time when comparing video conferencing to face-to-face interactions. How-ever, they reported a significant reduction in the variability of the ratings. This finding suggests that there are visual cues in face-to-face interactions that may not generalize while video conferencing.

Self-disclosure is typically valued in consultation, and Joinson (2001) found that the extent of spontaneous self-disclosure was actually higher in computer-mediated communications when compared to face-to-face interactions. Also found in the study, though, was that participants who were visually anonymous disclosed significantly more information than those who could be seen.

In a study of group problem solving, Habash (1999) found that decision making did not appear to be impaired when using distance technology. In this study, however, he also found that there was negligible impact when video was added to the audio conferencing.

The preceding studies are not intended to discourage your consider-ation of video conferencing as an alternative for technoconsultation. Video cues are an important consideration in online communications (Coursol & Lewis, 2000; Sampson, 2000), and video conferencing may provide a "close enough to real-life" communication experience.

A study of online test interpretation by Jones, Harbach, Coker, and Staples (2002) compared online text-chat with face-to-face modalities. Results indicated that ratings of session depth were equivalent if the text-chat included a video window showing provider and participant. Partici-pants whose video image was being broadcast did have higher ratings of discomfort during the session, a finding that may explain the decreased self-disclosure in the Joinson (2001) study cited previously. A follow-up study (Jones, Harbach, Coker, & Staples, 2001) was conducted in which the provider image was broadcast to all participants, and the participants were randomly assigned to groups in which their image was or was not broadcast to the provider. Results appear to confirm the hypothesis that seeing the person on the other end of the communication is desired, but being seen is not. The advantages of the visual cues may offset the discomfort, and anticipating the likelihood of some discomfort may ameliorate the effects.

Considering all available information, video conferencing certainly seems to warrant your consideration as a tool for distance interactions with a consultant. Our suggestion with current technology is that, unless you have direct access to the more sophisticated implementations, the video should be conceptualized as a supplemental tool to a text-chat interaction with the suggestions for that modality described earlier in this chapter.

If you are convinced that this is worth a trial, Brown (2000) provides some useful guidance for the professional who is just getting started. Jones, Coker, Harbach, and Stapes (2002) provide detail on implementing a text-chat system, with and without video conferencing capability.

☐ Going to Class Without Going to Class

Continuing to grow as a therapist obviously requires a commitment to continuing education, both in supervisory consultation and in more formal educational experiences. Online courses and CD-ROM products are increasingly available as technological alternatives to the standard classroom.

Online courses have been encouraged by institutions that may see these courses as revenue-enhancing strategies (i.e., the content may be created once and utilized numerous times), while also providing instruction at more convenient times and places for the learner. Early efforts in this direction took the form of "correspondence courses," where the learner was mailed curriculum units and replied with completed assignments via postal mail to the instructor. With the Internet, entire courses can be mounted online and communication with the instructor can take place via e-mail or live chats. Whether this pedagogy is sufficient for all forms of training as a therapist has been questioned by some (Albrecht & Jones, 2002), and it has created a variety of challenges for state education agencies and accreditation boards as they struggle to define minimum instructional requirements. Whether or not there are specific areas in which this modality is not sufficient, it certainly is a viable alternative for many content areas and more convenient in essentially call cases.

Sites sponsored by ERIC/CASS (http://ericcass.uncg.edu/) and the *Journal of Technology and Counseling* (http://jtc.colstate.edu) offer extensive professional development resources for counselors and therapists, ranging from refereed journal articles to downloadable files to be used with Microsoft PowerPoint presentations.

The availability of CD-ROM products has also grown rapidly in recent years. Isolated professionals who desire a "tune-up" in their basic counseling skills will find "Basic Counseling Responses" (Haney & Leibsohn, 1999) and "Basic Counseling Responses for Groups" (Haney & Leibsohn, 2001) to be particularly valuable resources for simulation training (as pilots learn to fly airplanes). A comprehensive review of historical attempts to create simulation training for counselors is available online in the inaugural edition of the *Journal of Technology in Counseling* (Casey, 1999).

☐ Closing Thoughts

Professional isolation and lack of professional development is a growing problem for therapists and other human service professionals across rural and urban settings. This chapter has illustrated selected samples of technoconsultation tools that hold promise for reducing isolation and enhancing professional development. Our examples were focused on a rural area in just one state, but the use of these tools is essentially identical whether communicating with someone down the hall or with a colleague in a distant part of the planet.

Many questions remain unanswered. An especially relevant challenge is illustrated in comments from a school counselor in rural Nevada who, despite being the first school counselor in northern Nevada to design a counseling Website, states:

> Technology is a great tool, but as a way to mentor and help new counselors in the field, it is still lacking. Email and technology cannot substitute for a friendly and empathetic face or word. Until technology gets better developed with video conferencing, many counselors in rural and isolated areas are going to feel left out of the loop. (D. Bryant, personal communication, 2001)

As hardware innovation begets software development, and software development begets adoption and utilization (Casey, 1995), our technoconsultation opportunities will grow with each new technological innovation. As videotape was the dominant training tool for the last half of the 20th century, the Internet and its associated tools are showing signs of becoming a lifeline for the 21st century. Judicious and prudent adoption of appropriate technologies will be a key ingredient in this growth.

☐ **References**

Albrecht, A.C., & Jones, D. G. (2002). *High tech/high touch: Distance learning in counselor preparation.* Alexandria, VA: Association for Counselor Education and Supervision.

Ball, C. J., Scott, N., McLaren, P. M., & Watson, J. P. (1993) Preliminary evaluation of a Low-Cost (LCVC) system for remote cognitive testing of adult psychiatric patients. *British Journal of Clinical Psychology, 32,* 303–307.

Brown, D. (2000). The odyssey of a technologically challenged counselor educator into cyberspace. In J. W. Bloom & J. R. Waltz (Eds.), *Cybercounseling and cyberlearning: Strategies and resources for the millenium* (pp. 51–64). Alexandria, VA: American Counseling Association.

Casey, J., Bloom, J. B., & Moan, E. (1994). *Use of technology in counselor supervision.* ERIC Digest ED372357 Apr 94. ERIC Clearinghouse on Counseling and Student Services, Greensboro, NC. Available online at http://www.ed.gov/databases/ERIC_Digests/ED372357.html

Casey, J. (1995). Developmental issues for school counselors using technology. *Elementary School Guidance and Counseling, 30,* 26–34.

Casey, J. (1999). Computer assisted simulation for counselor training of basic skills. *Journal of Technology in Counseling, 1.* Retrieved March 28, 2002, from http://jtc.colstate.edu/vol1_1/simulation.htm

Coursol, D. H., & Lewis, J. (2000). Cybersupervision: Close encounters in the new millenium. Retrieved February 10, 2002, from http://cybercounsel.uncg.edu/book/manuscripts/cybersupervision.htm

Delmonico, D. L., Daninhirsch, C., Page, B., Walsh, J., L'Amoreaux, N. A., & Thompson, R. S. (2000). The palace: Participant responses to a virtual support group. *Journal of Technology in Counseling, 1.2.* Retrieved May 25, 2002, from http://jtc.colstate.edu/vol1_2/palace.htm

Habash, T. F. (1999). The impact of audio- or video-conferencing and group decision tools on group perception and satisfaction in distributed meetings. *Psychologist-Manager Journal, 3,* 211–230.

Hackerman, A. E., & Greer, B. G. (2000). Counseling psychology and the Internet: A further inquiry. *Journal of Technology in Counseling, 1.2.* Retrieved February 5, 2002, from http://jtc.colstate.edu/vol1_2/cyberpsych.htm

Haney, H., & Leibsohn, J. (1999). *Basic counseling responses: a multimedia learning system for the helping professions.* Pacific Grove, CA: Wadsworth.

Haney, H., & Leibsohn, J. (2001). *Basic counseling responses in groups: a multimedia learning system for the helping profession.* Pacific Grove, CA: Wadsworth.

Hart, J. L. (2000). Mentoring without walls: Using cyberspace to enhance student-faculty guidance. Retrieved February 10, 2002, from http://cybercounsel.uncg.edu/articals/Hart's%20Last%20Break.htm

Joinson, A. N. (2001). Self-disclosure in computer-mediated communication: The role of self-awareness and visual anonymity. *European Journal of Social Psychology, 31*(2), 177–192.

Jones, W. P., Coker, J. K., Harbach, R. L., & Staples, P. A. (2002). Concept into practice: A case study in software design. *Journal of Technology in Counseling, 2.2.* Retrieved October 5, 2002, from http:// jtc.colstate.edu/vol2_2/jones/pauljones.htm

Jones, W. P., Harbach, R. L., Coker, J. K., & Staples, P. A. (2001). Text-chat test interpretation: Implications of visual cues. Retrieved October 5, 2002, from http://education.unlv.edu/EP/Faculty/Jones/nl6_2.htm

Jones, W. P., Harbach, R. L., Coker, J. K., & Staples, P. A. (2002). Web-assisted vocational test interpretation. *Journal of Employment Counseling, 39,* 127–137.

Lovell, K., Fullalove, L., Garvey, R., & Brooker, C. (2000). Telephone treatment of obsessive-compulsive disorder. *Behavioural and Cognitive Psychotherapy, 28,* 87–91.

Manhal-Baugus, M. (2001). E-therapy: Practical, ethical, and legal issues. *CyberPsychology and Behavior, 4,* 551–563.

Mannion, L., Fahy, T. J., Duffy, C., Broderick, M., & Gethins, E. (1998). Telepsychiatry: Keeping a link with the island. *Psychiatric Bulletin, 22,* 47–49.

Masi, D., & Freedman, M. (2001). The use of the telephone and online technology in assessment, counseling and therapy. *Employee Assistance Quarterly, 16,* 49–63.

McFadden, J. (2000). Computer-mediated technology and transcultural counselor education. *Journal of Technology in Counseling, 1.2.* Retrieved March 27, 2001, from http://jtc.colstate.edu/vol1_2/transcult.html

Muehlfelder, M., Klein, U., Simon, S., & Luczak, H. (1999). Teams without trust? Investigations in the influence of video-mediated communication on the origin of trust among cooperating persons. *Behavior & Information Technology, 18*(5), 349–360.

Sampson, J. P. (2000). Using the Internet to enhance testing in counseling. *Journal of Counseling and Development, 78,* 348–356.

Shepard, P. (1987). Telephone therapy: An alternative to isolation. *Clinical Social Work Journal, 15,* 56–65.

Springer, A., & Stahmann, R. F. (1998). Parent perception of the value of telephone family therapy when adolescents are in residential treatment. *American Journal of Family Therapy, 26,* 169–176.

Sussman, R. J. (2000). Counseling over the Internet: Benefits and challenges in the use of new technologies. Alexandria, VA: American Counseling Association/ERIC/CASS. Retrieved May 25, 2002, from http://cybercounsel.uncg.edu/book/manuscripts/internetcounseling.htm

Troester, A. I., Paolo, A. M., Glatt, S. L., Hubble, J. P., & Koller, W. C. (1995). Interactive video conferencing in the provision of neuropsychological services to rural areas. *Journal of Community Psychology, 23,* 85–88.

Wetchler, J. L., Trepper, T. S., McCollum, E. E., & Nelson, T. S. (1993). Videotape supervision via long-distance telephone. *American Journal of Family Therapy, 21,* 242–247.

10
CHAPTER

Stacey L. Sinclair
Gerald Monk

There's No "I" in Self:
A Discursive Approach
to Self-Supervision

Self-supervision has frequently been recommended as a universal goal for therapists; however, relatively little attention has been paid to the actual details, including the practical characteristics, which comprise self-supervision (Dennin, 1998; Morrissette, 1999; Todd, 1997). The general exclusion of a theoretical perspective has also contributed to the vague and enigmatic quality of the self-supervision process (Dennin, 1998; Morrissette, 1999). Perhaps most important, the bulk of the literature on self-supervision has failed to address the cultural location of the "self" in self-supervision, and has not advanced an approach to self-supervision that acknowledges and appreciates the complex, diverse, and fluid context in which we practice. Rather, self-supervision is generally located within a generic, individualistic framework, defined as a process whereby professionals work autonomously to monitor and guide their own professional development (Bernard & Goodyear, 1998; Donnelly & Glaser, 1992; Morrissette, 1999; Todd, 1992, 1997).

Broadly speaking, self-supervision has been conceptualized to promote future autonomous functioning, professional growth and development, and greater therapist competence, as well as provide benefits relating to cost, time, and convenience. Despite appearing straightforward and inclusive, self-supervision in fact requires specific reflexive and critical skills, and the process of becoming self-supervising can be quite challenging

161

(Lowe, 2000; Morrissette, 1999; Todd, 1997). Moreover, there does not appear to be sufficient preparation, guidance, or training in self-supervision (Bernard & Goodyear, 1998; Dennin, 1998; Morrissette, 1999; Todd, 1997).

To help clarify and explicate this particular avenue for improving clinical skills and professional competence, this chapter presents a social constructionist metaphor as a useful organizing framework for managing the challenging self-supervisory process and extends a discursive approach into the self-supervisory arena. First, we examine the assumptions underlying traditional notions of self-supervision, revealing the limitations and implications of self-supervision as it is currently regarded. Second, we outline a social constructionist approach that attends to the larger discursive context in which therapists are positioned. Last, we discuss a series of practical tools that can be used to assist therapists to become more intentional, reflexive, critical, and socially just. Throughout this chapter, we offer personal stories as illustrations of what we propose are innovative ways of conducting self-supervision. Ultimately, our hope is to inform a new paradigm for doing better.

☐ The Self in Liberal-Humanism: Rugged Individualism or Naïve Idolization?

For the last three decades, liberal-humanism has dominated mainstream counseling, psychology, and psychotherapy. Gaining momentum in the 1960s, the liberal-humanist tradition, pioneered by psychologists such as Allport, Maslow, and Rogers, has traditionally identified the individual as the central agent of all social phenomena, and has celebrated the self as independent, stable, and knowable, emphasizing an individual's capacity for choice, freedom, and self-development (Jenkins, 2001). Polkinghorne (2001) observed that, "the self became a cornerstone in their view of the development of the inherent possibilities of human existence and of the process through which positive changes occurred in their psychotherapeutic work with clients" (p. 82). A parallel process has occurred in the area of both formal and informal supervision. That is, the process and practices associated with doing better have been courted and influenced similarly by liberal-humanism. The dated but nonetheless popular notion of self-actualization, for instance, epitomizes the liberal-humanist position that individuals are capable of being in charge of their own lives and grants individuals the freedom to be self-guided, self-governed, and effective in their pursuits of personal growth and development.

Given the widespread popularity of liberal-humanist values in contemporary therapeutic practices (Corey, 2001; Kottler, 2002), it is no surprise then to discover that much of the literature published on self-supervision is primarily sourced in humanistic terms. For example, Morrissette (1999), who presented both a historical and current review of self-supervision, found it to be a process that encompasses introspection, self-awareness, self-evaluation, and an active self-regulating role to evaluate development. In addition, terms such as "internal supervisor" (Casement, 1985), "reflectivity" (Morrissette, 1999; Neufeldt, Karno, & Nelson, 1996), and "self-monitoring" (Borders, 1991; Bradley & Gould, 2001) have frequently been used to describe the process by which therapists make attempts to manage and improve their practice. Although they are not explicitly presented within a theoretical framework, we find these popular self-supervision practices to be inscribed with cultural assumptions concerning individuals as independent, rational, and moral agents responsible for self-control, assumptions that underpin the liberal-humanist tradition.

Interwoven with the liberal-humanist perspective of the individual as an independent, autonomous, and unitary being at the central core to any field of inquiry has been the notion that people are fundamentally separate from the social and historical world (Davies, 1993). That is, with its celebration of individualism, liberal-humanism has tended to locate human problems within individuals as distinct and separate from social, cultural, and political contexts in which they live (Neimeyer, 1998; Winslade, Monk, & Drewery, 1997). This dislocation of individuals and their problems from the larger cultural context reflects the humanistic focus on intrapsychic processes occurring within people (Kottler, 2002). From this viewpoint, the essence of individuality is the feeling self, whereby feelings are seen as products of nature and bearers of truth about the individual, not of culture. Accordingly, much time has been devoted to exploring one's feelings in both the area of counseling and supervision. For instance, a primary goal in self-supervision is identifying personal emotions and feelings during a therapeutic session (Morrissette, 1999).

Increasingly, liberal-humanism is being critiqued and challenged for its naïve and uncritical privileging of the individual and his or her inner process as distinct from the sociocultural context (Carter, 1995; Jenkins, 2001; Kottler, 2002; Sampson, 1988). In particular, the excessive individualism contained in the liberal-humanist movement has tended to ignore the larger sociocultural issues impacting on therapists and clients alike. Foreshadowing a contemporary criticism, Buss (1979) observed, "a theory that predisposes one to focus more upon individual freedom and development rather than the larger social reality, works in favor of maintaining that social reality" (p. 47). As a result, the effects of various oppressive practices have frequently been overlooked. For example, the relevance of the humanistic position to the situation of people of color has been challenged (Carter, 1995; Jenkins, 2001). Toward this end, skeptics maintain that because liberal-humanist doctrine has portrayed persons as autonomous beings who are primarily responsible for their plight, those practicing self-supervision within this framework may easily dismiss racism, sexism, and/or homophobia.

Indeed, there has been a growing recognition of liberal-humanism's overly individualistic and self-oriented focus by humanists themselves (Jenkins, 2001; Kottler, 2002; Polkinghorne, 2001; Wadlington, 2001). Present-day academics are actively making efforts to reformulate the insights of the "founding fathers" of the liberal-humanist movement with the aims of engaging contemporary (postmodern) understandings of the self. For instance, Jenkins (2001) advocates for expression of "an *evaluating mentality* to the process of living within the proscriptions of a sociocultural context" (2001, p. 43, italics added). He suggests that one's agency, uniqueness, and free will should not be subordinate to the influence of the cultural context and maintains that the self is developed through its active engagement with the environment. In arguing that a humanist approach is compatible with a multicultural world, Jenkins points out that individuals "by training themselves" are able to rise above the societal confounds and hardships presented to them (p. 43).

Despite this well-intentioned desire to embrace a sociocultural description of the self, there is still a fixation on an *individual in isolation* production of self-improvement. Within this framework, attempts of doing better in the self-supervisory arena would likely remain located within the individual versus within the collective world at large. For example, suppose a self-supervising therapist is working with an unemployed, uneducated woman who desires to leave her emotionally abusive husband. If the therapist privileges her "evaluating mentality" in her attempts to leave, it is possible that he or she will fail to consider fully the social and institutional barriers (i.e., patriarchal attitudes, stigma, financial dependency, legal needs, etc.) that impact on the process of her departure. In Jenkins' contemporary reformulating, the therapist's focus would remain on parceling the client's personal strengths.

Acknowledging the challenges associated with "postmodernizing" the self in liberal-humanism, Wadlington (2001) cautions against reformulating humanistic therapeutic approaches to fit new contemporary problems, as it "keeps us locked in an argument about what is worth salvaging from the past rather than attempting new strategies in the present" (pp. 493–494). Rather than attempting to translate familiar terms such as self, free will, and human potential into postmodern vernacular, it is suggested that practitioners accept invitations by postmodern approaches to do things differently. It is within this inviting spirit that we advocate a new approach for doing better.

We contend that the relatively uncritical and acontextual self-supervision approach supported by the liberal-humanist position produces therapists who, in our opinion, are ill equipped to consider, for example, the effects of patriarchal attitudes on their clients. Rather than emphasize the autonomous self, we conceive of the self in self-supervision as "dethroned" from the position of stability, independency, self-determination and self-regulation and instead is a collective of identities thoroughly dependent upon and impacted by the socially constructed world.

☐ Social Constructionism: Advancing a Discursive Approach to Self-Supervision

No man is an island entirely of itself; every man is a piece of the continent.
                                                                 John Donne

Social construction theory presents an innovative and alternative approach to understanding the theory and practice of self-supervision in comparison to the more dominant liberal-humanist approaches, providing what we believe is a refreshingly new approach to doing better in one's therapeutic practice. We do not want to get sidetracked into a lengthy exposition of social constructionist theory but we do need to cover some key assumptions of the theory to help us explain the lens through which we view self-supervision.

Social constructionist theory, in its most basic form, is grounded in four key assumptions, all of which build on one another (Burr, 1995). First, social constructionist theory invites a critical stance toward taken-for-granted knowledge (Burr, 1995). That is, social constructionists challenge the conventional knowledge that has historically guided our understanding of the world, and ourselves in it (Burr, 1995; Gergen, 1985). Second, social constructionists have proposed that the ways in which we commonly understand the world, including the categories, concepts, and language we use, are historically and culturally specific (Bayer & Shotter, 1998). This means that all knowledge is time- and culture-bound and cannot be taken as once-and-for-all "truth" or understanding (Burr, 1995; Gergen, 1985). Third, social constructionist theory asserts that knowledge is constructed through social processes; namely, it is fabricated through daily interactions between people (Bayer & Shotter, 1998; Burr, 1995). Thus, our current accepted ways of understanding the world, or what we commonly regard as "truth," are products of the social interactions people engage in on a daily basis (Burr, 1995; Parker, 1998). Finally, it is posited that these negotiated meanings, or "social constructions," carry a number of possible actions or responses. In other words, knowledge and social action go together (Burr, 1995).

In paying special attention to the multiplicity, contextuality, and active construction of meaning, social constructionist theory offers itself as a useful framework for understanding the cultural location of the "self" in self-supervision. Specifically, this theory recognizes that, in fact, the self is socially constructed and positioned within particular social and historical cultural settings. This view comes in contrast to more established and conventional conceptions of the self as a naturally occurring, independent object, devoid of cultural significance. In so much that the self is deeply penetrated by the (often complex and shifting) cultural milieu in which it is surrounded, a therapist's "self" is also dependent on the social world. In fact, this is a notion of the self that is far from being stable and singular and instead is a multiple of selves surrounded by a "polyphony of voices—not all of which are singing in the same key" (Neimeyer, 1995, p. 30).

If you are feeling a bit disoriented by this hurried explanation of the social constructionist agenda, do not fret! Indeed, one frequently experiences "conceptual vertigo" (Neimeyer, 1998) when engaging with constructionism. The aim is not to reject our familiar sense of self for its own sake but rather to clear a space for alternative methods of social reality, which offer fresh possibilities for the process of doing better in general, and for self-supervision specifically. An understanding of the term discourse is a basic starting point for the remainder of the chapter.

The term discourse refers to a set of meanings, concepts, images, and/or statements that produce a particular representation of an event, object, person, etc., to the world (Burr, 1995). The things that people say or write are examples of discourse and at any given moment, a variety of discourses will be in circulation. Discourses are not simply abstract ideas; they construct meaning and shape behavior, as individuals perceive the world and their experiences in it through discourse. So, who we are depends upon the circumstances we are placed in and the discourses available in the setting we find ourselves. One example, albeit simple and brief, may provide greater clarity. I (Stacey) recently experienced the separation of my parents. This separation came as quite a shock and I experienced it with considerable distress and sadness, despite being an "adult." I was positioned within the discourse that "when your parents separate as a child, it's deeply distressing; however, as an adult, the impact is not as great." A consequence of this discourse is that I have felt embarrassed and ashamed that I have been as troubled by their separation as I have. Had I not been so captured by the aforementioned discourse, I would likely have experienced the separation differently and with different emotional responses.

One might ask how this discursive analysis is different from a humanistic one? Our point here is that instead of seeing embarrassment and shame as a normal universal human experience, we see Stacey's response as being produced within a specific social-cultural context where the cultural meanings invite her to evaluate herself as inadequate in some way. We argue that Stacey did not make up this idea on her own; instead, we consider that there were compelling cultural reasons why she should do well in adjusting to parents separating and divorcing because she is an adult.

The consequences for a discursive understanding of the self for improving clinical skills and professional competence are great. To be more precise, we have found that the theory of social constructionism, and its focus on discourse, afford us opportunities to engage with a high degree of reflexivity about our practice as therapists. It invites the therapist to explore a more focused, intentional, and socially responsible means of improving their practice, and encourages therapists to examine and renegotiate various value-laden beliefs and meanings. For example, I (Gerald) remember working with a Samoan male client who was insisting that his child, of whom he did not have custody, take his surname. At the time, I was unaware of the larger cultural meanings associated with surnames. I was positioned within a Western discourse of democracy and equity that suggested that the child keep the surname of his mother, who did have custody. On discursive reflection, or examining the "assumptions underlying the assumptions," I was able to acknowledge and appreciate the discursive positioning of my client. Rather than essentialize my client's actions and conclude that he was "resistant," "angry," or "domineering," I explored the possible discourses that were shaping his behavior, such as the Samoan idea that a conscientious and committed father has children who share his surname. Identifying the larger cultural framework from which he was operating enabled me to see him in more positive ways. This example illustrates that different discourses offer people a variety of divergent positions to speak from, and that to the extent that therapists know the discourses that are significant to the client, the more likely they are to identify what counts for the client. The next section provides more guidance regarding "how to" do self-supervision from a discursive perspective.

☐ The Self in Context, or "It's Not All About Me"

From a discursive, social constructionist viewpoint, the liberal-humanistic view of the self is both overly idealized and insufficiently contextual. In order to better assist therapists in monitoring, reflecting, and improving their practice, we offer several practical tools that provide an entry point to assist therapists to address some of the more complex discursive issues arising in the self-supervisory arena. We also give accounts of personal experiences to demonstrate how these practices work.

Deconstruction

Deconstruction, a term developed within the social constructionist movement, refers to the practice of exploring the taken-for-granted assumptions and influential discourses underpinning our conversation, behavior, and emotional expression. The therapist utilizing a deconstructive approach to self-supervision is interested and curious about how their work is influenced by possible prejudices, dogmatism, biases, and therapeutic certainty that shuts down avenues of exploration and inquiry with their clients. When using deconstructive approaches in self-supervisory processes, therapists ask themselves, "What interactions am I having with my clients that demonstrate I am jumping to conclusions and too easily accepting prior assumptions about the nature of the problem?" and "What limitations are produced from my own cultural frameworks of meaning that are influencing my understanding of the cultural contexts impacting upon my client and their difficulties?" In other words, the therapist reflects on how the dominating discourses shaping their interactions are impacting on themselves and their clients. Further, when therapists identify the discourses impacting themselves and their clients, they can then begin the process of naming alternate discourses, thus providing more options for each to consider.

Deconstruction invites a tentative, curious, deliberately naïve posture. For example, it has us asking of any therapeutic engagement, "What was left out? What was covered over? What was privileged and what was not?" Discursive self-supervision focuses on the contextual staging of problems to assist us to keep things moving and become less preoccupied with seeking definitive and objective answers that fail to consider the larger background of our lives as well as the lives of our clients. During self-supervision, practitioners are invited to engage in the deconstruction process that challenges the ways in which cultural systems maintain the status quo. When deconstruction is applied successfully, the therapist questions his or her own preoccupations and preferred points of reference, familiar habits, social practices, beliefs, and judgments, which are often regarded as common sense.

I (Stacey) recall using deconstruction during a case involving a female client who was experiencing resentment due to her great difficulty communicating feelings of anger with her family. Initially, I was quite frustrated with her, and spent considerable time in session trying to "convince" her that open, honest, and direct expression of emotions produces desirable outcomes. When this wasn't working (i.e., she didn't "come my way"), I began to reflect and take apart the assumptions we were both working from. I asked myself the question, "What constrains women from expressing anger assertively?" and this question opened up an investigation of the effects of gender discourse on the expression of emotion. For example, I explored how widespread cultural norms prescribe passivity, compliance, and sensitivity for women, all in the name of "femininity." I also asked myself, "What do I consider to be appropriate expressions of emotion for women?" and "Are there other alternate discourses that support greater flexibility in emotional expression for women?" These discursive understandings led me to change my focus in session. Emphasizing the larger context, I facilitated a discussion, marked by curiosity and interest, about how women are invited to silence feelings of anger and outrage and instead privilege the expression of more inwardly expressed feelings such as depression and resentment. The result of this deconstructive process was that the therapeutic conversation was expanded, existing assumptions about gendered behavior were challenged, and I was more intentional and socially responsible in recognizing the dominant cultural narratives that had been internalized. Ultimately, as the client and I renegotiated the gendered discourses around suppressing anger, she successfully voiced her feelings to her family with positive effects.

Power

Intimately interwoven with the practice of deconstructing discourses in self-supervision is the notion of how power is understood in social constructionist terms. In order for therapists to be appropriately self-critical and socially just in their practice, an understanding of how power relations impact on the therapeutic process is an important issue to attend to in self-supervision. We argue that doing better in therapy is closely tied to the extent to which therapists become aware of the systematic marginalizing and alienating discourses that produce power relations that constrain clients' actions and choices. We don't want to present the view that power is a commodity that people possess to greater or lesser degrees. This way of thinking often produces a simplistic analysis about people's resourcefulness and ability to act and results in an oppressed and oppressor binary. Power as commodity suggests that in societal organization, the holder of power is the oppressor who may or may not share their power with those without it—and the oppressed are completely at the mercy of the power holder.

The idea of commodity power is expressed in the supervisory process and is most noticeably present when therapists talk about empowering their clients. Implied in this notion is the concept that the therapist is a more influential person in the social hierarchy and has the resources, professional potency, and influence to empower their clients. In the self-supervisory process, we invite therapists to think differently about how they exert power on, over, or with their clients. From a social constructionist perspective, power is not a commodity but operates relationally. Power shifts in a context-dependent fashion rather than being inherent within categories of people. It cuts across individual lives in a variety of ways that can entail privilege and oppression for the same person in different respects. In other words, individuals have more power or less power in different situations. Power viewed from this perspective opens up possibilities for developing a more complex analysis of therapeutic moves in session, as well as client engagements outside of session. It is not a tidy package that is owned.

Because of the fluidity and dynamic nature of power, it is possible to imagine that the therapeutic relationship has junctures where the therapist and client occupy both oppressive and oppressing positions. That is, power relationships are constantly changing and fluctuating in every counseling interaction. The preceding story involving Stacey's client provides a good illustration of the implications of this standpoint for self-supervision. Early on in my work with this client, I (Stacey) was positioned within a discourse that suggested that as the therapist, I had the influence (power) to empower my client. Alongside this discourse was the idea that she was powerless to express her anger and it was my duty and obligation to free her from her silence. After several sessions when it was becoming clear that my noble attempts at liberation and empowerment were not having their intended outcomes, I spent time analyzing the aspects of power in my work with this client. I began to see that in fact my client did have power, recalling a story she recounted of demanding apartment repairs promised to her from her male landlord. Her account of this situation provided several examples of her expressing anger quite eloquently, forcefully, and compellingly. In addition, I had observed her presenting herself vigorously with the receptionist when she received a parking ticket in the counseling center's parking lot.

I also began to see that I did not have the ownership on power I originally thought. In particular, this client had established a routine of arriving at least 10 minutes late to each session. Despite the irritation, annoyance, and inconvenience it had caused me, I had not yet "confronted" her about it. Analyzing power within this fluid framework invited me to acknowledge the multiple identities and positions that my client and I were engaged in and helped me to stay curious about the power and influence we both held at times. I realized that power was "exercised rather than possessed" (Foucault, 1977, p. 27) by both my client and myself. On this self-supervision, I approached our next session differently. I pointed out the unique outcomes of using her voice and expressing anger and then explored how she could extend these skills when interacting with her family (and I eventually shared my feelings about her tardiness!). Although this example is quite basic and unsophisticated, it does underscore how a social constructionist analysis of power in self-supervision opens up possibilities and options in session.

Temporary Essentialism

We propose that the social constructionist metaphor invites the therapist to create a space where "knowing and doubting are balanced; ignorance is dangerous, but so is knowledge, if that knowledge is narrowly specialist" (Williams, 1995, p. 212). The self-supervising interactions of the therapist can neither be guided by "universalizing notions" of a human experience nor can the therapist seek refuge in a series of assumptions of a correct treatment. The therapist guided by such essentialist theorizing privileges the establishment of facts, values certainty, and requires the practitioner to be guided by established knowledge. A therapist using a constructionist understanding of self-supervision, however, is guided by the ability to embrace ambiguity and indeterminacy, and nurture a spirit of wonder and naïveté. From this perspective, there are no universal truth-based approaches to rely on in guiding the therapist's actions; instead, the therapist has to ask him- or herself, "How can I do better in being curious and respectful about the client's experience and the meanings they associate with this experience?" "What are the client's truth-based assumptions that guide their behavior?" "What expertise does the client have that can be drawn out and used to assist them with their difficulties?" and "What are the local knowledges that might be relevant to this client's needs in this context at this time?"

   Indeed, remaining curious and open-minded is essential during the self-supervision process. Accordingly, the therapist is invited to view professional knowledge as provisional, temporary, limited, and tentative. This professional attitude is part of the process of self-examining one's practice. This stance allows the therapist to hold his or her professional knowledge lightly and through the encounters with his or her clients be prepared to revise the therapeutic efforts, and perhaps in some instances, examine and then change preciously held assumptions about some aspect of one's viewpoint or approach. Self-supervision from a social constructionist framework involves a therapist demonstrating a willingness to review, critique, and if necessary, change his or her stance in the face of new information. We refer to this practice of remaining curious and open-minded as temporarily essentialism. In other words, although we start from an identifiable position that shapes how we practice, this position or orientation is constantly under review and is modifiable in the light of new experiences and challenges.

For example, in the past, I (Gerald) have been easily agreeable with colleagues and clients who might challenge my whiteness and suggest that because of my privileged racial status in the United States, I am not able to understand the nuances of racism and the subtlety of the abuse and humiliation that comes with it. I have been quick to acknowledge and challenge racism when it is exhibited by whites toward other ethnicities. However, I have tended to be inattentive to racist interactions exhibited by members of underrepresented ethnic groups toward whites, believing that only those in the majority can perpetrate such abuses. Despite my previous position, a recent experience during an unstructured counseling group led me to speak out and support a women identifying as Euro-American who was attacked by two people who identified themselves as being members of an oppressed ethnic group. The participants cut off the white woman and told her that she could not experience oppression because she was white. They interrupted her and paid no attention to her efforts to respond to their challenges. This was a deeply disrespectful interaction toward a woman who had a distressing story to tell about her own oppression. Seeing this injustice led me to revise my earlier understandings of racism. I chose as a white man to support this white women, and she was finally heard by those that initially invalidated her experience.

Rather than adhere to a specific essentialist description of ethnic and racial relations, I chose to be flexible and learn and be changed by one participant's experience. After this experience, I became more willing to take risks and challenge what I would regard as oppressive interactions from those who have different phenotypical characteristics than myself despite the fact that my whiteness might be perceived by other ethnicities as a source of prejudice and racial bias. This example illustrates a self-supervisory process based on a temporary essentialist position.

Discursive Empathy

Liberal-humanism invites us to believe that empathy and understanding are present if the therapist is able to connect with his or her own humanity. Because the reference point for empathy is the universal human condition, therapists utilizing a humanist approach are likely to believe that everyone has the capacity to "walk in another's shoes." One of the important factors in the self-supervisory process must surely be the ability of the therapist to monitor the extent to which he or she can engage in an empathetic understanding of the client. However, we argue that from a social constructionist perspective, there are domains of human experience that may not be understood or translated between therapist and client. We suggest that there are discourses that position the client that cannot be known, shared, or understood by the therapist. If this is the case, this has implications for how a therapist comes to understand his or her role. For example, in the self-supervisory process, we suggest that therapists allow themselves the right to not always know what to do and in some instances be thoroughly confused by the client's account of his or her struggles. When the therapist is self-supervising, we invite him or her to be openly tentative, respectfully curious but not attempt to gain some form of finality about the client's experience.

We advocate for therapists to develop discursive empathy where they on a constant basis review the dominant cultural discourses that are helping shape the relationship they have with their clients. This may assist therapists to avoid inappropriate cultural impositions on their clients. We acknowledge that this is easy to say and hard to do. Therapists who have spent much of their lives positioned in discourses that are predominantly racist, classist, or sexist, for instance, may experience a difficult challenge being empathetic with clients who have been targeted by those very discourses. In fact, one of the difficulties of self-supervision is that, by oneself, it is difficult to identify discourses if one is coming from a completely unconsidered and unexamined framework.

I (Gerald) will never forget the challenge I faced when working a Maori elder and his daughter in a therapy session when I was working as a therapist in New Zealand. In many traditional Maori communities, it is the responsibility of the eldest daughter in a Maori family to present her first-born child to her parents. With European nuclear family patterns of child care beginning to dominate Maori caregiving practices, many young parents have abandoned this practice of offering their first-born child to the maternal parents. In this case, the daughter had invited her father to attend the session. Because I was a trained professional to help families deal with conflict, she was hoping that there was some way that I could communicate with her father that not letting her parents have the child was not an act of disrespecting and devaluing her parents. Rather, it was about the changing child caregiving arrangements that were followed by many other Maori of her generation. Despite my gentle persuasions to the father about these changing traditions, as the session progressed it was apparent that her father began to feel more distressed, dejected, and troubled. I became frustrated and rather helpless. The session ended with the woman's father saying he understood the reasons for the change but he clearly was as distressed as he was at the onset of the session.

In a period of self-supervising following this session, I realized that I had discursive empathy for the daughter but clearly had exhibited little empathy for the father's position. I shared the same discourse with the daughter about nuclear family values and shared her distress about the prospect of giving up her child. There was no understanding demonstrated by me toward the father's discursive position. Since this time, I have become much more sensitive to working with clients who have very different discursive positions than my own. The practice of discursive empathy in my self-supervision has me becoming much more open to the cultural assumptions that clients hold that are initially difficult for me to grasp.

☐ Doing Better: Self-Supervision From the Outside In

The act of self-supervision takes many forms according to the beliefs that therapists have about human nature, therapeutic change processes, and the nature of the helping profession itself. In order to grow and develop as practitioners and do better in our work, we take the perspective that we must reflect on what we have done with our clients according to our epistemological assumptions. Being intentional, self-reflexive, and socially just requires of us the ability to name the assumptions that guide our practice. Haley's question, "What is your theory of change?," which he said so often it was put on his birthday cake (Todd, 1997), underscores for us the centrality of epistemology in the self-supervision process.

In this chapter, we committed ourselves to outlining a social constructionist theory of knowledge and change that underlines our practice of "outside in" self-supervision. A discursive approach to self-supervision as we have advocated involves demonstrating sensitivity to the larger cultural backdrop of our lives, as well as the lives of our clients. Self-supervision from this vantage point invites reflexivity where we can give an account of the discourses that inform our work, and at the same time it encourages us to review, critique, and if necessary, change our approach. In doing so, this discursive approach to self-supervision challenges us to be changed by our encounter with others. Finally, we proposed that practices involving deconstruction, power, temporary essentialism, and discursive empathy provide an entry point to assist therapists in monitoring, reflecting, and improving their practice.

☐ References

Bayer, B. M., & Shotter, J. (1998). *Reconstructing the psychological subject: Bodies, practices, and technologies*. Thousand Oaks, CA: Sage.

Bernard, J. M., & Goodyear, R. K. (1998). *Fundamentals of clinical supervision*. Boston: Allyn & Bacon.

Borders, L. D. (1991). A systematic approach to peer group supervision. *Journal of Counseling and Development, 69*, 248–252.

Bradley, L. J., & Gould, J. L. (2001). Psychotherapy-based models of counselor supervision. In L. J. Bradley & N. Ladany (Eds.), *Counselor supervision: Principles, process, and practice* (pp. 147–182). New York: Brunner-Routledge.

Burr, V. (1995). *An introduction to social constructionism*. New York: Routledge.

Buss, A. R. (1979). Humanistic psychology as liberal ideology. *Journal of Humanistic Psychology, 19*, 43–55.

Carter, R. T. (1995). *The influence of race and racial identity in psychotherapy: Toward a racially inclusive model*. New York: Wiley.

Casement, P. (1985). *On learning from the patient*. London: Tavistock.

Corey, G. (2001). *Theories and practice of counseling and psychotherapy*. Pacific Grove, CA: Brooks/Cole.

Davies, B. (1993). *Shards of glass: Children reading and writing beyond gendered identities*. St. Leonards, NSW, Australia: Allen & Unwin.

Dennin, M. K. (1998). *Effects of a method of self-supervision for counselor trainees*. Doctoral dissertation, State University of New York at Albany, Albany, NY.

Donnelly, C., & Glaser, A. (1992). Training in self-supervision skills. *The Clinical Supervisor, 10*(2), 85–96.

Foucault, M. (1977). *Discipline and punish: The birth of the prison*. Harmondsworth: Penguin.

Gergen, K. (1985). The social constructionist movement in modern psychology. *American Psychologist, 40* (3), 266–275.

Jenkins, A. H. (2001). Humanistic psychology and multiculturalism: A review and reflection. In K. J. Schneider, J. F. T. Bugental, & J. F. Pierson (Eds.), *The handbook of humanistic psychology: Leading edges in theory, research, and practice* (pp. 37–45). Thousand Oaks, CA: Sage.

Kottler, J. A. (2002). *Theories in counseling and therapy: An experiential approach*. Boston: Allyn & Bacon.

Lowe, R. (2000). Supervising self-supervision: Constructive inquiry and embedded narratives in case consultation. *Journal of Marital and Family Therapy, 26*(4), 511–521.

Morrissette, P. J. (1999). Family therapist self-supervision: Toward a preliminary conceptualization. *The Clinical Supervisor, 18*(2), 165–183.

Neimeyer, R. A. (1995). Constructivist psychotherapies. In R. A. Neimeyer & M. J. Mahoney (Eds.), *Constructivism in psychotherapy* (pp. 11–38). Washington, DC: American Psychological Association.

Neimeyer, R. A. (1998). Social constructionism in the counseling context. *Counselling Psychology Quarterly, 11*(2), 135–149.

Neufeldt, S., Karnot, M., & Nelson, M. (1996). A qualitative study of expert's conceptualization of supervisee reflectivity. *Journal of Counseling Psychology, 43*, 3–9.

Parker, I. (1998). *Social constructionism: Discourse and realism*. Thousand Oaks, CA: Sage.

Polkinghorne, D. E. (2001). The self and humanistic psychology. In K. J. Schneider, J. F. T. Bugental, & J. F. Pierson (Eds.), *The handbook of humanistic psychology: Leading edges in theory, research, and practice* (pp. 81–99). Thousand Oaks, CA: Sage.

Sampson, E. E. (1988). The debate on individualism: Indigenous psychologies of the individual and their role in personal and social functioning. *American Psychologist, 43*, 15–22.

Todd, T. C. (1992). Self-supervision? A goal for all supervisors. *The Supervision Bulletin, V,* 3.

Todd, T. C. (1997). Self-supervision as a universal supervisory goal. In C. L. Storm & T. C. Todds (Eds.), *The reasonably complete systemic supervisor resources guide* (pp. 17–25). Boston: Allyn & Bacon.

Wadlington, W. (2001). Performative therapy: Postmodernizing humanistic psychology. In K. J. Schneider, J. F. T. Bugental, & J. F. Pierson (Eds.), *The handbook of humanistic psychology: Leading edges in theory, research, and practice* (pp. 491–501). Thousand Oaks, CA: Sage.

Williams, A. (1995). *Visual and active supervision: Roles focus techniques.* New York: Norton.

Winslade, J., Monk, G., & Drewery, W. (1997). Sharpening the critical edge: A social constructionist approach in counselor education. In T. L. Sexton & B. L. Griffin (Eds.), *Constructivist thinking in counseling practice, research, and training* (pp. 228–248). New York: Teachers College Press.

CHAPTER 11

David D. Chen
Matt Englar-Carlson

From Self-Regulation to Self-Supervision: Lessons from Sport Psychology to the Practice of Therapy

Mark Plaatjes, a native South African and United States citizen, always had a dream of becoming the best runner in the world. After many years of planning, training, and reflecting, his dream became a reality in 1993 when he won the men's marathon at the Track and Field World Championship in Stuttgart, Germany. His victory was not a chance occurrence, but a plateau that he actively planned to reach. He was self-directed and knew that he had to be both physically and psychologically prepared if he wanted to win the race. Before the race, Mark ran in all kinds of weather conditions and trained with the assistance of a training partner. Prior to the World Championships, Mark ran four races in humid and hot conditions just to get used to the expected weather conditions in Germany. Guided by mental notes of the Stuttgart Marathon course, Mark visualized his opponents, anticipated pains and fatigue, and outlined ways to deal with potential difficulties. He did all of this when he was not physically running, but resting. Mark felt well prepared when he got to the World Championship. During the race, Mark dipped into his cache of psychological tricks and used calming and affirmative self-talk to help him relax and remain positive. With that type of complete preparation, it was no surprise that he won the marathon.

High achievement in athletics is impossible without the development of self-regulation skills and the commitment to self-selected long-term goals. Self-regulation can be understood as the process during the performance of a cognitive task that allows individuals to control or direct their own activity through self-imposed rules or regulations in order to tailor performance to circumstances or surroundings (Ferrari, Pinard, Reid, & Bouffard-Bouchard, 1991). In the same way that successful athletes utilize a variety of cognitive skills to calculate efficient and effective sport behavior, successful therapists utilize self-supervision skills to monitor their reactions and create effective interventions for clients. The concept of self-supervision has been recognized as an important skill in helping a therapist learn to be self-sufficient as a more effective professional (Todd, 1997). It is our belief that therapists looking to improve their self-supervision skills could benefit from the ideas about self-regulation taken from the discipline of sport psychology. The skills and theories that assist athletes' adherence to self-regulation may help therapists develop strategies to promote self-supervision in the practice of therapy. In this chapter we hope to highlight the links that tie these two concepts together. This chapter contains four sections. The first section examines some of the parallels between sports and therapy. The second section examines theories related to self-regulation in sport psychology. The third section reviews research examining the effectiveness of self-regulation training and the relationship between self-regulation and environmental factors. The final section focuses on the application of strategies and theories developed to promote peak performance in sport participation to the practice of self-supervision. For the most part, this chapter explores how the concept of self-regulation relates to the practice of therapeutic self-supervision. When links between the two concepts exist, we use examples to explore parallel experiences.

☐ Parallels Between Sport Participation and Practice of Therapy

Sport participation has been defined as a type of self-regulated behavior performed in the relative absence of immediate external constraints (Crews, 1993; Kanfer & Karoly, 1972; Zimmerman & Kitsantas, 1997, 1999, 2001). Athletic success is patient work requiring the best mental and physical conditioning. Similarly, psychotherapy is a process in which therapists continually self-supervise and sort internal reactions that have few external constraints. Successful athletes endure long and lonely hours of training in order to reach peak performance during competitions. Although physical training is an essential component to success, psychological training focused on managing the stress of laborious training and intense competition additionally contributes to peak performance. The development of self-regulation skills is at the core of psychological training.

Much like athletes, therapists endure long training programs to develop their therapeutic skills and become effective clinicians. At the core of clinical training is clinical supervision in which less experienced therapists learn about professional competence and clinical skills from more senior colleagues. Supervision is viewed as evaluative, extending over time, and having the effect of enhancing the professional functioning of the supervisee (Bernard & Goodyear, 1998). One of the universal goals of supervision is the development of self-supervisory skills (Todd, 1997). Self-supervision methods are hypothesized to enhance professional development and competence (Bernard & Goodyear, 1998; Hawkins & Shohet, 1989), and contribute to more autonomous functioning for therapists (Bernstein & Lecomte, 1979).

Certain commonalities exist between the process of self-regulation training in sport and self-supervision training in therapy. The inherent conditions in both endeavors lend themselves easily to the concepts of self-regulation and self-supervision. These conditions include: (a) uniqueness; (b) unpredictability; (c) the need for evaluation, assessment, and quick decision-making; and (d) a process that is oriented toward producing effective results.

Uniqueness addresses the reality that no two sports scenarios or clinical situations are identical. Both sporting events and clinical sessions contain an element of unpredictability in which therapists and athletes often do not know what could be coming next. The complexity (i.e., the number of intertwining elements) in both encounters puts athletes and therapists in the situation of always remaining alert, focused, and aware in order to respond properly to incoming situations. Former basketball player and coach Phil Jackson (Jackson & Delehanty, 1995) reflected on the importance of awareness:

> I knew from experience that I was far more effective when my mind was clear and I wasn't playing with an agenda of some kind, like scoring a certain number of points or showing up one of my opponents. The more skilled I became at watching my thoughts, the more focused I became as a player. (p. 50)

Whereas being alert and aware helps athletes respond to the changes in play and games, therapists experience the moment-to-moment changes as clients reveal and unravel their concerns. Therapists help clients tell their stories; as such, therapists often do not know what clients will say next or where a session will end once it has begun. In addition, because therapy assists clients in connecting with disconnected emotions, most therapy sessions progress with a sense of unpredictability.

Whereas both athletes and therapists have automatic responses (e.g., nonverbal behavior, instinctual behavior) to their respective scenarios that may pass as unconscious processes, athletes and therapists both encounter a conscious cognitive process of evaluating what to do next. Before athletes respond to a situation, they go through a quick process of evaluation and judgment, and then execute their decisions (Weinberg & Gould, 1999). Therapists encounter a similar process as they self-examine what could be the best therapeutic invention and reaction to a client. This process can be seen as incorporating ideas around selection of efficient and effective counseling strategies (Nelson, in press) or simply asking clients, "How can I be of help to you right now?"

Finally, both sport participation and therapy are goal-directed endeavors focused on producing effective and efficient results. Because both sport and therapy are dynamic encounters involving many factors outside of the present setting, ideas about success and solution become increasingly complex and ambiguous. It is during these times that the skills of self-regulation and self-supervision come to bear on keeping athletes and therapists grounded and focused on the tasks at hand. Jackson (Jackson & Delehanty, 1995) recalls the process of formulating a vision for the Chicago Bulls when he was named head coach:

> I started by creating a vivid picture in my mind of what the team could become. My vision could be lofty but it could not be a pipe dream. I had to take into account not only what I wanted to achieve, but how I was going to get there. (pp. 98–99)

In therapy, establishing realistic, attainable, and clear goals helps both the therapist and client remain focused as therapy becomes more complex. If therapists use therapy goals as a constant beacon, therapy can proceed in multiple directions without ever going off course. Numerous techniques, such as Erickson's (1954) crystal ball technique, Adler's (1956) question, and de Shazer's (1988) miracle question, all have the same purpose of identifying preferred possibilities for clients and establishing therapy goals.

☐ Self-Supervision and Self-Regulation Defined

What Is Self-Supervision?

One of the central tasks of being a supervisor is to help supervisees become self-sustaining and self-sufficient practitioners who are able to manage their resources to effectively to meet the needs of their clients. Whereas some have viewed the process of self-supervision as simply a useful form of preparation for more formal supervision (Bramley, 1996), Carroll (1996) notes the strength of self-supervision as encouraging therapists to be pro-active and reflexive, which also tends to help enhance a therapist's confidence in their self-reflections. Training therapists to self-supervise can ultimately serve the goal of helping a therapist become self-sufficient. In this sense, self-sufficiency is not viewed as total independence. Instead, self-sufficiency includes the ability to decide when additional consultation or supervision is necessary (Todd, 1997). Lowe (2000) offers the alternative term of "self-sustaining" as opposed to self-sufficient to represent therapists who feel confident to practice in the absence of formal supervision but also have the awareness to know when their reflections need to be enhanced through consultation from others.

Self-supervision has been identified as a process in which therapists use self-reflection to generate appropriately tailored interventions for clients while being aware of when to ask for consultation and how to get help. In this sense, therapists are aware of the demands of the clinical environment and able to adapt their interventions to the needs of clients. The self-supervising therapist, much like the self-regulating athlete, has the self-motivation to practice and hone therapeutic and athletic skills, the self-reinforcement and confidence to take proactive responsibility to know when they are able to work alone and when they need the consultation of colleagues or coaches, and the self-education to know their own limits. Whereas self-supervision has been recognized as an important process in the training of therapists, Lowe (2000) points out that the concept of self-supervision often lurks in the background of the literature about supervision and is rarely directly addressed. Self-regulation, however, is a concept widely addressed in the sport psychology literature. Because these two concepts share many commonalities, examining the self-regulation literature can provide a unique window into self-supervision.

What Is Self-Regulation?

Over the past two decades, researchers (Ferrari et al., 1991; Hardy & Nelson, 1988; Kirschenbaum, 1984; Orlick, 2000; Ungerleider, 1996; Zimmerman & Kitsantas, 1999, 2001) have recognized the importance of self-regulation in achieving success in sports and reaching exercise goals. Achievement in competitive sport situations is dependent to a large extent on the ability to organize one's effort to accomplish definite and clear athletic objectives. Such ability may account for the success of some athletes and the lack of success for others. Even though an athlete may be highly skilled and well conditioned, talent alone cannot guarantee success. The world of athletics is littered with stories of athletes who could have been, were "sure things," and had the physical gifts to be peak performers only to end short of their goals and objectives. Mental toughness and psychological factors have been implicated as factors conducive to peak performance (Ungerleider, 1996). Coping skills during a performance, such as the process of self-regulation, have been linked to positive sport outcomes (Gaudreau, Blondin, & Lapierre, 2002).

Four-time Tour de France winner Lance Armstrong (Armstrong & Jenkins, 2000) reflected on his early professional races where he learned about self-regulation, noting:

> At first, I never evaluated my races. I'd think, "I was the strongest rider out there; those guys couldn't keep up with me." But when I lost several races, I was forced to think again, and one day it finally occurred to me: "Wait a minute. If I'm the strongest guy, why didn't I win?" (p. 58)

Armstrong remembers his coaches telling him, "There are moments when you can use your energy to your benefit, and there are moments when you use it to no avail" (p. 58). Learning self-regulation skills helped propel Armstrong from a very good single-day racer to achieving the highest honor in professional cycling, winning the Tour de France. Armstrong noted how winning the Tour required more than sheer physical skill:

> My reputation was as a single-day racer: show me the start line and I would win on adrenaline and anger, chopping off my competitors one by one. I could push myself to a threshold of pain no one else was willing to match, and I would bite somebody's head off to win a race. But the Tour was another thing entirely. If you raced that way in the Tour, you would have to drop out after two days. It required a longer view. The Tour was a matter of mustering the right resources at the right time, of patiently feeding out your strength at the necessary level, with no wasted motion or energy. It was a matter of continuing to ride and ride, no matter how uninspired you felt, when there was no rush of adrenaline left to push you. (p. 67)

Self-responsibility, dedication, hard work, perceptions of self-control, and the ability to manage problems and situations all contribute to athletic success.

Self-regulation is a process of comparing the status quo with the desired objective or goal to ensure that proper progress is being made to reduce the gap. Competition demands that athletes train under optimum conditions in order to prepare to meet any competitive challenge. Further, self-regulation is a process that assists athletes in managing stress (Ravizza, 1986). Life stress can be a disruption in an athlete's ability to focus and perform. Few athletes reach success without being able to manage life stress. Sporting events provide a unique window through which we can understand how athletes combine mental processes and cognitive and metacognitive strategies to achieve athletic goals.

As far as self-regulation and learning are concerned, psychologists have identified three key subprocesses that are important to self-regulated learning: metacognitive, motivational, and behavioral (Zimmerman, 1986). Zimmerman points out that metacognitively, self-regulated learners plan, organize, self-instruct, self-monitor, and self-evaluate during various stages of the learning process; motivationally, self-regulated learners view themselves as competent, self-efficacious, and autonomous; and behaviorally, self-regulated learners select, structure, and create environments that optimize learning.

In summary, self-regulation requires a performer to possess the following qualifications:

1. Knowledge about oneself in such areas as personal goals
2. Resources for achieving goals and their barriers
3. The ability to acquire the necessary skills and knowledge related to specific tasks
4. The ability to monitor oneself and identify the existing gap between the status quo and the goal

The self-regulation process runs smoothly when all the preceding conditions are present. It can be interrupted or aborted when some key information or skills are absent. The following exploration of self-regulation theories expounds on the intricacies of this process.

☐ Optimal Self-Regulation in Sports and Therapy

The process of self-regulation may consist of multiple steps (e.g., Carver & Scheier, 1981; Kirschenbaum, 1984; Zimmerman & Kitsantas, 1999, 2001). When one of these steps is not managed properly, the process may experience a temporary failure or breakdown. The following factors have been hypothesized to be important in the self-regulation process: goal setting, standard of comparison, feedback, and environmental support.

Goal Setting

If an athlete has not clearly set goals and feels bored by the daily routines, he or she will eventually feel dejected and call it quits. The more clearly one can set goals, the more motivated he or she will be in daily activities. The lack of goals may also reflect low ambitions or lack of incentives. In therapy, goal setting is indicated as a crucial early step in brief therapy. For a therapist, a lack of goals may lead to confusion about what needs to happen in therapy to help a client reduce discomfort. Goals allow therapists to select appropriate interventions and to establish an accepted end point for the therapeutic work. For therapists in supervision, the establishment of supervisory goals is essential to ensure that progress on areas of growth is accomplished. During early supervision sessions, I always ask supervisees about their growth edges and pose the question, "What would have to happen during our supervision time together so that at the termination of supervision, you would view supervision as having been helpful?"

Clear Standards of Comparison in Daily Activities

The establishment of goals starts the process of self-regulation. This goal should be supported with clear environmental standards to assess the progress of goal-achieving activities. For instance, an athlete's performance may suffer if the athlete fails to process the feedback received from an external source as well as from internal sensors by comparing it with what was intended. An example of using feedback to monitor progress can be seen when track runners get splits for each lap that is completed. Runners often have goals set in terms of time; by receiving splits during a race, a runner can determine if the pace is too fast or slow in terms of reaching one's goal. In terms of training, many athletes use heart rate monitors to keep workouts at predetermined levels to help reach training goals. This type of self-directed attention toward attaining feedback is necessary for the functioning of the comparator of the feedback loop. This process allows self-regulation to be possible.

If a problem is identified through the feedback process, for example, determining that a runner is off pace, a plan that is effective and possible can be used to remediate any deficits. Similarly, therapists also need to have clear feedback from clients and supervisors to determine if progress is being made toward goals. One way therapists determine progress toward goals and preferred outcomes is by using scaling questions that indicate incremental change. Scaling questions allow a scale to be created from which comparisons can be drawn on a consistent basis (Bertolino & O'Hanlon, 2002). A therapist might say to a client, "On a scale of one to ten, with one being the worst the problem has ever been and ten representing the best, where would you rate things today?" A similar question can be used by supervisees to track their progress through supervision. In addition, the establishment of predetermined evaluation points (e.g., midterm evaluation) can serve the function of providing consistent feedback to supervisees.

Using Feedback from Prior Mistakes as a Lesson

Mistakes are not avoidable in sports or practice of therapy. The important thing is to learn from them, reflecting and deriving lessons that can be applied to dealing with similar situations in the future. Some athletes make the same mistake over and over again because they fail to learn a lesson from previous mistakes. Athletes sometimes expect to be told by a coach that they made a mistake or are so concerned about mistakes that their focus becomes on predicting what a coach wants rather than conscious self-evaluating what an athlete is doing wrong. Learning moments occur when an athlete is able to take personal responsibility for mistakes and reacting to oneself much like a coach would. Phil Jackson (Jackson & Delehanty, 1995) talked about this when he began coaching the Chicago Bulls, noting:

> At the core of my vision was getting players to think more for themselves. Doug Collins (the Bulls former coach) had kept the younger players, especially Scottie Pippin and Horace Grant, on a tight rein, frequently yelling at them when they made mistakes. Throughout the game they'd look over at the bench, nervously trying to read his mind. When they started doing that with me, I immediately cut them off. "Why are you looking at me?" I'd ask. "You already know you made a mistake." (p. 105)

Therapists also understand that exploring therapeutic mistakes within supervision is one way to learn not to repeat the same mistake again. Further, Hoyt (2000), in exploring the therapeutic failures of Milton Erickson, recognized that it is possible to learn from the mistakes of "master therapists" in the same way that we learn from their successful cases. He states:

> Perhaps I am not the only one, at times, who has felt "disempowered" by reading one miracle success after another. Even if we cannot always explain *why*, I find it encouraging to know that even "The Master" did not hit a home run every time. (p. 193)

Unsupportive Environment

Self-regulation depends on the presence of a healthy and supportive environment. A healthy environment is one where athletes receive support and praise from coaches and teammates, whereas an unhealthy environment is one where athletes receive negative feedback and are often distracted by conflicts and disharmony among teammates. Timely feedback from the environment, coaches, or teammates, or supervisors and colleagues is important for continual regulation. Immediate and accurate feedback information allows individuals to make quick corrections or reinforce their proper behavior. For therapists, this could be seen as feedback from supervisors and other collogues that allows a therapist to regulate his or her behavior based on the standards reflected in the feedback. Supervision dyads or groups that feel safe and supportive allow supervisees to feel encouraged about their work while providing the space for constructive feedback. Nicholas (1989) suggested that it is the task of supervisors in the early stages of group supervision to provide "nurturant" energy to help supervisees feel supported enough to take early risks.

☐ Feedback, Dependency, and Self-Regulation Disruption

Feedback is essential to acquiring and performing sports skills (Chen, 2001) and can be defined as the information provided externally to a learner. When feedback is provided too frequently or too fast, it can lead to a type of learner dependence in which a person cannot operate independent of feedback from others (Salmoni, Schmidt, & Walter, 1984; Winstein & Schmidt, 1990). This dependency effect is believed to affect self-regulatory processes in acquiring information. Therefore, when working with athletes or supervisees, coaches or supervisors must be sensitive not only to the content of feedback, but also to what is the best way and time to deliver it. In this sense, providing and using feedback can be understood as an acquired skill requiring expertise and training. As athletes and therapists understand how to best use feedback given to them by outside sources, it is hoped that through the process of self-regulation and self-supervision, athletes and therapists can then provide internal feedback that guides their endeavors. This process of learning is not easy, however, because the overuse of feedback can distort the perception of the learner and sometimes become too manipulative. Therefore, athletes and therapists must learn how to be thoughtful consumers of feedback, knowing what to use and what to discard.

An important question around feedback relates to how long a teacher or coach should wait before offering feedback to a potential learner. The answer to this question can be found by understanding the length of the feedback delay interval (i.e., the time interval between the completion of a movement and the presentation of augmented feedback). Common sense suggests that feedback should be delivered as soon as possible. However, the validity of this view has been challenged (see Magill, 2001; Swinnen, Schmidt, Nicholson, & Shapiro, 1990). Swinnen et al. suggested that a minimum amount of time is required before offering feedback, noting that giving knowledge of results instantaneously generates a detrimental effect on learning. An interpretation of this observation is that learners who receive feedback too quickly have been deprived of the opportunity to process learner-generated, intrinsic feedback.

Giving a learner, athlete, or supervisee extra time before receiving feedback can provide a window for self-reflection and a better opportunity for feedback to be integrated. This extra time can help the learner develop an internal error-correction mechanism that sustains self-correction (Magill, 2001). Thus, to answer the question posed at the beginning of this paragraph, when providing feedback with the goal of improving learning, first give a learner the time and opportunity for self-evaluation, self-judgment, and self-regulation, then give feedback.

☐ Conditions Leading to Self-Regulation and Supervision

Various strategies have been developed to help improve the ability for self-regulation. Some strategies examine a combination of self-regulation strategies (Hamilton & Fremouw, 1985; Mace, Eastman, & Carol, 1987; Rushall, Hall, Roux, Sasseville, & Rushall, 1988; Wrisberg & Anshel, 1989), whereas others examine specific self-regulation strategies (Martin & Hall, 1995). These strategies have the goals of increasing self-confidence, controlling anxiety and physical arousal, managing attentional resources, and setting appropriate goals for the purpose of achieving independence in self-regulation during sport participation. In the following, we discuss a variety of self-regulation strategies with the idea that therapists developing self-supervision skills and awareness could effectively employ these strategies.

Self-Awareness and Self-Monitoring

Self-awareness refers to a sense of oneself in terms of who we are and how we are doing. Self-monitoring is a frequently employed behavioral management or reinforcement technique (Weinberg & Gould, 1999). It refers to the "processes by which individuals plan and enact their behavioral choices in social contexts" (Snyder, 1983). Ken Ravizza, a veteran sport psychologist who has served as a consultant for many professional sports teams, such as the Anaheim Angels baseball team and the University of Nebraska football team, strongly believes in the importance of athletes increasing self-awareness, because "awareness is the first step to gaining control of any pressure situation" (Ravizza, 1986, p. 149). He suggests that awareness plays an important role in skill acquisition, emotional management, reaching peak performance, and stress management.

Ravizza proposes three techniques to build self-awareness and the ability to self-monitor. These techniques are journal keeping, performance feedback sheets, and group discussions. The sport journal method allows the athlete to systematically reflect on the experience gained during a specific performance episode. For the performance feedback method, coaches provide athletes well-designed feedback sheets, on which athletes can analyze their performances and learn from their mistakes before the next performance episode. This method has been found to be particularly helpful in situations where athletes play many matches in a short period of time (Ravizza, 1986). Finally, group discussions can offer another opportunity for athletes to improve their self-awareness through feedback from other players and coaches. Group discussion should be suggested not enforced. When properly conducted, these techniques promote self-awareness and increase team cohesion. These techniques closely parallel learning strategies supervisors use to help counselors-in-training better understand themselves and the impact people are having on others.

In a similar vein, sport psychologist Terry Orlick has worked with elite athletes to help achieve peak performance during competition. His approach on peak performance and self-growth is based on the improvements athletes make when they develop greater self-awareness. His six-step procedure for self-growth has been tested and found effective in sport psychology consulting (Orlick, 2000). The six-step approach is follows:

1. Select an area of focus that needs to be improved.
2. Complete a self-directed interview to identify the strengths and weaknesses in performance.
3. Reflect on what may have worked and select those strategies that may have the best potential of assisting self-growth.
4. Experiment with one or more of the strategies first in a nonthreatening situation, and then in a more stressful situation.
5. Keep a log to record the strategies that are effective for you, and make a note of what needs to be done to make them work.
6. Get together with friends or teammates who are also working on self-growth to discuss the effectiveness of various strategies and the best ways to execute them.

We believe that adopting Orlick's six-step approach in supervision could help supervisees tailor their supervision to their specific growth areas. The six steps clearly identify the processes of identification, self-reflection, experimentation, monitoring, and discussing progress with others. We believe that in a supportive and encouraging supervisory setting, this process is ideal for both addressing growth edges while developing self-supervision skills.

Self-Talk

Self-talk can be positive and negative. It has been established that positive self-talk used extensively by athletes can enhance performance for both experienced and novice athletes (Landin & Herbert, 1999; Mahoney & Avener, 1977; Ziegler, 1987). Self-talk is believed to help performers shift their attention to appropriate targets. These targets range from a vast external area to the management of one's internal fears, allowing information to processed most effectively (Nideffer, 1993).

Rushall (1984) identified three primary categories of self-talk that athletes might use in practice and competition: (a) task specific self-talk ("Just slow down and keep your rhythm and timing"); (b) positive talk for encouraging increased effort ("If I work hard today, then the next workout will be easier"); and (c) mood words that describe the nature of the performance ("Hang in there"). Rushall suggested that a combination of task specific self-talk and positive self-talk is very effective. Weinberg and Gould (1999) stated that positive self-talk can be used to enhance skill acquisition, break bad habits, initiate action, and sustain effort. In the therapeutic arena, negative self-talk can be related to a lack of confidence in one's abilities and doubts about one's ability to be effective. Supervisors working with entry level counseling supervisees often note anxiety related to negative self-talk and self-evaluation (Bernard & Goodyear, 1998). Kottler (1993) identified multiple self-talk strategies that could be effective for therapists, such as: when one's mind starts to drift elsewhere during a session ("Concentrate, concentrate"), when a client becomes abusive ("Oops. I'm letting him get to me"), and when a therapist feels blocked in session ("What is getting in the way of my being helpful?").

Goal-Setting

Goal setting is an effective technique for high achievement in sport settings (see Kyllo & Landers, 1995, for a review). Every mental training program has goal setting as its first requirement (Ungerleider, 1996). Without clear goals, there are no incentives for actions and therefore no incentives for self-regulation and self-supervision. Benji Durden, Olympic marathoner and coach, advocates thorough planning for himself and other athletes he coaches. He helps athletes set precise and thorough goals constantly and requires that they check in on their goals regularly through e-mail, phone, or fax. The most common reason for goal setting is to provide direction and develop a stronger focus on the task at hand. Kyllo and Landers (1995) demonstrated that with athletes, setting goals that are moderately difficult, yet realistic, often work best. Locke and Latham

(1985) hypothesized that athletic goal-setting is effective because it: (a) directs our attention to important elements of the skill; (b) mobilizes performer effort; (c) prolongs performer persistence; and (d) fosters the development of new learning and performance strategies. We believe goal setting in therapy operates in the same manner. Even though sometimes the goals for a therapist are less clearly defined, the ultimate target is still clear. That is, clients want to feel better and lessen discomfort. Sometimes, "feeling better" means accepting who they are and embracing their strengths and weaknesses; at other times, clients need to eliminate or add elements that are not conducive to reaching their goal. Therapy goals may be different, but all therapy needs to have a direction. In the current environment of brief therapy, Levenson (1995) notes that finding a focus in therapy is often the first step.

Mental Imagery

Imagery is a powerful mental technique enabling us to simulate what we are about to do and re-create what we have gone through. It is hailed as a facilitator for performance as well as for learning (Hardy & Nelson, 1988). Strong anecdotal evidence suggests that many athletes practice imagery (e.g., Nicklaus, 1976; Orlick & Partington, 1988; Ungerleider, 1996). Research has indicated that the practice of imagery in sport may boost self-confidence (Moritz, Hall, Vadocz, & Martin, 1996), improve concentration (Weinberg & Gould, 1999), control emotional responses (Vadocz, Hall, & Moritz, 1997), facilitate skill acquisition (Wrisberg & Anshel, 1989), and assist in coping with injuries (Ievleva & Orlick, 1991). Specifically, the connection between imagery and self-regulation can be found in research suggesting that imagery may enhance intrinsic motivation. Martin and Hall (1995) argued that imagery could promote self-efficacy, self-evaluative cognitions, and goal setting. Their research suggests those who use imagery tend to spend significantly more time practicing tasks, set higher goals, and have more realistic self-expectations.

In the same way mental imagery can help athletes prepare for competition and develop greater focus, imagery also can be used by therapists to prepare for therapeutic encounters. In beginning each therapy session, Keat (1999) writes about the process of epochè as a form of mental imagery that prepares therapists to connect with clients by focusing attention on being present and open when a session begins. Epochè is a Greek word meaning to stay away from, or abstain. In epochè, therapists set aside prejudgments, biases, and preconceived notions about things (Moustakas, 1988).

Moustakas views epochè as a rare event in which therapists prepare for an experience with clients with deliberate focus and attention on seeing clients anew through unfettered lenses. Keat (1999) notes that before each session he spends 5 to 10 minutes clearing his mind so that he can enter a client's world. In his state of self-hypnosis, Keat focuses on becoming reacquainted with issues from last session, being aware of ideas that could arise in the upcoming session, and finally leaving a mental "note" to meet clients in their world when the session begins. This form of mental imagery can be used by therapists in self-supervision to better understand how they can best establish rapport with clients, while mentally preparing to enter a client's frame of reference. It can also assist in self-supervision by helping the supervisee focus on the time and task at hand.

Modeling and Self-Regulation

Modeling is defined as "the use of demonstration as a means of conveying information about how to perform a skill" (Magill, 2001, p. 353). Self-regulation as a skill can be taught by a teacher, coach, or therapy supervisor through modeling techniques (Kitsantas, Zimmerman, & Cleary, 2000; Zimmerman & Kitsantas, 1997, 1999). It has been assumed that experts in a sport skill could demonstrate a skill for a novice learner and that repetitive viewing of an expert player demonstrating a skill live or on tape could enhance skill acquisition. However, recent investigation showed no evidence to support this claim (see Druckman & Swets, 1988). This result is consistent with the previous notion that errorless practice and rote repetition are poor learning strategies (Lee, Swinnen, & Serrien, 1994; Magill, 2001), because these activities may not encourage the learner to engage in problem-solving activities or self-regulatory processes.

Lee and White (1990) postulated that the use of correct or perfect models might not be the most effective means of conveying movement skill information. Instead, an alternative approach is to have a learner watch an unskilled or learning model repeatedly perform a skill. The process of watching a learning model can engage learners in problem-solving and other cognitive activities, making the learning more proficient. McCullagh and Caird (1990) further demonstrated the effectiveness of watching a learning model. Compared to those who watched an expert model, they found that participants who watched learning models were able to learn more accurately and could transfer this learning to other tasks. Even though inconsistent findings exist, Lee et al. (1994) believe that "observing a learning model will be no less effective than observing an expert model" because "a learning model more actively engages the observer in the problem-solving processes that characterize learning" (p. 331).

Two points are made in this section. First, self-regulation can be taught through modeling. Second, the best kind of modeling may be a learning model, instead of viewing experts. For instance, a coach can teach a learning athlete to think on his own feet during a competition. A good way to teach this skill is through the use of an example where a former athlete struggled to get started and managed to succeed eventually in preparing herself for competitions. Another idea is for athletes to watch videotapes of other athletes trying to perfect a skill. For therapists in training, whereas it can be helpful to view and explore therapeutic successes, it can be just as helpful to hear about mistakes that were made. In my experience working with first-year counseling students, my students tend to appreciate my stories of therapeutic failures and hearing about the anxiety I experienced as a beginning counselor. Students like to know that their models and professors have experienced many of the same thoughts and emotions that they are experiencing. In addition, students like to hear that I still struggle with my clients and theoretical concepts as part of being a lifelong student of the profession. The best way to demonstrate and encourage this lifelong commitment to learning is to demonstrate it to students.

Discovery Learning Aids Self-Regulation

Discovery learning is an alternative technique used to construct a learning environment. Discovery learning is a process in which withholding explicit instructions or modeling encourages learners to discover optimal solutions to problems independently; this often leads to equivalent or more efficacious learning and retention (van Emmerick, den Brinker, Vereijken, & Whiting, 1989; Vereijken & Whiting, 1988; Whiting, Bijlard, & den Brinker, 1987). Green and Flowers (1991) suggested that providing learners with instructions or rules could lead to an increase in processing load and high attentional demands during acquisition, which is subsequently harmful to learning. Hodges and Lee (1999) postulated that discovery learning enables learners to demonstrate a more exploratory learning strategy, thereby learners become more familiar with the dynamics of the task and variations in intrinsic information sources.

If discovery learning facilitates acquiring motor skills, it may also be practiced by therapy supervisors to encourage supervisees to engage in more independent thinking and personal development. Instead of providing answers and solutions, supervisors may be more effective if they ask their supervisees to come up with their own solutions and ideas. Discovery learning can be made more effective if the supervisor provides clear goals and the possibility of assistance when the supervisee gets into a predicament. This model mirrors the core of counseling, in that clients need to discover their own solutions rather than have a therapist tell them exactly what to do. Therapists help clients uncover solutions, but clients retain the responsibility to create change and the ownership of changes that do occur.

☐ From Self-Regulation to Self-Supervision: Implications for the Practice of Therapy

We have attempted in the previous sections to lead you to the conclusion that self-regulation, which is essential to achieving peak motoric performance, can also contribute to the practice of therapy. We believe that the concept of self-regulation is synonymous with the concept of self-supervision as defined by Pond (1997):

> As supervisors we can commit ourselves to behaviors that elicit energy from supervisees, helping to produce therapists who may be described as self-confident, able to generate appropriate custom-made interventions, and who know when to ask for help and how to get help. (p. 167)

We have written this chapter from the assumption that the processes of self-regulation with athletes who are being guided by coaches can operate in a similar manner for therapists working under supervision. We assume that both athletes and therapists want to improve their skills in their respective domains of practice. In the following we offer suggestions taken from the work on self-regulation that we feel may be help in facilitating self-supervision for supervisors and supervisees.

Suggestions for Creating Supervision That Fosters Self-Supervision

1. Create an environment conducive for beginning supervisees to ask for help whenever they need it. We live and work in a community and our behaviors are greatly influenced by everything in it. An environment where supervisees may solicit help from others must be a friendly and nonthreatening one. Athletes and students often do not ask for help because of fear of being discriminated against or belittled by their teachers or coaches. Likewise, supervisors who are not sensitive to the needs of beginning therapists may turn away eager students. The key to creating a supportive environment is for supervisors to take the initiative to create "nurturant" spaces for supervision (Nicholas, 1989). Encouragement goes further than criticism. Supportive environments serve as the basis for

discovery learning and enable supervisee to ask for help without the fear of being judged.

2. Supervisors need to evaluate how they give feedback and how they interact with supervisees. Evaluate the time interval when feedback is given to allow the supervisee to respond first, note how much feedback is given, and in terms of how to integrate feedback, supervisors can model effective ways of integration.

3. Profit from learning models. It is as important to learn from the most skilled therapists as well as learning from young and unskilled ones. Supervisors can take advantage of some unsuccessful cases where the clients and therapists did not reach their common therapy goals. Supervisors can reflect on the times when they sought supervision and consultation.

4. Offer feedback but not crutches. Supervisors can provide feedback for beginning therapists following some simple guidelines. First, feedback should be specific and task-oriented, rather than person-oriented. Second, feedback should not be provided too frequently and too fast. Third, it is advisable that self-evaluation techniques be implemented earlier in supervision with established evaluative checkpoint. During the evaluation process, any discrepancy between self-evaluation and supervisor-evaluation should be addressed immediately. Talk about self-supervision at the onset, rather than the termination of supervision. Then, as supervision enters the frame of evaluation, discuss how supervisors and supervisees are seeing the process of supervision from their own unique perspectives.

5. Allow a beginning therapist the opportunity to make mistakes and learn from them. Learning occurs when a person learns from mistakes, does not dwell on them, and has the opportunity to try again. Using a golf metaphor, Hoyt (2000) notes to "keep it in the fairway and seek progress, not perfection," mirroring the golf adage "it's not how well you hit it; it's how well you mis-hit it" (see Lardner, 1960 as cited in Hoyt, 2000). Take the time to explore what mistakes, or mis-hits, but always move ahead. To minimize the impact of their mistakes on clients, a supervisor should provide some guidance yet take the time for the process of learning to emerge. Following the model of discovery learning, a safe supervision environment encourages supervisees to seek answers and explore the process of supervision. For instance, before a consultation session starts, the supervisor may have studied the case first and then offer some advice as to the potential problems that may ensue during the consultation. At the end of the consultation, the supervisor may provide immediate feedback and conclusions from the session.

6. Be an effective model in terms of using goal setting, mental imagery, self-talk, and self-awareness in supervision. From the onset, establish goals for supervision that address a supervisee's growth areas. Examine the tar-

gets that supervisees are trying to reach and how supervision can assist this process. Practice visualization or epochè at the beginning of supervision with a supervisee. Explore the type of self-talk that supervisees encounter and work to create positive self-talk when appropriate. Finally, consistently ask supervisees to reflect on their experiences either verbally or in a supervision journal.

Suggestions for Beginning Therapists Working Under Supervision

1. Monitor yourself and learn to identify conditions that require external help. What do you think you can handle and what are your blind spots? In sports, athletes need their coaches' assistance when the situation is considered risky and difficult, like the performance on the uneven bars for female gymnasts or during a tense and pivotal point in a game. In these situations, many athletes call a timeout to consult with coaches and establish a plan of act. For therapists, the credo "when in doubt, consult," holds true whenever a supervisee encounters situations that involve risk. Consultation can be viewed as a therapeutic "timeout." During these moments, don't be afraid or hesitate to call a timeout and consult with your supervisor. Other tough times are when athletes encounter mental or emotional barriers. Coaches do not always know what athletes are going through in their personal life. Likewise, supervisors might not know the personal situations of supervisees. It is important to let supervisors know your personal concerns that may be influencing clinical work.

2. Set clear goals for self-development and self-regulation. Just like athletes who use goal setting for peak performance, such as the track athletes who monitor lap splits, supervisees need to establish what they want out of supervision and how progress will be monitored. Again using a golf metaphor, Hoyt (2000) notes "it's a long day on the course if you don't know where the hole is. Have a specific goal and be purposeful on every stroke" (p. 6). It is important to remember that self-regulation cannot occur if goals and reference points for regulation are not established.

3. Consider how you mentally prepare for your therapy and supervision sessions. Is your mind clear enough to enter a client's world and the world of supervision? Are you able to clear away personal concerns and stressors to the point that you are wholly there for your clients, supervisors, and yourself? Self-supervision and self-regulation are only possible when athletes and supervisees can focus clearly on the situation and have the mental space to self-reflect. Consider the use of mental imagery, such as the process of epochè, as a preparation exercise.

☐ Conclusion: A Word of Caution

The practice of therapy is clearly different from achieving success in athletics. In addition, we clearly understand sports occur on the field of games and competition, whereas therapy occurs in the realm of real human lives that are often accompanied by real pain and suffering. The analogies drawn from our understanding of human performance and counseling literature are an attempt to bridge two very different disciplines of study. It is our understanding that little research exists to empirically support the transfer of knowledge between these areas. This bold step to compare these two areas may be controversial, yet also may be refreshing to those who need a breath of fresh air to knock down some barriers for creativity and the maintenance of therapeutic skills.

☐ References

Adler, A. (1956). *The individual psychology of Alfred Adler: A systematic presentation in selections from his writings* (H. L. Ansbacher & R. R. Ansbacher, eds.). New York: Basic Books.

Armstrong, L., & Jenkins, S. (2000). *It's not about the bike: My journey back to life.* New York: Putnam.

Bernard, J. M., & Goodyear, R. K. (1998). *Fundamentals of clinical supervision* (2nd ed.). Boston: Allyn & Bacon.

Bernstein, B. L., & Lecomte, C. (1979). Self-critique technique training in a competency-based practicum. *Counselor Education and Supervision, 19,* 69–76.

Bertolino, B., & O'Hanlon, B. (2002). Collaborative, competency-based counseling and therapy. Boston: Allyn & Bacon.

Bramley, W. (1996). *The supervisory couple in broad-spectrum psychotherapy.* London: Free Association.

Carroll, M. (1996). *Counseling supervision: Theory, skills and practice.* London: Cassell.

Carver, C. S., & Scheier, M. F. (1981). *Attention and self-regulation: A control theory approach to human behavior.* New York: Springer-Verlag.

Chen, D. D. (2001). Trends in augmented feedback research and tips for the practitioner. *Journal of Physical Education, Recreation, and Dance, 72,* 32–36.

Crews, D. J. (1993). Self-regulation strategies in sport and exercise. In R. N. Singer, M. Murphey, & L. K. Tennant (Eds.), *Handbook of research on sport psychology* (pp. 557–568). New York: MacMillan.

de Shazer, S. (1988). *Clues: Investigating solutions in brief therapy.* New York: Norton.

Druckman, D., & Swets, J. A. (1988). *Enhancing human performance: Issues, theories, and techniques.* Washington, DC: National Academy Press.

Erickson, M. H. (1954). Pseudo-orientation in time as a hypnotherapeutic procedure. *Journal of Clinical and Experiential Hypnosis, 2,* 261–283.

Ferrari, M., Pinard, A., Reid, L., & Bouffard-Bouchard, T. (1991). The relationship between expertise and self-regulation in movement performance: Some theoretical issues. *Perceptual and Motor Skills, 72,* 139–150.

Gaudreau, P., Blondin, J. P., & Lapierre, A. M. (2002). Athletes' coping during competition: Relationship of coping strategies with positive affect, negative affect, and performance-goal discrepancy. *Psychology of Sport and Exercise, 3,* 125–150.

Green, T. D., & Flowers, J. H. (1991). Implicit versus explicit learning processes in a probabilistic, continuous fine-motor catching task. *Journal of Motor Behavior, 23,* 293–300.

Hamilton, S., & Fremouw, W. (1985). Cognitive-behavioral training for college free-throw performance. Cognitive *Therapy and Research, 9,* 479–483.

Hardy, L., & Nelson, D. (1988). Self-regulation training in sport and work. *Ergonomics, 31,* 1573–1583.

Hawkins, P., & Shohet, R. (1989). *Supervision in the helping professions.* Milton Keynes, UK: Open University Press.

Hodges, N. J., & Lee, T. D. (1999). The role of augmented information prior to learning a bimanual visual-motor coordination task: do instructions of the movement pattern facilitate learning relative to discovery learning? *British Journal of Psychology, 90,* 389–397.

Hoyt, M. F. (2000). *Some stories are better than others: Doing what works in brief therapy and managed care.* Philadelphia: Brunner-Mazel.

Ievleva, L., & Orlick, T. (1991). Mental links to enhanced healing. *The Sport Psychologist, 5,* 25–40.

Jackson, P., & Delehanty, H. (1995). *Sacred hoops: Spiritual lessons of a hardwood warrior.* New York: Hyperion.

Kanfer, F. H., & Karoly, P. (1972). Self-control: A behavioristic excursion into the lion's den. *Behavior Therapy, 3,* 398–416.

Keat, D. B. (1999). Counseling anxious male youth. In A. M. Horne, & M. S. Kiselica (Eds.), *Handbook of counseling boys and adolescent males* (pp. 249–277). Thousand Oaks, CA: Sage.

Kirschenbaum, D. S. (1984). Self-regulation and sport psychology: Nurturing an emerging symbiosis. *Journal of Sport Psychology, 6,* 159–183.

Kitsantas, A., Zimmerman, B. J., & Cleary, T. (2000). The role of observation and emulation in the development of athletic self-regulation. *Journal of Educational Psychology, 92,* 811–817.

Kottler, J. A. (1993). *On being a therapist* (rev. ed.). San Francisco: Jossey-Bass.

Kyllo, L. B., & Landers, D. M. (1995). Goal setting in sport and exercise: A research synthesis to resolve the controversy. *Journal of Sport and Exercise Psychology, 17,* 117–137.

Landin, D., & Herbert, E. P. (1999). The influence of self-talk on the performance of skilled female tennis players. *Journal of Applied Sport Psychology, 11,* 263–282.

Lee, T. D., Swinnen, S. P., & Serrien, D. J. (1994). Cognitive effort and motor learning. *Quest, 46,* 328–344.

Lee, T. D., & White, M. A. (1990). Influence of an unskilled model's practice schedule on observational motor learning. *Human Movement Science, 9,* 349–367.

Levenson, H. (1995). *Time limited dynamic psychotherapy.* New York: Basic Books.

Locke, E. A., & Latham, G. P. (1985). The application of goal setting to sports. *Journal of Sport Psychology, 7,* 205–222.

Lowe, R. (2000). Supervising self-supervision: Constructive inquiry and embedded narratives in case consultation. *Journal of Marital and Family Therapy, 26,* 511–521.

Mace, R., Eastman, C., & Carroll, D. (1987). The effect of stress-inoculation training on gymnastic performance on the pommelled horse: A case study. *Behavioral Psychotherapy, 15,* 272–279.

Magill, R. A. (2001). *Motor learning: Concepts and applications* (6th ed). New York: McGraw-Hill.

Mahoney, M. J., & Avener, M. (1977). Psychology of the elite athlete: An exploratory study. *Cognitive Therapy and Research, 1,* 135–141.

Martin, K. A., & Hall, C. R. (1995). Using imagery to enhance intrinsic motivation. *Journal of Sport & Exercise Psychology, 17,* 54–69.

McCullagh, P., & Caird, J. K. (1990). Correct and learning models and the use of model knowledge of results in the acquisition and retention of a motor skill. *Journal of Human Movement Studies, 18,* 107–116.

Moritz, S. E., Hall, C. R., Vadocz, E., & Martin, K. A. (1996). What are confident athletes imaging? An examination of image content. *The Sport Psychologist, 10,* 171–179.

Moustakas, C. E. (1988). *Phenomenology, science and psychotherapy.* Sydney, Nova Scotia, Canada: Family Life Institute, University College of Brenton Press.

Nelson, M. L. (in press). An assessment-based model for counseling strategy selection. *Journal of Counseling and Development.*

Nicholas, M. W. (1989). A systemic perspective of group therapy supervision: Use of energy in the supervisor-therapist-group system. *Journal of Independent Social Work, 3*(4), 27–39.

Nicklaus, J. (1976). *Play better golf.* New York: King Features.

Nideffer, R. N. (1993). Attention control training. In R. N. Singer, M. Murphey, & L. K. Tennant (Eds.), *Handbook of research on sport psychology* (pp. 542–556). New York: Macmillan.

Orlick, T. (2000). *In pursuit of excellence: How to win in sport and life through mental training* (3rd ed.). Champaign, IL: Leisure Press.

Orlick, T., Partington, J. (1988). Mental links to excellence. *The Sport Psychologist, 2,* 105–130.

Pond, C. (1997). Highlighting success in groups: Empowering and energizing supervisees. In T. C. Todd & C. L. Storm (Eds.), *The complete systemic supervisor: Context, philosophy, and pragmatics* (pp. 165–167). Boston: Allyn & Bacon.

Ravizza, K. (1986). Increasing awareness for sport performance. In J. M. Williams (Ed.), *Applied sport psychology: Personal growth to peak performance* (pp. 149–162). Palo Alto, CA: Mayfield.

Rushall, B. S., Hall, M., Roux, L., Sasseville, J., & Rushall, A. C. (1988). Effects of three types of thought content instructions on skiing performance. *The Sport Psychologist, 2,* 283–297.

Salmoni, A. W., Schmidt, R. A., & Walter, C. B. (1984). Knowledge of results and motor learning: A review and critical appraisal. *Psychological Bulletin, 95,* 355–386.

Snyder, M. (1983). The influence of individuals on situations: Implications for understanding the links between personality and social behavior. *Journal of Personality, 51,* 497–516.

Swinnen, S. P., Schmidt, R.A., Nicholson, D. E., & Shapiro, D. C. (1990). Information feedback for skill acquisition: Instantaneous knowledge of results degrades learning. *Journal of Experimental Psychology: Learning, Memory, and Cognition, 16,* 706–716.

Todd, T. C. (1997). Self-supervision as a universal supervisory goal. In T. C. Todd & C. L. Storm (Eds.), *The complete systemic supervisor: Context, philosophy, and pragmatics* (pp. 17–25). Boston: Allyn & Bacon.

Ungerleider, S. (1996). *Mental training for peak performance: Top athletes reveal the mind exercises they use to excel.* Emmaus, PA: Rodale.

van Emmerick, R. E. A., den Brinker, B. P. L. M., Vereijken, B., & Whiting, H. T. A. (1989). Preferred tempo in the learning of a gross cyclical action. *The Quarterly Journal of Experimental Psychology, 41,* 251–262.

Vereijken, B., & Whiting, H. T. A. (1988). A comparison of echokinetic and synkinetic paradigms in the learning of a complex cyclical action. *Pre-proceedings of the Second Workshop on Imagery and Cognition.*

Vereijken, B., & Whiting, H. T. A. (1989). In defense of discovery learning. In P. C. W. van Wieringen & R. J. Bootsma (Eds.), *Catching up: Selected essays of H. T. A. Whiting* (pp. 155–169). Amsterdam: Free University Press.

Vodocz, E. A., Hall, C. R., & Moritz, S. E. (1997). The relationship between competitive anxiety and imagery use. *Journal of Applied Sport Psychology, 9*, 241–253.

Weinberg, R. S., & Gould, D. (1999). *Foundations of sport and exercise psychology*. Champaign, IL: Human Kinetics.

Whiting, H. T. A., Bijlard, M. J., & den Brinker, B. P. L. M. (1987). The effect of the availability of a dynamic model on the acquisition of a complex cyclical action. *The Quarterly Journal of Experimental Psychology, 39*, 43–59.

Winstein, C. J., & Schmidt, R. A. (1990). Reduced relative frequency of knowledge of results enhances motor learning. *Journal of Experimental Psychology: Learning, Memory, and Cognition, 16*, 677–691.

Wrisberg, R. S., & Anshel, M. H. (1989). The effect of cognitive strategies on the free throw shooting performance of young athletes. *The Sport Psychologist, 3*, 95–104.

Ziegler, S. G. (1987). Effects of stimulus cueing on the acquisition of groundstrokes by beginning tennis players. *Journal of Applied Behavior Analysis, 20*, 405–411.

Zimmerman, B. J. (1986). Becoming a self-regulated learner: Which are the key subprocesses? *Contemporary Educational Psychology, 11*, 307–313.

Zimmerman, B. J., & Kitsantas, A. (1997). Developmental phases in self-regulation: Shifting from process to outcome self-regulatory goals. *Journal of Educational Psychology, 89*, 29–36.

Zimmerman, B. J., & Kitsantas, A. (1999). Acquiring writing revision skill: Shifting from process to outcome self-regulatory goals. *Journal of Educational Psychology, 91*, 241–250.

Zimmerman, B. J., & Kitsantas, A. (2001). Self-regulation differences during athletic practice by experts, non-experts, and novices. *Journal of Applied Sport Psychology, 13*, 185–206.

Laurie Carty
W. Paul Jones

Self-Supervision in Medical Settings

A female nurse walked into the room of a 24-year-old hospitalized woman who had attempted suicide. The patient refused to speak to anyone and hid her face behind her long dark hair. The nurse noticed that her patient wrote poetry and asked if she could read some of the poetry. The feelings expressed in the poetry were many of the same feelings expressed by survivors of sexual abuse. The nurse, herself a survivor of sexual abuse, thought she had a good idea of what her patient needed.

Over the next few days the nurse worked with her patient to establish trust and safety. The nurse brought in some of her poetry to share with her patient. The patient began to talk to the nurse about the meanings in her poetry. Just as the nurse asked her patient, "Has anyone ever hurt you?" the physician walked into the room. He said, "Don't go there. . . . It's none of our business."

The nurse became silent as a wave of powerlessness enveloped her. The nurse knew that she was disempowering herself in relationship to the greater status of the physician. Inside the nurse was struggling with herself, hoping to find her voice. Inside she said, "Speak up. At least protest this avoidance behavior. You know he's wrong. This young patient needs you to advocate for her. I'm a gutless wimp. I need a supervisor to talk to but there is no one available. I am on my own." The nurse remained silent and the physician left.

The nurse felt disappointed with herself. She was flooded with feelings of shame, inadequacy, and a diminished self. Reflecting on her experience the nurse asked herself the following questions:

1. Have I resolved my issues about my own sexual abuse?
2. How can I help my patients work through their abuse issues when I haven't worked through mine?
3. How can I advocate for my patients when I feel so powerless when confronted by physicians?
4. How can I make a difference when I feel helpless and trapped within rigid structures and huge systemic barriers?

In a different hospital, a male marriage and family therapist was surprised at the persisting symptoms of anxiety experienced as he entered the room of a client who had requested his services. Providing therapy in a hospital setting was not a brand-new experience. Since attaining his "health professional affiliate" status, several physicians had written orders for him to provide a therapy session for one of their patients. He could now, with reasonable ease, navigate the hospital corridors to find a patient's room. He no longer felt a complete novice about recording his visit in the patient's chart.

Not far from conscious memory, however, were the feelings associated with the very first experience. Who were all of those people at the nurse's station? To whom was he supposed to announce his presence? Should he ask about his "client" or his "patient?" There was no privacy in the patient's room and the day room was not much better, with a constant stream of people going in and out. He found a room identified for consultation, but persons with disapproving looks continued to open the door after the session began. Where exactly is therapy supposed to occur in a hospital setting?

The therapist was more than a little perturbed and disappointed that the anxiety evident in his first inpatient therapy sessions continued to be evident. He could not completely escape feelings of inadequacy and diminished self. Reflecting on his feelings, he asked himself the following questions:

1. Why did I leave the comfort of familiar surroundings to provide therapy in a hospital setting?
2. Do I really belong in this setting?
3. Can I deliver a high quality of service in this setting?
4. Why, as a well-trained and experienced practitioner, do I feel so powerless?

The circumstances, practice specialty, gender of the practitioners, and severity of the problems are obviously quite different in the preceding scenarios. There is, though, an important common feature. In both instances, the practitioner feels helpless, trapped in a system, concerned at feeling powerless to perform the health care tasks for which each was trained.

The questions being asked by the nurse and the marriage and family therapist illustrate the beginning of the process of self-supervision. Reflective practice activities and self-supervision are necessary for professional competence, and this nurse, for example, needs to evaluate her practice in relation to nursing practice standards (Stuart & Laraia, 2001). Practice standards are developed by the official licensing body (College of Nurses of Ontario, CNO) and define the behaviors necessary for professional competency. Self-supervision is defined as performance appraisal by Stuart and Laraia (2001) and defined as self-assessment by the CNO (1996).

The therapist also is being confronted with questions associated with standards of practice. Providing services outside the scope of professional competence is most often identified in reference to a specific technique or client problem area. It could easily be argued, however, that attempting to practice in a setting that elicits feelings of helplessness or makes it difficult to maintain standards of privacy might also warrant identification as being outside the boundaries of appropriate practice.

Recognizing that enhancing clinical skills must include consideration of the environment in which the professional practice occurs, our focus in this chapter is on features associated with practice in the hospital setting. Given the lengthy history of hospital-based health care and the variety of outside forces to which hospitals must respond, it is not surprising to learn that self-supervision has been formalized into self-assessment tools, machine-scored questionnaires to monitor compliance with professional standards. In the last section of this chapter, we will examine an illustrative self-assessment tool, prepared in Ontario, Canada for use by nurses, with particular attention to features that may be valuable in application to other health care specialties.

We also recognize, however, that for those of us identified as "second-tier" professionals in medical settings, there can be a dark side to practice in a hospital setting, features that, if left unaddressed, can make it difficult to maintain the personal and emotional characteristics necessary for effective practice. These features are examined using a template of our own experiences as a nurse and psychologist, respectively.

☐ The Nurses' Experience

The nurse in our story was affected by a great many factors in the hospital culture. She was aware of some factors but there were others of which she was not aware. Four critical factors contribute to the dark side of the hospital culture.

The Nurse–Physician Relationship

In spite of changes toward equality in the general culture, the hospital has remained a male-dominated environment (McDonald, 1999). Nursing in the hospital is viewed as women's work, and women's work is not valued. The relationship between nurses and doctors is hierarchical and disconnected. Physicians have developed identities based on separation and individuation. Nurses have developed identities based on connection and relationship. Bevis (1983) says that if care of patient were considered a pie, one piece of the pie for physicians would be concerned with the relationship and life experience of the patient. The rest of the pie would be made up of symptoms of illness, disease, and medical treatments. The opposite is true for nurses. One piece of the pie would be symptoms of illness, disease, and medical treatment, whereas the rest of the pie for nurses is relationship and life experience of the patient. For the physician, autonomy and control are required at all times. Connection with nurses about decision-making, dialog, and shared problem solving are experienced as threats to physicians' autonomy and control (Chandler, 1992). Response to the threat often has been to ignore the nurse and/or attack the intrusion.

A study by Katzman and Roberts (1988) about nurse–physician interaction patterns on a busy inpatient unit noted that nine out of 18 physicians came and left without speaking to a single nurse. Cox's study (1991) reported that 96.7% of staff nurses experienced verbal abuse from a physician. Nurses reported that verbal abuse affected the patient care, morale, productivity, job security, and turnover. Because of a lack of administrative and collegial support, the nurses' response to abusive episodes was passive acceptance. The young nurse in our story experienced herself being dismissed and silenced by the physician. The path this nurse chose was the traditional path. Gray (1994) states that the traditional path results in subordination of women. Gray also says that when she chooses a different path she is harassed, ignored, criticized, and shamed by both women and men in the hospital environment.

The Nurse–Nurse Relationship

When nurses are ignored, reprimanded, devalued, and dismissed, they experience a diminished sense of self. Their powerlessness results in anger, and angry nurses in the hospital culture are not acceptable. When anger is not allowed, depression, apathy, withdrawal, and burnout occur. This results in horizontal hostility, infighting, and rejection of ones' colleagues. This anger, frustration, and mistrust are directed toward other members of the same group. This feels safer than confrontation with the dominant physician group. These nurses identify with those in power (Chandler, 1992). Roberts (1983) calls this process oppressed group behavior. Oppressed group behavior is toxic for individuals and the environment. This behavior is destructive in work groups. Horizontal hostility prevents cohesion and alienates members who are different from the traditional group. Infighting, backstabbing, and unfair criticism occur daily, resulting in a toxic, isolating, and alienating environment (Chandler, 1992; McDonald, 1999). Internal division within the nursing profession keeps the profession helpless and powerless.

The History of Nursing

The story about our young nurse reflects many of the ongoing issues and systemic barriers faced by all nurses. This nurse struggled with her role as a woman doing women's work in an environment that devalues the work of women. There was little support for this young woman. Nursing has done little to nurture and direct young members (McDonald, 1999). McDonald states, "It is only recently that issues of professionalization and collegiality with physicians have been addressed openly from a feminist perspective" (p. 34).

Two historical trends have isolated nurses from women in other professions:

1. Formal nursing organizations have only recently supported the contemporary women's movement (Allen, 1985; Vance, Talbott, McBride, & Mason, 1985).
2. Feminists labeled nursing as a ghetto profession and only supported high-status professions such as medicine and law (Gordon, 1991).

These two trends have resulted in a profession that, until recently, has been isolated from the inside and the outside (Hoff & Ross, 1993).

Personal Abuse History

Hoff and Ross (1993) identify the importance of nurses with a history of abuse working through these issues. Russell (1990) believes that because physical/sexual abuse is high in the general female population, it is highly probable that many nurses carry abuse histories. Because a "cloak of silence" has perpetuated women's "secrets" until very recently, many abuse issues remain hidden.

The young woman in our story had a history of abuse. Because she was able to use this history to connect with her patient, she had a level of awareness of her history. Her awareness was fragile and she was easily silenced by the physician. There was no supervisory support and this young nurse was alone.

☐ A Psychologist's Experience

Earlier we suggested that feelings of helplessness may be elicited in practitioners working in medical settings. An even better description of the elicited feelings may be evident in the concept of self-efficacy. In simplest terms, self-concept can be defined as "who I think I am," and self-efficacy defined as "what I think I can do." Bandura (1989) notes that persons with a high sense of self-efficacy tend to visualize success scenarios and cognitively rehearse viable solutions to potential problems. A low sense of self-efficacy is associated with diminished motivation and impaired performance.

The premise here is that working in unfamiliar surroundings or in new roles can and often does directly affect a practitioner's perception of efficacy. Certainly we've all spent time in physicians' offices, and most, if not all, have at least some experience in the hospital setting. But, for most of us, that experience is primarily based on being the receiver not the provider of services. Usually we went to a hospital to visit a friend or relative, and typically we were more than a bit overwhelmed by the surroundings. Unless some part of our practicum or internship experience was in a medical setting, we have entirely different roles to play when we enter the medical world as visiting practitioners. With the new roles, we find new expectations, challenges, fears, and doubts.

The history of the psychologist in medical and other hospital settings is, of course, not nearly as long as that of the nurse. Neither, though, could it be described as a new phenomenon. For at least one-half of a century, stimulated by actions of the Veteran's Administration following World War II, the psychologist's scope of practice has included providing evaluations and/or therapy in the hospital environment. Although periodic turf squabbles between psychiatrists and psychologists are reported in the literature (e.g., prescription privilege, evaluation versus therapy focus), there is very little extant literature focused directly on the interactions of physicians and psychologists working together in hospital settings.

This section, thus, is purposefully entitled "a," rather than "the" psychologist's experience. The material that follows comes from my own experience in delivering psychological services in medical settings.

As I begin my story, there are some important disclaimers. Through the decades of my practice, I've been granted hospital privileges in several states, typically with a title along the lines of allied health professional. During this time, physicians and the nurses have consistently treated me with respect and dignity. Administrative personnel have taken appropriate steps to ensure that I feel welcome and to communicate that my work is valued. Working in medical settings has been sometimes financially rewarding and always personally rewarding. However, without a single exception, in each of the several settings, I have felt periodically uncertain, often concerned about whether my behavior was "correct," and frankly sometimes just in fear of the setting. The diminished self-efficacy described in the preceding, and the feelings of powerlessness discussed earlier have at times been clearly evident in my feelings about practice in the medical settings.

Inappropriate, condescending behavior by physicians and/or nurses has to be ruled out as the underlying cause. This is not, by the way, a suggestion that I've never encountered a physician with a condescending manner. Instead, it is just that those individuals have been "equal opportunity egotists," no more or less inappropriate in their attitudes and interactions with me than with their peers. Physicians and nurses just don't provide the etiology for the problems in my story.

Perhaps the next most likely hypothesis is that I just have problems with self-esteem and perceptions of self-adequacy in most settings, and that those problems simply generalized into my work in medical surroundings. Although I'm certainly not the most objective reviewer of this hypothesis, it does not appear consistent with other information and also needs to be rejected as the probable cause.

If it's not my colleagues and it's not me, what's left? In this case, what's left is the setting itself. Perhaps more specifically, what's left is at least a plausible hypothesis that non–medical mental health providers have gaps in our training that make it more difficult to deliver our services with maximum effectiveness in medical settings.

My story begins with what seems the most mundane of issues. What do we call the people we serve? Early in my career, I was offered an opportunity for a part-time assignment, working with three pediatricians in an urban setting. They provided office space, 1 day per week, including use of receptionist and waiting area. They provided all referrals. For an academic seeking additional part-time practice and experience working with children, it was a dream assignment.

Still fresh in my ears were the words I had heard in classes and from my clinical supervisors. We do not have patients. We have clients. It is very important to avoid use of the term patient. That is the medical model. It is not ours! After all, the one who names, defines, and chooses the language is the one in power.

Although perhaps never really grasping why my supervisors felt this was so important, I certainly had accepted it as an ultimate truth. So, before my first day on the job, I visited with the receptionists, and politely (but firmly) asked them to please use the term "client" when announcing my appointments. All agreed to do so.

It's my first day of appointments. It's a Saturday. All three of the pediatricians also accepted appointments on Saturdays. Picture the scene, Saturday morning in a busy multiprovider pediatric practice. The waiting room is crowded with children and accompanying adults. Many of the children are coughing. Some are crying. Some are just noisy. And, the hyperactive ones are mostly mine. The office staff is frantically trying to maintain some semblance of order in the chaos, keeping the appointments moving along at least close to the scheduled time while coping with walk-ins, insurance problems, and so forth.

The receptionist and a nurse, at the same time, come to the door of my office, which opens into the waiting area. The nurse says, "Could you possibly make time for an unscheduled patient? Doctor ___ would like your consultation." The receptionist, remembering my request, fumbles with her words: "your first patie . . . , I mean your client is already here and doesn't like to be kept waiting." The receptionist continues, confronting the nurse with: "He doesn't want his people to be called patients."

They say that a picture is worth a thousand words. The look on the nurse's face spoke volumes (and none of them particularly flattering to the new person on the block). The receptionist was embarrassed about not responding correctly and annoyed with the nurse for her reaction.

Somehow we got through that day, and at day's end, I found time to thank the receptionists for their efforts in trying to do what I had asked and suggested that we forget trying to make the distinction. It really wasn't necessary and wasn't worth the bother. They quickly agreed (with obvious signs of relief). I also made time to visit briefly with the nurse who had come to my door earlier, acknowledging the source of my suggestion, admitting that it was just a bad idea. She accepted graciously; we had a good visit about gaps between what we were trained to do and the realities of actual practice.

Obviously in this setting, the distinction made no sense. The person had already been a "patient" in the office, otherwise the referral would not have been made. Changing from "patient" to "client" contingent on which door you enter from a waiting room was, at best, absurd.

One could perhaps argue that this was just much ado about nothing. It's only a word. What difference does it make? The difference in this case was more than trivial. The ensuing confusion raised, in my mind, that bothersome question of whether I belonged in this setting. And questions about whether one belongs lead directly to questions about efficacy. And questions about efficacy eventually result in higher odds of diminished performance. That is a big deal, over just a simple term.

The issue about designation, of course, is not limited to special practice settings like the preceding one. Assume that in your own office, you prefer the term client. Assume further that one of your clients attempts suicide and is admitted to the hospital. The psychiatrist knows of your past relationship with the individual. You have allied health privileges at the hospital. The psychiatrist invites you to continue therapy sessions while the individual is hospitalized. So far, so good. Now, which terminology will you use while in the hospital? And does the fact that there is even a question serve to increase, even slightly, your discomfort in practicing in the hospital setting?

My story continues with perhaps a more troubling and significant event, failing to remember the boundaries. This scene, for reasons that will become apparent, requires some disguise. A number of years had passed since the incident described in the preceding. I'd become much more comfortable working in medical settings. The circumstances of my work at that time were such that a significant portion of my part-time practice was in evaluations and therapy in one particular hospital. I was on a rotational call for new patients admitted to the psychiatric ward.

Responses from other providers and the hospital staff had made it clear that I was especially well thought of in that setting. I'd made many friends among the staff. I was attentive to my beeper. I was prompt and complete in charting the sessions. My recommendations in patient staffings were always considered and almost always followed to the letter.

The case to be described came from the rotation list. I was pleased that the psychiatrist had written orders for an evaluation and a series of therapy sessions. The psychiatrist assigned to the case, however, did not have an especially robust reputation for expertise. That's the kind way to say it. More specifically, his reputation and my previous experience with him on shared cases indicated that he was only barely competent. There was no evidence that he was doing harm; there was just very little evidence that his skills were anything but marginal.

I completed the evaluation with the patient and found no evidence of current or underlying clinical pathology. My chart notes reflected this perception. I had two therapy sessions with the patient that completely reinforced the assessment, again noting the findings in the chart. As far as I could see, there was absolutely no reason for this individual to be treated in an inpatient setting. The spouse of the patient happened to be in the waiting area when I completed the second session. I asked if we could visit for a few minutes, wanting to be sure that there wasn't something going on that I was missing.

The spouse confirmed what the patient had told me. There had been a death in the family. They had made an appointment with the psychiatrist because the patient was having trouble sleeping. No suicidal ideation had been expressed. During the appointment, the psychiatrist informed them that inpatient treatment was essential, and that they could expect hospitalization for a minimum of 2 weeks.

With this confirmation and wanting to be responsive to the pleas of spouse and patient to be allowed to go home, I told the spouse that I could see no reason for continuing the inpatient treatment. I said that I would inform the treatment team the following morning, and that they could expect a discharge by the afternoon.

Okay, in retrospect that was a really dumb move on my part. At the time, though, it seemed completely appropriate. I was proactively working in the best interests of the patient. There was nothing in the chart suggesting anything contrary to my appraisal of the situation.

I went confidently to the treatment team meeting, expecting to be acknowledged as a hero. Bed space was at a premium. This patient should be discharged immediately. My professional judgment had never been challenged in that setting and certainly would be viewed as superior to that of the psychiatrist who admitted the patient.

As you have probably already guessed, that meeting was a nightmare that I hope never to repeat. Before the meeting, the patient had informed the attending nurse that a discharge was imminent. The nurse had informed the psychiatrist. I will never forget the psychiatrist's words as the meeting began: "Who in hell gave you authority to talk to my patient about discharge?" To say that he was angry wouldn't even come close to capturing the emotion evident in his words. I looked around the room for support. After all, I was the published academic clinician; my work in that hospital had been above reproach. Everyone knew he was mediocre, at best. But, no support was forthcoming. In fact, I couldn't find anyone in the room with whom to make eye contact.

The psychiatrist went on, citing some obscure and irrelevant rationale for another day of observation. He stopped glaring at me; instead it was as if I ceased to exist while there was discussion by the treatment team of the need for the bed. The psychiatrist's position was never directly confronted by the team. A face-saving compromise resulted in the patient's being discharged early the following morning instead of later that afternoon.

I escaped without a formal reprimand. The psychiatrist left the city a month or so later. Until I moved on, I continued to receive referrals for work at the hospital but could not escape the feeling that the other psychiatrists were now wary when I came up in the rotation. With the wisdom of hindsight, of course, I should have talked to the psychiatrist before talking with the patient or family member about discharge. There is no good excuse for that error.

The more important lesson, though, a lesson that has served me well since then, was the recognition that hospitals are just not "level playing fields" in reference to psychologists and physicians, even when skill and/ or experience with a specific case favor the psychologist. In the preceding case, I crossed a boundary, clearly exceeding my authority. I had violated a cultural rule related to who has the power, who has the control.

Psychologists and other therapists play an important role in hospital settings and that role is both acknowledged and respected by most physicians. But the rules are clear, and success in a hospital-based practice requires understanding and acceptance of the boundaries. We are valued guests, but we are only guests. It is not "our house."

Two questions conclude this section. Are there features in hospital and other medical settings that may make it more difficult for a therapist to maintain a quality practice? And, from the title of this chapter, are there things we can learn from practice in medical settings to enhance the overall level of practice?

For the first of these questions, my experience certainly suggests that the answer is Yes. There are factors that, if not addressed, are likely to impair performance. For example, to state the obvious, hospitals are intended for people who are ill. If your theoretical frame of reference cannot accept this definition, then hospital practice should be avoided at all costs.

Hospital settings are not designed to emphasize patient comfort. Despite the elaborate brochures that may suggest the contrary, the fact is that the procedures and the setting have treating of illness as the ultimate goal. Patient comfort is secondary to that goal.

Consider the contrast to the office you've designed for your practice. You've most likely taken every affordable step to be sure your client feels safe, secure, and comfortable in a therapy session in your office. To conduct therapy sessions in a hospital setting, you need to be willing to use whatever space is temporarily available, and, as a member of a health care team, sacrifice some of the confidentiality features you've come to hold so dear, and not become rattled when you are interrupted one or more times during a session.

And, particularly evident in one of the preceding examples, you need to keep paramount the understanding that you are not, and will never be, the one "in charge." You may be encouraged to provide input about the types of intervention needed by the patient; you may be asked to express an opinion about when a patient is ready for discharge. You may be asked to offer your suggestions about what kinds of aftercare will be most helpful. The key words in the preceding are: input, opinion, and suggestion. In the hospital environment, you do not make the decisions.

With all of the inherent limitations, it seems reasonable for a person to wonder why it makes sense to even bother with practice in a hospital setting. Aside from financial considerations, there is a good answer. Patients in hospitals have need for the services we have been trained to provide. Inpatient settings allow service delivery modes that are essentially precluded in the outpatient, managed care world. For example, we really have no strong evidence that a 40- to 50-minute session, once or twice per week, is the optimal frequency to reduce discomfort and/or resolve problems. Hospital settings allow for more frequent interactions and easy integration of individual and group modalities.

To the second question, what do we have to learn, two particular factors come to my mind. The first is actually related to the impairing issue discussed in the preceding. It could easily be argued that much, if not nearly all, of the discomfort that we as therapists experience in delivery of service in hospital settings is simply a lack of experience. Nurses and doctors are not born with a genetically coded comfort zone for practice in such a setting. Through their training, such settings became the "natural" place for their practice. If your course in counseling techniques had been taught with a view toward how to practice in a hospital, and if either your practicum, internship, or both had been in a hospital setting, then feeling like an "outsider" would probably be more likely in the place where you now practice.

This is not an argument for restructuring the training model (although practice in a hospital setting might be easier if therapy trainers would lighten up a little on the long tirades about the medical model). It is instead to suggest that your first experience in delivering therapy in a hospital setting might be enhanced if you conceptualized that experience as a self-supervised, paid internship. Recognize going in that this is a different environment and expect some discomfort while habituating to the setting. Let go of some of ingrained constraints about what is necessary for a "good" therapy session. A session that helps a patient is a good session, regardless of where it occurs, how many times you were interrupted while providing it, or even whether someone else might have overheard some of the conversation. The practice of confidentiality in the hospital is different from the experience of most therapists. The treatment team has access to the patient's chart. In team conferences the information that is discussed would be considered confidential and is not explored, as it is in the hospital. Therapists working in a hospital need to adapt to this more open team approach.

Finally, there seems to be at least one feature typically evident in medical practice that we should perhaps learn to emulate. As therapists, we spend what seems to be an inordinate amount of time emphasizing our differences. Knowing that someone is an MFT, a psychologist, an LCSW, etc., alone is an extremely poor predictor of what kinds of therapeutic approaches will be used and how effective the individual is as a therapy provider.

Perhaps even to an extreme, persons in the medical professions have worked effectively in presenting a united front to the public they serve. We could perhaps profit from that example. There are more than enough problems, more than enough misery, to go around for all of us. In the bigger scheme of things, the academic department in which we happened to earn a degree seems much less important than the skill with which we provide the services for which we were trained.

☐ A Formal Tool for Self-Assessment

The questions being explored in this chapter by the therapist and nurse demonstrate the beginning of self-supervision. Self-supervision is a skill that must be taught and nurtured through the entire process of professional education. The CNO are developing a system of reflective practice that includes a tool for self-assessment and peer assessment (CNO, 1996). This tool could be adapted for use by other professions. In the next section I discuss this Self-Assessment Tool.

Before describing the tool it is important to understand who developed the tool and why it was developed. The CNO developed the tool in response to government legislation that requires a licensed profession to have a quality assurance program. The CNO is a self-regulating body that develops and implements the final examination for all graduate nursing students. All nursing students are required to pass this licensing exam in order to be registered in the province.

The other responsibility of the CNO is to protect the public from harm caused by incompetent nursing care. The Self-Assessment Tool is one part of the quality assurance program developed to meet the reflective practice requirements of the CNO. A description of the tool follows.

☐ Overview

Nurses are required to complete a self-assessment at least once a year. Peer evaluation is part of the assessment and a learning plan also must be developed. The tool includes questions related to the Professional Standards for Registered Nurses in Ontario. The tool itself includes most nursing roles but other roles may be added.

The Structure of the Self-Assessment Tool

The Self-Assessment Tool includes five professional standards practiced in four roles expressed in five skill areas. The six standards are related to:

1. Professional service to the public
2. Knowledge
3. Application of knowledge
4. Ethics
5. Continued competence (p. 4)

The four roles are "direct practice, administration, education, and research" (p. 4). Behavioral indicators have been developed for the standards expressed within the roles expressed in five skill groups: communication, leadership, critical thinking, job knowledge, and legislation and standards (CNO, 1996). An example of an assessment for the skill communication item follows: "Improve professional service by listening to and learning from my clients" (p. 9). The professional standard this refers to is the application of knowledge. The role is direct practice and the skill is communication. A number of behavioral objectives descriptors follow each item. A checklist follows for each of the behavioral objectives. The categories of the checklist are: "Expert, Highly Developed, Refining, Developing, Not Applicable" (p. 9).

☐ Process of the Self-Assessment Tool

The nurse selects the questionnaire that most reflects her or his practice as a direct practitioner, administrator, educator, or researcher. The questionnaire includes the skill groups of communication, leadership, critical thinking, job knowledge, and legislation and standards. The nurse completes a copy for her- or himself and one for peer feedback.

The nurse meets with a peer that he or she has chosen. The peer should be a person the nurse works with. The nurse and her or his peer review the questionnaires. Feedback is discussed and recorded on a peer feedback sheet. Each nurse prepares a learning plan and discusses its application to practice with the peer partner. The goal is that these paired nurses will give each other feedback on an ongoing basis. The goal is also that the paired peers will meet to formalize their growth in a written format the next year.

This Self-Assessment Tool has potential to change some of the darker aspects of the hospital environment. Earlier we looked at four critical factors that contribute to this darker side.

1. Nurse–physician relationship
2. Nurse–nurse relationship
3. History of nursing
4. Personal abuse history

This self-assessment process assists nurses to establish a practice based on reflection. There is increased self-awareness, awareness of others, understanding how nursing's history and the history of abuse have all influenced the hospital environment. Working with a peer begins the process of connection, dialog, and support among nurses. The silence is broken, the isolation changed.

☐ Concluding Thoughts

In this chapter we have explored some self-supervision features peculiar to practice in a medical environment. We've noted the importance of solidarity within the medical profession and how empowering this solidarity can be. We've examined the levels of hierarchical communication in the hospital, recognizing that our intervention strategies have to adapt to this culture. A self-assessment tool developed by nurses was included as an excellent model of both self-assessment and peer assessment that could be effectively used by therapists as well.

We also believe that there are a number of things that therapists should not learn from nurses and doctors. We should not learn to repeat the dysfunctional environment of the hospital. In relationships with colleagues, we should not create the dysfunctional relationships between nurses and doctors.

We in the therapeutic community should make every effort to use the lessons from the medical environment, keeping only what is effective, not repeating the evident problems. Self-supervision is obviously a critical factor for all professionals who strive toward an effective, reflective practice. Our professional relationships and work environment should be growth promoting, not self-impairing. Positive relationships with the self, patients, and coworkers are essential elements of effective practice.

Toward that goal, we offer three simple admonitions. Always:

- Be who you are.
- Speak with your own voice.
- Respect and honor yourself and others.

☐ References

Allen, M. (1985). Women, nursing, and feminism: An interview with Alice J. Baumgart. *The Canadian Nurse, 81*(1), 20–22.

Bandura, A. (1989). Regulation of cognitive processes through perceived self-efficacy. *Developmental Psychology, 25,* 729–735.

Bevis, E. M. (1983). *Curriculum building in nursing.* Toronto: Mosby.

Chandler, G. E. (1992). Revolution looks at clinical practice: Power through relationships: A natural for nurses. *Best of Revolution: The Journal of Nurse Empowerment,* Winter, 87–89.

College of Nurses of Ontario. (1996). *Self-assessment tool.* Toronto: Author.

Cox, H. (1991). Verbal abuse nationwide; part II: Impact and modifications. *Nursing Management, 22*(3), 32–35.

Gordon, S. (1991). Fear of caring: The feminist paradox. *American Journal of Nursing, 89*(2), 45–46.

Gray, P. D. (1994). Feminism and nursing. In O. I. Strickland & D. J. Fishman (Eds.), *Nursing issues in the 1990s* (pp. 505–527). Albany, NY, Delmar.

Hoff, L. A., & Ross, M. M. (1993). *Curriculum guide for nursing: Violence against women and children.* Ottawa: University of Ottawa Faculty of Health Sciences.

Katzman, E., & Roberts, J. (1988). Nurse and physician interactions as barriers to the enactment of nursing roles. *Western Journal of Nursing Research, 10*(5), 576–590.

McDonald, C. (1999). Promoting the power of nursing identity. *The Canadian Nurse,* February, 34–37.

Roberts, S. J. (1983). Oppressed group behaviors: Implications for nursing. *Advances in Nursing Science,* 21–30.

Russell, D. (1990). *Rape in marriage.* New York: Collier Books.

Stuart, G. W., & Laraia, M. T. (2001). *Principles and practice of psychiatric nursing.* Toronto: Mosby.

Vance, C., Talbott, S., McBride, A., & Mason, D. (1985). An uneasy alliance: Nursing and the women's movement. *Nursing Outlook, 33*(6), 281–285.

CHAPTER

Shirley Emerson
W. Paul Jones

Licensing Boards and Continuing Professional Growth: Friend or Foe?

The focus throughout this book is on "doing better." A variety of perspectives are used to explore how and when self-supervision can contribute to continuing professional growth. Suggestions are offered to avoid or overcome conditions that often limit or impair the ongoing delivery of quality clinical services. This chapter is about an often-overlooked partner in this process, your state licensing board.

Most therapists have, at best, mixed feelings about their state licensing boards. The board became part of their vocabulary while still in graduate school, with their professors telling them that "the board says you must. . . . " or "the board doesn't allow. . . ." It seems fair to assume, though, that few therapists know the details about what a state board actually does, particularly the activities related to continuing professional growth.

In this chapter we examine the role of the licensing board from two perspectives. First, Shirley details the various roles and functions of such boards from the perspective of a marriage and family therapist board member. Paul follows with thoughts about the utility of such boards from the perspective of a licensee.

☐ Through the Eyes of the Board

Noted in the preceding was our belief that few students and therapists have a clear idea about what really goes on in their licensing boards. And should they care? As a member of a state marriage and family therapist licensing board for over 14 years, I suggest that practicing, as well as aspiring therapists should know exactly what their board does and does not do, and yes, they should care! To understand how licensing boards contribute to maintaining and/or improving the level of practice in the professions they oversee, an overall review of board functions may be helpful.

Structure and Regulations

Let's start with structure. In most states, the legislature passes a law that legitimates and structures the board, with members of the board appointed by the governor, usually with some intent to achieve diverse membership representative of geography, ethnicity, gender, age, and whatever political agenda the governor has on his or her plate that day (Cohen & Mariano, 1982). Licensed therapists comprise the majority of most boards, along with representatives of the lay public. The mandate from the governor, for all licensing boards, no matter the profession, is "to protect the public." Thus, the "public" or lay members represent that protected group. In some states, an omnibus mental health board serves psychologists, drug and alcohol counselors, mental health counselors, marriage and family therapists, professional counselors, and sometimes social workers (Sturkie & Paff Bergen, 2001). Other states have individual boards for each group. Members serve for varying, usually staggered terms, and may be reappointed at the discretion of the governor.

Board members elect their own officers, usually a rotating arrangement. Most boards hire an executive secretary or director to manage the actual work, including records, correspondence, budget, and general running of the operations. Board members set policy, but because they are volunteers with other responsibilities, they typically leave the day-to-day operations to the executive secretary, or in large states, to the office staff.

Most boards operate under a set of "regulations" that must be consistent with the statutory guidelines, but expand the details of just how the licensing and disciplinary functions are to be carried out. The regulations are usually written (and amended as necessary) by the board, but must undergo public review and hearings before being ratified by a legislative council. States differ in their procedures, but in general this is the way boards come into being and operate.

The Licensing Function

The primary function of a board is to protect the public, and setting minimum guidelines for licensure is key to this function. Specific requirements will vary by state and discipline but typically include at least a master's degree, passing written and oral examinations, and successfully completing a post-degree internship. Once all these hurdles are jumped (whew!) the applicant presents her- or himself, with duly signed documentation in order, and is blessed by the board with a license.

So, now you are licensed, you pay your fee every year, and you're through with the board. Right? 'Fraid not! That was only the entrance exercise. Now we will begin. Remember: The board's job is to protect the public, and now that one is out there practicing, usually without regular or prescribed supervision, the real protective function is even more important. Two other safeguards of the public now come into play: required continuing education and monitoring of ethical charges.

Continuing Education

Continuing education: Why do we need it? In any profession that is active in practice and research, theories, approaches, methods, and results are constantly evolving. A therapist could sit in his or her office for years, seeing the individuals and families who come for help, using the same approaches and techniques he or she was taught in graduate school. Although those ways of helping people may still be all right, if the practitioner adds nothing from current research findings, the client may be cheated of the advanced help that the therapist could provide—if he or she had continued to learn and to upgrade skills. If therapists continue to learn and grow both professionally and personally, the opportunities for burnout lessen, and the risk to the client diminishes too. Some boards do not mandate specific continuing education experiences, but most licensing boards generally mandate so many hours per year of continuing education workshops and courses (Sturkie & Paff Bergen, 2001). This is not to make for "busy work," but to assure the public that the therapist has attempted, at least minimally, to continue to learn and to grow.

When Things Go Wrong

The other protection of the public takes a little more frightening direction when therapists stop to think about it. This is the necessity for self-discipline in any profession, which means simply that peers (in this case, licensed board members) take on the responsible task of ensuring that therapists know the ethical rules of conduct and that they follow them. In recent decades, the entire field of psychotherapy has been called on to self-discipline within the profession; this has come about in large part because of the increased awareness of some therapists' ineptitude, duplicity, exploitation, and abuse (Hermann, 1992; Peterson, 1992; Pope, 1990; Sturkie & Paff Bergen, 2001). To better understand how "policing the profession" works, let's look at two examples of ethical violation charges and follow them through the total process.

"Beth" was a client of "Dr. Jim" (a real case, with details masked to respect privacy), a therapist who had been in practice for many years. He worked in a private office, with no secretary and no nearby colleagues. Beth called the state licensing board office in tears and told the secretary that her therapist had done some terrible things to her, but she didn't know what to do. She felt guilty for her initial participation in his activities and was too embarrassed to tell the secretary just what had happened. After being informed by the secretary that a written complaint would be required for board action and assured that her privacy would be respected, Beth agreed to mail a complaint form with all the instructions. The secretary also suggested that Beth consult with an attorney or a friend, or another therapist whom she trusted, to get support emotionally and to get help in telling her story carefully and accurately. About a month later, the written complaint arrived at the board office.

Beth alleged in her complaint that Dr. Jim had made sexual advances toward her during her therapy sessions. She was initially flattered, and they were soon having a full-blown affair—during her therapy sessions, in his office. She further said that he continued to bill her insurance company for the sessions and to charge her the co-pay amount.

The secretary read the complaint and immediately informed the Deputy Attorney General assigned to the board, giving him a rough outline of the complaint. He said to have it investigated and keep him posted. Dr. Jim was also informed with instructions that he had 30 days in which to respond in writing. Within the month, Dr. Jim's answer came back, denying everything. The secretary then made a copy of the complaint for the state private investigator to whom she assigned the case. The investigator made appointments with both parties and with other potential information sources. He then wrote a report for the Deputy Attorney General who informed the board that it seemed probable that there had been unethical behavior by the therapist, and a disciplinary hearing would be necessary to determine the facts.

Up to this point, board members knew nothing of the complaint. The secretary scheduled a hearing presided by the president of the board. The Deputy Attorney General's role was similar to that of a prosecuting attorney with Dr. Jim's legal representative in a role comparable to a defense attorney.

The process at this point is for the board members (also allowed to ask any questions they wish of both parties) to go into closed session and deliberate the facts and decide what should be done. They then return to public hearing and announce their verdict and any action to be taken. This action may be of differing levels of severity, ranging from probation, to suspension of license for a prescribed period, to total revocation of the license. Suspension and probation are almost always accompanied by actions that the defendant must take, such as completing a prescribed class or training, or practicing only under supervision, or any other reasonable rehabilitation measures that board members think might be helpful, including personal therapy. The severest action is revocation of the license.

In this case the investigator had found two more women, former clients of Dr. Jim's, who had experienced surprisingly similar actions on his part. The board members had little trouble deciding that Dr. Jim no longer would have a license in our state. The action became public information and was sent to the national ethics-clearing house, published for use by all state boards.

A second example describes a scenario for which even the most ethical counselor may be at risk. "Janet" specializes in treating children. She is also a registered art therapist. A mother brought her 4-year-old daughter, "Patti," to Janet with concerns about the child's nightmares and showing fear of going to her father's apartment when the custody arrangement of the parents' divorce mandated that she spend some nights with him. Patti was unable to verbalize why she was afraid, but she showed her fear in most of her artwork. Janet's training made her very suspicious that someone at dad's home was sexually molesting Patti. She asked questions from which Patti recoiled, but in many nonverbal ways indicated that Janet's suspicions were probably well grounded.

Janet discussed the matter with Patti's mom, who immediately called her attorney. The attorney filed to reopen the custody agreement in court and requested that Janet submit her findings. Janet knew she had seen only one side of the story, so she requested, and received, permission to invite the dad to come in and talk with her. He did; he spoke very negatively about his former wife, degraded therapy, and accused Janet of making up wild things in order to take his daughter away from him. Janet tried very hard to convince him that she had invited him to talk precisely because she did not want to take sides and wanted to give him the right to tell his side of the story—or even, she suggested, indicate if there might be anyone else at his apartment who could be abusing Patti. He stormed out of her office, saying he would see her in court.

Janet was upset. The dad's attorney called her and tried to intimidate her and influence her report to the court. A complaint from the dad went to the licensing board, charging Janet with breach of ethics by "inventing" a way for his wife to get custody of Patti.

The process went just as the previous case, in that Janet was sent a copy of the complaint and given 30 days to respond in writing. The Deputy

Attorney General again requested a full investigation. So the investigator spoke with Janet, looked over her records, questioned the mom, met with Patti, and visited the dad in his office. He then wrote his report, giving the Deputy Attorney General his opinion of what Janet's role had been and if she had acted ethically. The Attorney General then suggested to the board that the charge be dropped. After their reading and deliberation, they invited Janet to meet with them and asked her some questions. They dismissed the case.

Whew! Janet sighed! But the time, the emotional anxiety, the calls to her attorney, and some sleepless nights were still a considerable price to pay for doing her job. The father had also threatened a suit against Janet, but once the board dismissed the complaint, his attorney convinced him he had no case. Again, a relief for Janet and her insurance company, but only after a period of severe anxiety.

The point here is that board members make every effort to give fair consideration to all sides in every case. As a result of their decision, they actually protected Janet from further difficulty, although that was not their assigned job.

Licensing Boards and Professional Associations

There is sometimes confusion between the definitions and functions of boards and professional associations. Most therapy-based groups have a voluntary association, for example, the American Association for Marriage and Family Therapy, American Psychological Association, American Counseling Association, and National Association of Social Workers, that provides continuing education opportunities, legislative lobbying functions, research forums, and publicity functions. They have differing membership requirements, and do perform ethical enforcement functions, but have no control over licensing. One need not be a member of the professional association in order to practice the profession, but most therapists choose to join one or more groups that keep them informed of research results and current trends in the profession, through journals, newsletters, and conferences, on both state and national levels.

The licensing boards, as described, act as gatekeepers to the practice of the profession, and as arbiters in cases of misconduct. Licensing board members do not usually directly lobby for legislation or advocate for particular causes—at least not in their position as board members. However, the professional members of the boards are usually also members of the association, and may act in that capacity. Sometimes boards cooperate with the state associations to share the costs of educational or research projects. With the considered opinion of our Deputy Attorney General, our board contributed to the state association's lobbying fund when a crucial issue was coming before the legislature. The board members believed the proposed law change could have a direct influence on the "protection of the public" mandate.

Licensing Boards and National Regulations

Each state and each specialty of therapy has its own methods for admission to the practice, as indicated. In the case of Marriage and Family Therapy, for example, a national organization, the Association of Marital and Family Therapy Regulatory Boards, is composed of one delegate and an alternate delegate from each state licensing board. The state boards select their delegates and the Association selects its officers and functioning committees. This group took on the responsibility for standardizing the examination process for all states that wished to participate. Although there is no reciprocity per se for MFT licenses, all states have regulations whereby a licensed therapist can move from one state to another without sitting for the examination again—providing that he or she has passed the exam at the new state's passing score. (States differ slightly in what they consider passing.) Additional requirements may be enforced by the new state, but the transition is now greatly simplified. At last count, 44 states were members of this national association, and 43 of them use this examination. California, the first state to license MFTs, requires its own state exam.

Licensing Boards and Academic Training Programs

When you were in graduate school, you probably heard your professors talk about accreditation standards. These standards are set by a division of the national professional associations. These divisions (e.g., CACREP for American Counseling Association, AAMFT Commission on Accreditation, and the Committee on Accreditation for the APA) set minimum acceptable course requirements (content, credit hours, practicum, and internship experiences) that the program must offer in order to be accredited. As with all the other requirements mentioned, there are minor differences within the professions, and fairly obvious differences between the disciplines. Most state boards use these training standards as minimum for applicants. Most also require that the academic degrees be earned at regionally accredited universities. This is again an attempt not to be elitist or exclusive, but to ensure to the public that the particular therapist one may consider working with has a reputable training background, as opposed to the (unfortunately seen, sometimes!) kooky techniques taught by mail order from East Cupcake U.

Possible Future Trends

All living systems are constantly evolving, and the profession of therapy is no different. Research is continual and productive; new ideas are born and tried daily. The profession is a large and dynamic one, with the licensing boards occupying only one part of the larger system. As the parts of the system evolve, and we hope improve, so must the boards. Our state board, for instance, decided several years ago that one function we could contribute to therapists, and thereby the public, was to present workshops on timely issues, free to therapists and interns. Ethics received considerable attention, and we all hope that the intent to prevent ethical violations has been helpful. A workshop on supervision was popular and definitely changed the approach to the larger issue of governing the activities of interns. Out of that workshop came a total change in our state's structure of the post-degree internship, which has been well received by both supervisors and interns. Mentioned earlier, the closer working alliance with the state association has been helpful to the association and to the board members, and we hope, to the welfare of clients as well. It would be my prediction that there may be even closer working possibilities in the future, where everyone wins. Certainly legislation is always crucial and sometimes frightening, when legislators who cannot be expected to know a great deal about the practice of therapy tend to meddle with laws that may not be helpful to therapists or clients. Therapists have always occupied the role of educators, in that one educates one's clients to better ways to cope with their life situations. Educating of the public, and especially of legislators seems a logical, and crucial, role for all therapists, but especially board members. Associations have always worked at this effort, and I predict that more state boards will support and assist in this effort in the future.

☐ Through the Eyes of the Licensee

My perspective on licensing boards and personal clinical growth has acknowledged limitations. Although I suspect there are more similarities than differences, my licensing experience has been only with state psychology boards in three states, and I have no direct experience with comparable boards for marriage and family therapists, licensed professional counselors, or clinical social workers. Although I've never been disciplined by a state board, I have been called to testify about practice standards in disciplinary hearings involving other clinicians. I've learned from the experience of others to be especially cautious about practice areas (e.g., child custody evaluations) in which clinicians seem most likely to get in trouble. It would appear that general principles of board operation are fairly consistent across geographic boundaries, but my experience is limited to states in the western United States.

From that background, I would first want to reinforce the underlying theme in the material preceding about state licensing boards. This book is about maintaining and enhancing clinical performance, and state licensing boards have a clear vested interest in this function. We tend most often to identify their "gate-keeping" role in reference only to that initial license, the demonstration of a level of clinical performance sufficient to be allowed to practice in that state. The mandate "to protect the public," however, goes further than just initial license. Licensing boards also have been delegated the task of "pushing back out through the gate" when there is evidence that either a mistake was made in the initial assessment of clinical competence or that clinical performance has deteriorated to a level below appropriate standards.

As described, there is no question that boards have evolved significantly over the years, finding more efficient ways to identify initial levels of competence and, through continuing education requirements, to monitor and encourage continuing professional development. Board members serve without pay and have to take responsibility for often onerous tasks, work that most of us are only too happy to delegate to someone else. The thoughts that follow are thus not intended to question the integrity or motivation of those who serve on such boards. The intent, instead, is to raise some questions about the outcomes, particularly related to an individual clinician's attaining, maintaining, and enhancing clinical performance.

Who Is Really Minding the Store?

Identification of requisite knowledge and clinical skills for practice as a therapist clearly goes beyond the scope of any single entity and appears to be jointly held by three groups: licensing boards, the accrediting arms of professional associations, and academic training programs. In theory, this appears to work well; each has a primary protection focus: the public, the practitioners, and the disciplines, respectively. But, how well does this work in actual practice? Are there not some inherent conflicts of interest?

Consider, just for the sake of argument, what would happen if a fresh new training model were to be developed that eliminated unnecessary duplication in current course requirements with clinical skills evaluated on the basis of demonstrated mastery rather than accumulation of supervised hours. On its face this seems a goal to which we should aspire. But, what are the odds that such a development would provide anything other than frustration and disappointment?

If a model like this were to be championed by licensing boards, think of the hue and cry from the academic training programs. Fewer required courses results in fewer student credit hours, which means less funding, which means less money available for travel and materials, and so forth. With fewer faculty members needed, the influence in the university by departments providing the training programs would decrease catastrophically. Unemployment ranks would be swelled by displaced faculty members. (Readers who might be thinking that this predicted reaction is a gross exaggeration have probably not sat in on many university department meetings.)

It is unfair to suggest that academic training programs have a corner on the "maintaining status quo" market. When we pay the ever-increasing dues to professional associations, a primary benefit we expect is that the associations will be vigilant in protecting the investment we made to be able to practice. Another concern is protecting boundaries from encroachment by other clinical specialties. We could anticipate immediate and vocal concerns about reduced training time, resulting in flooding the market with competing therapists.

The question is whether the current reciprocal, symbiotic, and perhaps incestuous, relationships among licensing boards, professional associations, and training programs have elements that may limit skill development. Who really sets the initial standards of practice?

An academic program may assert that a certain course must be completed because "our accreditation requires it." Accreditation boards appear inextricably linked to professional associations. Accrediting boards or professional associations may assert that "it is required for your license" or "it is required by the academic program."

This apparent decision by most licensing boards to delegate to accrediting bodies the identification of minimal standards is advantageous in moving decisions about professional practice standards from lay boards who may not have clinical expertise. The motive appears noble. A side effect of the outcome may be, however, that self-interest and maintaining the status quo have the highest priority.

Think about how many of the current initial standards for clinical practice were the result of decisions by a committee. What, for example, drove the actual decision about the length of post-degree supervised experience required for licensure? Was it a carefully informed, data-based decision by a board with primary interest in protecting the public from inept clinicians? Or, was it just a compromise in the accrediting arm of a professional association committee enabling the members to get out in time for dinner?

Is It Continuing or Coercive Education?

A valid argument could be made that the concern about reciprocal relationships described in the preceding should not be placed at the feet of the licensing boards. Perhaps boards bear no more responsibility for the issues of concern than do the other stakeholders. Mandated continuing education requirements, however, are the sole province of the boards, and those requirements are directly related to enhancing clinical practice. A cursory view of the tangled web of requirements certainly raises questions about whether there is any "method to this madness" and could easily lead to the conclusion that the latter is much more evident than the former.

To acknowledge credit where credit is due, licensing boards were among the earliest of those who recognized a need to address the issues that are the topic of this book. Boards recognized the reality that the knowledge and skill levels evident at initial licensure might not be maintained and were proactive in responding to this concern. Mandatory continuing education (CE) requirements quickly became the norm for renewing a license. The current situation, however, appears replete with confusion, particularly associated with unnecessary turf battles, trust issues, and unnecessarily narrow criteria.

Consider, for illustration, what would happen if I were to recognize that the quality of my practice would be enhanced with a better understanding of family systems theory. A noted family systems theorist is presenting a weekend workshop in a location nearby. Seems like a no-brainer. I will get good information and also pick up CE hours to renew my license.

The reality, though, is quite different. I may well pick up valuable information, but my board may or may not recognize the CE units because the primary presenter on the topic of family systems theory would be more likely to be an MFT, not a licensed psychologist. From the published requirement forms it appears obvious that psychology boards prefer that psychologists receive CE training from psychologists; social work boards prefer that social workers receive continuing education from other social workers; and so forth. It would be hard to think of a process more likely to discourage thinking "outside the box" of our original training.

Should clients trust their therapists? Boards often suggest to the general public that trust is better placed in those who have attained licensure than in those who practice with titles using the language loopholes in state statutes. It seems to follow, then, that boards trust the therapists they have licensed.

Consider the history. We (the board) believe you (the therapist) participated in a CE program because you said you did. That apparently didn't work, so we believe you participated in a CE program only if you have a certificate that says you participated. Those certificates were apparently too easy to obtain, so we believe that you participated in a CE program only if you have a certificate, and only if the grantor confirms that you "signed in" prior to each morning and afternoon session and that you "signed out" only after the program was completed.

Now we (the board) have too much paperwork to contend with so we are back to accepting you (the therapist) at your word. Almost, that is, because this is accompanied by a warning that some percentage of renewal applications will be audited with dire consequences if all claims cannot be confirmed. Sounds like the Internal Revenue Service, and I'm not sure many of us would associate the IRS with the word "trust."

The situation appears even more muddled when we examine the typical boundaries of continuing education defined by state licensing boards. If I just sit in an approved workshop, my board will approve a CE award. I don't actually have to do anything, just sit there, and with several such workshops I can finish my complete CE renewal requirement.

If I instead select individual self-study courses, either traditional or online, I can meet only some predetermined percentage of my CE requirement. Boards apparently have determined that there is some inherent instructional value in "getting folks together" that overides the fact that self-study requires some intellectual engagement, whereas conferences only require a physical presence.

If I read an article in a profession-related newsletter, answer a few simple questions (and pay the fee), my board will approve a CE award. But, were I to develop and teach a new advanced clinical training course at my university, my board would not recognize this task worthy of CE award.

Is there not something wrong with this picture? Is it surprising that many, if not most, therapists conceptualize the CE renewal requirements as just a game, selecting activities for convenience with little consideration of actual individual need for enhancing clinical skills?

It is an interesting paradox that, although outside forces are encouraging if not insisting that therapists use data-based interventions, board determinations of what does and does not define appropriate continuing education has apparently no empirical basis. For example, is there any evidence that the now ubiquitous requirement that CE units for renewal include some activity associated with malpractice and/or professional ethics has resulted in any measurable impact on quality of practice? There has been a benefit to some individual therapists in reduced insurance costs and perhaps to state professional associations in increased attendance at annual conferences, but is there any other demonstrable value?

Outside the United States, for example in Canada, there is evidence of recognition that continuing professional development may be better served with procedures other just attending a workshop. Described in another chapter in this book are self-assessment guides and professional development plans for nurses that appear to focus directly on maintaining and enhancing clinical performance. Perhaps it is now time for state licensing boards in the United States to step away from continuing efforts to reactively "fix" the current plans, and rethink the power available to them to actually serve as monitors of quality clinical performance.

Who Identifies and Helps the Impaired Therapist?

It would be extremely difficult to fault the state licensing boards in their efforts to respond when a licensed therapist's quality of practice has been challenged. As described in the first section of this chapter with therapists "Dr. Jim" and "Janet," boards have established procedures designed to protect the public from inept and/or unethical behavior by therapists while also protecting therapists from unwarranted charges. As noted in that section, any one of us could at any time be subject to a claim of improper behavior by any of our clients. The larger your practice and the more difficult your cases, the more likely it is that you will some time be the target of such a charge.

If or when this occurs, the steps taken by boards as outlined in the first section of this chapter to ensure due process will be of potentially immense value. Those steps appear to be generally consistent among licensing boards and encompass among the most important roles served by licensing boards both for the general public and the practitioner.

The questions to be raised in this section of the "licensee's view" are thus more focused on obligations of the therapist than roles of the board. None of us are immune to the problems, both emotional and physical, confronted by the rest of the population. In fact, as detailed elsewhere in this book, the very nature of our work seems to increase the chances of experiencing some impairing conditions.

What will you do with your practice if you find yourself trying to cope with emotional and/or physical concerns that make it difficult to provide quality services for your clients? The correct answer is transparent. You will recognize those limitations and adjust your practice activities accordingly. Most of us, I suspect, would choose not to make our licensing board aware of the circumstances, particularly if we anticipated full recovery and expected a reasonably short-term recovery period. Although we might thus be ignoring a specific board regulation, no harm to clients would be likely, and we could rationalize easily that there was no reason to "bother the board" with this temporary condition.

Changing this question only slightly results, though, in a much more complex dilemma. What would you want others around you to do if the impairing condition was evident, but you were either unaware of the clinical limitations it was causing or unwilling to admit them to others or even to yourself? Our first step as colleagues is clear; we are ethically obligated to confront you directly. How many of us would be willing to take that step unless your colleague's limitations were impacting clients you serve?

What if you did confront your colleague and he or she either refused to acknowledge the impairment or agreed in conversation with you to take personal responsibility to limit the practice, but no action was forthcoming? You have an obligation to protect the public. You have an obligation to protect the profession. But, you are afraid that bringing a "charge" to the board will jeopardize the future of your colleague, who may have a history of exemplary clinical practice. There is no question about what *should* be done. In reality, what *will* you do?

The medical profession has provided a model that may warrant consideration for our professional groups as well. Through programs often identified as "physician assistance," procedures are in place that involve mandatory reporting of colleagues with substance use or abuse problems (Welsh, 2001). These programs are designed to protect the public with a simultaneous objective of rehabilitating rather than punishing the physician. Comparable programs for our shared professions, perhaps with a broader problem definition, would help to resolve what can be a vexing problem. If such programs are already available through our licensing boards, a licensee "awareness" initiative is clearly needed.

☐ A Shared View

Our intent in this chapter has been to provide a view of the role of licensing boards in helping therapists to "get better" from perspectives of a board member and a licensee. It is our belief that increased understanding of the structure, roles, and functions of licensing boards enables enhanced appreciation of the magnitude of their tasks. Board policies are always a "work in progress," and it is our hope also that pointing out some possible flaws in the current policies and procedures can serve to encourage revisions to even better address the continuing need to improve the quality of clinical practice.

We share a strong belief that licensing boards are really not "out to get you!" They exist to set minimum standards to protect the public—and we are all members of that public. Board meetings are open meetings and you are welcome to attend and learn.

Agendas for meetings are posted in numerous public places, by law, in advance of meetings—usually about a week ahead. You are permitted to speak at most state board meetings, if you request a place on the agenda in advance.

Go to a board meeting; know who your board members are, and let them know you are interested and watching. Feel free to make constructive suggestions for board consideration. Think about volunteering to serve as a board member. The work is time-consuming and often intense, but rewarding.

☐ References

Cohen, R., & Mariano, W. (1982). *Legal guidebook in mental health*. New York: Free Press.

Hermann, J. (1992) *Trauma and recovery*. New York: Basic Books.

Peterson, M. (1992). *At personal risk: Boundary violations in profession-client relationship*. New York: Norton.

Pope, K. (1990). Therapist-patient sexual involvement: A review of the research. *Clinical Psychology Review, 10*, 477–490.

Sturkie, K., & Paff Bergen, L. (2001). *Professional regulation in marital and family therapy*. Needham Heights, MA: Allyn & Bacon.

Welsh, C. J. (2001). *Substance abuse disorders in physicians*. Retrieved December 8, 2001, from http://www.alcoholmedicalscholars.org/physician-out.htm

Maryam Sayyedi
Kathy O'Byrne

Therapist: Heal Thyself!

Mental health therapists are considered experts in the helping professions. People turn to therapists for help when they face relational challenges, unexpected losses, existential conundrums, and a myriad of other human plights. But the very qualities that make therapists effective helpers can also make them more vulnerable to stress. Every person we help may sensitize us to issues that are personal and provocative. These become opportunities to learn more about us but also add to our day-to-day struggles and stressors in general.

The constant vigilance to be aware of "our" issues by and of itself can be distressing and impact our psychological adaptation as therapists. Another source of distress for therapists is being in contact with others' pain and turmoil and feeling responsible at some level to bring relief to others. One of the primary sources of burnout for therapists has been to feel the pressure of solving the clients' problems and feeling overly responsible (Grosch & Olsen, 1994; Horner, 1993; Kottler, 1993).

One body of literature suggests that a significant number of mental health professionals experience serious mental health problems and problems with psychological adaptation to workplace demands. The range of problems reported includes depression, anxiety, relationship problems, burnout, substance abuse, and suicidal thoughts and attempts (Coster & Schwebel, 1997; Guy, 2000; Mahoney, 1997; Sherman, 1996; Sherman & Thelen, 1998).

Professional burnout has been the focus of research at least since Herbert J. Freudenberger, a psychoanalyst in New York City, wrote an article on occupational exhaustion among volunteer workers in social service agencies in 1974. Since then, there has been a general agreement among researchers that the risk of burnout is inevitable in the helping professions. Attempts are then made to understand this multifaceted problem and its underpinnings. Personality and environmental factors and their interactions have been studied in professional burnout, and ways of addressing or preventing burnout have been detailed in the literature (Grosch & Olsen, 1994; Kottler, 1999).

In this chapter we will discuss the issues of psychological adaptation of therapists from a different angle. We are interested in exploring when and why we may reject help and even avoid self-reflection in dealing with our life challenges in general and to what extent our own professional expertise and theories can help us to heal ourselves. We have interviewed several colleagues of various theoretical orientations and backgrounds to tell us their stories of dealing with their life challenges and how they used their expertise in helping themselves. We hope the stories that are interspersed throughout this chapter motivate you to attend to your own stories and take some time for self-reflection and self-care.

With difficult and challenging clients, the ethical standards of our profession require that we seek supervision and consultation with more experienced colleagues. The same standards also demand that we seek therapy when we find ourselves overwhelmed with our own life and its issues (Gladding, Remley, Jr., & Huber, 2001; Herlihy & Corey, 1996; Pope & Vasquez, 1998). It may seem obvious and quite rational to seek professional help when we need it, but it is more complicated than that. Is it harder for us (the therapists) to recognize and admit to having problems or needing "other" experts' help? Do we experience stress and life challenges differently than our clients? How do we recognize that we do need help? Does our knowledge and expertise as professional helpers help us dealing with "our" own issues? Finally, what are some of the things we can do to live a balanced life caring for others as well as for ourselves?

☐ Is It Harder for Us to Seek Help?

One might argue that therapists should easily overcome and adjust to stressors given their training and expertise in helping others overcoming life's problems. Most therapists, however, know well that therapists are no different than other people in becoming overwhelmed by life's challenges (Kottler, 1993, 1999; Mahoney, 1997). We are trained to believe that our perpetual and neverending self-growth is an integral part of our professional competency (Kottler, 1999; Kuyken, Peters, Power, & Lavender 1998; Kuyken, Peters, Power, Lavender, & Rabe-Heketh, 2000) and this leads us to self-reflect and perhaps analyze our issues more than lay people or nontherapists. This also means that we should be identifying and addressing our problems and issues promptly and diligently, not allowing them to fester and overwhelm us. Thus, we may not have the luxury of self-neglect, denial, or poor adjustment. Or do we?

We became therapists for different reasons, not all of which reflect our interest in our own self-actualization (Grosch & Olsen, 1994). Perhaps we wanted to help others in order to forget our own problems and create some distance from them. Or perhaps we devoted our life to understanding how others cope with the ambiguity and "gray areas" of human relationships as a fascinating, intellectual pursuit. Perhaps we played the role of "helper" in our original family system, and we want to now help all of humanity resolve its issues.

The choice of a career is a complex and multifaceted process that encompasses the person's early experiences, family history, and aptitudes as well as cultural and contextual factors of one's genre (Malach-Pines & Yafe-Yanai, 2001). Whatever our reasons, it took us many years of studying and training as well as personal sacrifices and soul searching to become professional helpers. We believed that we could make a difference in our world by helping others find their ways and help ourselves to heal our wounds and reach our potentials. Here, we explore our ways of dealing with our own life and its stressors as professional helpers. We take a look at us and how we are coping after years of working and helping others cope with their problems. We ask if our expertise makes it more likely that we will resolve our own issues and conflicts easily.

We find this exploration necessary because many of us have the inclinations that make us *less* likely to seek others in time of need. Perhaps this is a good time to tell one of our stories of self-neglect and loss. This is my story of how I came to be for "others" (i.e., my family, friends, colleagues, and clients) to the extent that I totally lost sight of "myself" and began to experience depression, weight gain, and sleep difficulties.

I (Maryam) hope by sharing my story, I can encourage you to take a moment to think about your own needs and self-care. When I was approached to write this chapter, I realized that I was unmotivated to take on a task that several years ago I would have given my arm to be a part of. Before this, I was becoming aware that I might have too much on my plate, and here it was one more thing to add. I became quite irritable and found myself withdrawing from everyone and was getting lost in feeling sorry for myself.

As a Middle-Eastern, married woman, mother of two, caring for my in-laws (who were visiting us for over 4 months), I did not have any cultur-ally sanctioned time for myself anyway. However, in trying to keep everyone happy I was becoming disenchanted and alienated. I did self-reflect and was aware of "overfunctioning" in all areas of my life; how-ever, I could argue intelligently and justify my unhealthy ways of being with others. I convinced myself that I should be able to do it all and be the "superwoman"; in fact, I believed that without me nothing would get done. At least, this was one of the reasons for being where I was, stressed out, isolated, and feeling overwhelmed, yet not asking for help.

It was an absolute feeling of despair that pressed for my attention. I recalled that once upon a time, not so long ago, I loved writing and had a thirst for learning about the human condition and functioning that I thought would never be quenched. However, I found myself unmoti-vated, anxious, and worried, not able to sleep at nights, taking inventory of all the unfinished projects and my other responsibilities. My life stress was beginning to impact my work with my clients. I found myself nudg-ing my female clients with marital dissatisfaction toward separation and divorce rather than reconciliation. I was also having a difficult time help-ing my depressed clients challenge their negative schemas.

I did not feel burnout per se, because I loved my work; it was not that I was questioning the meaning of my life or profession as is common in a professional burnout (Malach & Yafe-Yanai, 2001). It was that I was drown-ing slowly and not screaming for help. I tried to use whatever I knew to control the sense of doom that was overcoming me at a high speed be-cause of this project. As a clinical psychologist and cognitive-behaviorist, I specialize in the treatment of anxiety disorders, and my sessions often have a relaxation episode where I instruct my clients to take deep breaths, relax their shoulders, sit back comfortably, and allow their mind to think of peaceful or relaxing images. I have also challenged my clients when they process information "irrationally" (i.e., exaggerating the negatives and minimizing the positives, overgeneralizing, etc.). When they franti-cally share their list of stressors, I validate and normalize their feelings of frustration and helplessness while empowering them to think of creative solutions and new ways of facing their challenges. We then address the negative automatic thoughts or all those negative schemas that maintain one's self-destructive tendencies and fulfill our negative prophecies.

None of the preceding interventions worked for me, however. This was a different, situation I rationalized. I said this was a "true catastrophe," not an "irrational" processing. Yet, there was no time to feel sorry for myself, albeit every cell of my body was bellowing "take a break or you will not make it." I had not taken a vacation for the past 5 years, had committed to four other projects equally as important as this chapter, and had my chaotic family situation to attend to while maintaining a full-time academic job and a small private practice. There was no doubt that I was overwhelmed but as yet no one could tell; I maintained my sense of humor and showed up for life as usual.

We have likely been told that people find us easy to talk to, or that we are "good listeners." We are naturally empathic, perceptive, and insightful; understanding others' intentions and struggles is perpetually fascinating to us. In general, we nurture people and we like to help others solve problems, organize their challenges, or reach their goals. We are such good listeners that we may rarely volunteer much about ourselves, or become selective about sharing personal information with friends and colleagues. We are also very apt in rationalization and intellectualizations, employing them with such grace that Freud himself would begin to doubt they are "defense mechanisms." Some have even found us to be openly narcissistic, offering profuse suggestions unsolicited, believing in our superiority and powers dealing with life issues. Or we might be closet narcissists, believing in others' inability to help us in a meaningful way (Grosch & Olsen, 1994). Our inclinations and talents erroneously may have led us to believe that we are somewhat different than others who are not as proficient in matters of insight, reflection, and empathy. We even may feel superior about our level of insight onto our own issues and way of resolving them, which in turn tend to isolate us from family and friends when we need them the most. One of the colleagues whom we interviewed provided a beautiful example of just this issue. He is a licensed psychologist and has been a therapist for over 15 years. He stated, "I know I should, but I always balk at looking inward and initially want the same quick fixes my clients do. Eventually, I relent—since there are no quick fixes—and will have a conversation with my wife or friend where I can look deeply into my issues."

We may have come to believe that since we have studied so long and learned so much about human behavior in general, that there is nothing others can tell us or help us with when we are in distress. Our knowledge of therapy's imperfections and shortcomings may itself be a barrier to revealing our distress to other professionals. Colleagues may have demonstrated an insensitive or demeaning way of discussing their issues with their clients; we ourselves may have had moments of impatience and insensitivities with our own clients, which may then discourage us from seeking therapy or sharing our feelings with other experts. We may fear being exposed as imposters or being misdiagnosed as impaired. Unfortunately, the high expectations we have of ourselves, and distrust in others' ability to understand us may gradually build impermeable walls of isolation for the embryos of burnout and maladjustment to grow. That was where I (Maryam) found myself. I was alienated from my social support system and not willing to seek professional help. Although we might not be willing to seek professional help readily, we do not have the luxury of repressing or denying our issues for long, either. Our struggles with our own life stressors can seriously compromise our ability to empathize and ultimately work effectively with our clients (Sherman, 1996). Although we have been told, through years of training and supervision, that our issues will come to haunt us if we push them away, we believe in our ability to compartmentalize professional and personal feelings. How else could we manage to not take home the crises, abuse, and chronic challenges our clients bring to us each day? Further, as busy professionals, we are often too busy caring for others, juggling multiple roles, and walking a tightrope between meeting clients' expectations and family or friends' expectations, to engage in self-care.

Here another colleague helps us understand such a struggle and how she overcame her stressors. She is also a clinical psychologist by education and training who has been more active in the academic arena and is currently pursuing her license in order to start her part-time practice. She has been teaching, training, and researching the field for the past 10 years.

After graduate school, I began a full-time teaching job, with clinical training responsibilities, maintained my ties to my church, our family business, and my family simultaneously. I went to my office, and found myself unable to move. Not only was I stuck mentally, I was stuck physically. I made the cognitive decision to change things in my life. In fact, my doctor helped me to make that decision by telling me I was harming myself by wearing so many different hats. I did not deal with this situation very well, because it is my value to help everyone, especially my family, even when family can be the most demanding. When I could no longer handle this situation on my own I had to seek the assistance of my own personal therapist. She helped me to put things in perspective, and I was forced to reprioritize my life. This was very helpful because I realized that I could say no and not be a bad person. Personal therapy can be very beneficial for therapists, because many of us are in this profession because of our need to help and take care of others. I would also suggest that therapists create time for relaxation and fun. That has been wonderful for my family and I, because I am a much better person to live with.

I think my way of dealing with the stress was rather dysfunctional (smile). However, I am beginning to rely more on the systems around me to assist me in this area, which is true of the systems model I ascribe to. Also, I tend to rely heavily on cognitive behavioral strategies such as self-talk and I actively confront faulty maladaptive thinking and behaviors that keep me in a stressful condition. I also am finding ways to rescript my story. But the truth is, I still fall into the rut of being overwhelmed and stressed out from time to time. I do *backslide!*

We cannot stop life from happening, but we can change the way we react to life challenges and stressors. We can also identify the ways we contribute to life challenges and stressors. It was really important for me to recognize how I contributed to or allowed stress to enter into my life. I feel much more powerful now that I know I can stop some of the stress from coming to my house, whereas in the past I felt powerless.

☐ How Do We Recognize That We Need Help?

We need to take time regularly for serious self-care and reflections to address our own issues, and inventory the quality of our lives (Guy, 2000; Mahoney, 1997; Malach-Pines & Yafe-Yanai, 2001). We need to continually ask ourselves: Are we experiencing a general state of satisfaction with our life and relationships? What stressors are under our control? What changes seem attractive in meeting our needs? Or are we so busy that we have lost a sense of purpose and meaning (Sapienza & Bugental, 2000)? Can we point to satisfaction from our work and relationships? Are weekend excursions and planned vacations helpful to "recharge" and refresh one's overall quality of life? Where should we start?

Any work toward healing should start with appraisal of the problem investigating our original intentions to become a therapist, our expectations of our role, inventory of self-doubts and insecurities, as well as an inventory of one's strengths and resources (Kottler, 1999). The extent and duration of self-neglect is related to the extent of our burnout. Some signs are obvious, such as sleep disturbances, appetite disturbances, fatigue, and a state of restlessness, concentration problems, and problems with irritability and being generally dissatisfied (Grosch & Olsen, 1994). Others, such as loss of meaning, are more sophisticated signs that manifest when our soul is thirsty for and is calling for help (Amundson, 2001; Heery, 2001). Relationships begin to show the wear and tear of your neglect as well. Partners begin to complain about your unavailability, psychological distance, or absence from the relationship. You may find yourself more immersed in your work. You may begin to physically experience the weight of your projects and deadlines, after a few sessions of overeating and being too busy to exercise. Your back begins to ache, headaches or neck aches become everyday occurrences, and you begin to get sick with a perpetual upper respiratory problem (i.e., common cold) (Spiegel, 1999).

For those of us who may continue to neglect, ignore, or deny these signs, a total breakdown may result; we may find ourselves unmotivated to get out of bed or talk to anyone. How do you listen to the mind and body's cry for help and respond in the early stages of distress? How do you go about caring for yourself and facilitate your own growth and actualization once you notice that you are experiencing problems?

Kottler (1999) provides some helpful strategies and ways of caring for ourselves, from reviewing our expectations and the meaning of our profession in our lives to less philosophical practices such as traveling, exercising, eating well, and taking time off to care for our mind and body. Other writers, such as Guy (2000) and Sapienza and Bugental (2000), invite us to acknowledge our own needs for "mirroring" and to be "in communion with our own aliveness," respectively. Ellis (1997) tells us his personal story of dealing with the adversities in his life caused by his chronic medical problems, and encourages us to implement rational thinking and problem solving as well as time management in overcoming such challenges.

Some of the colleagues whom we interviewed had similar recommendations. One young colleague, who recently completed her doctoral degree, has an academic position as a full-time lecturer and has been practicing biofeedback therapy. She talked about her awareness of mind–body issues and how that helps her to develop a self-care regimen and avoid undue stress. She says,

> First, I take care of myself in a behavioral way by vigorous (almost obsessive) exercising, by eating healthy, and by making sleep a priority in life. I engage in a regular meditative practice and journal occasionally when things get rougher than usual. In addition, I talk with friends when I just need to vent. Mostly, I learned how to say "no" so that I don't get myself overcommitted.
>
> I practice what I preach. I'm a biofeedback therapist, so it's important for me to always be cognizant of the stress in my life. In addition, when I feel the need to cry, I just do it whether alone or with others. However, I have to admit that emotional expression is what's most difficult for me, and most healing. I think that's why I was attracted to gestalt. Getting Roger's conditions is an unrealistic expectation, so I sometimes have to do it for myself (i.e., I more often cry alone than with others). What make this most complicated for me is that my support system all live far away.

A senior colleague who is an associate professor of counseling and has been in private practice for over 20 years tells us that he also has tried to create a balance among all spheres of his life.

> I believe in holistic health, which means I am doing those kinds of things that are healthy for me in all spheres of my life: emotionally, physically, mentally, and spiritually. At a physical level, I engage routinely in exercise and in the past year I made a commitment to run my first marathon. The physical exercise is complemented by a focus on diet. What you take in serves as the sustenance for how you cope with and handle life's stressors.

If you survive on a fast food diet, those ingredients are going to impact you negatively. Mentally, I try to clear my thoughts at the end of the day. I engage in prayers and at the beginning of the day to center and open myself for guidance. Emotionally, I try to be with those people who are close to me like my family, friends, and colleagues on some routine basis so that there is a check in about who I am and how I meet others' needs besides those of my own. Spiritually, I have developed a prayer life and a meditation life that helps me remain centered.

If you are someone who is somewhat resistant to experts' suggestions, if you like to reinvent the wheel because you do not trust the others' wheels, if you are a drummer dancing to the beat of your own drum and have your own theories of therapy, you may want to ask yourself, as I did, How can I help myself? Can I help myself by using what I offer to my clients? Numerously, I told my anxious-depressed, hardworking, stressed-out female clients, who were struggling to maintain their balance while walking a tightrope between incompatible responsibilities of family and career, that they needed to prioritize and be assertive. I encouraged them not to try so hard to please everyone, to learn to say "No, I am sorry I need a break," or "No I am not able to take on this new project no matter how exciting it is," and learn to delegate. I told them, "Be for yourself" even if it is for a short time. I encourage them to choose a percentage of the day they feel comfortable devoting to themselves. But how could I ask them that or confront them with their codependencies when I had a hard time with disappointing the significant people in my life?

Yes, although assertiveness training, efficient time management, learning relaxation techniques, and cognitive restructuring are highly effective and reasonably supported by research as treatment interventions for stress management (Rowe, 2000), I was failing, as a cognitive-behavioral therapist, to help myself. I was failing to apply what I was preaching to my clients. Or perhaps it was the cognitive-behavioral therapy that was failing me and I was beginning to feel like a total hypocrite.

I recalled, however, that when clients did not respond to cognitive-behavioral interventions it was partially caused by not having had yet their needs for validation met. So did I need validation and understanding? I found myself responding affirmatively. I was isolated and disconnected emotionally from my family and good friends because I did not want to admit to my helplessness. I did a lot for my family but was emotionally disconnected and lost in my thoughts about my career.

After three sleepless nights, I finally had to stop and face my problems because I find myself too tired to meet everyone's expectations. I had canceled clients 2 weeks in a row and that could not continue. I was trying to buy time, somewhat ineffectively. I started by being honest with myself, realizing that I needed to be able to do what I preached, not only to help myself but also to be able to confront my clients with their resistance to change. If what I preached was not helpful to me, then how could it be helpful to my clients? I realized that I am not that different than my clients; my struggles are similar, albeit my defenses might be somewhat more sophisticated. I had to confront my narcissism that without me, the people around me could not function, that everyone needed me to manage his or her life. I also needed to accept that my problems were not so unique that no one would understand.

☐ What Do Therapists Do When They Are Dealing with Life Challenges?

Many theories have offered explanations for preventing and treating burnout. Psychoanalysis has devoted its attention to therapists' personalities and vulnerability to burn out more than others. The analysts' need for perfection, devotion to the tenets of the theory, and narcissistic tendencies have been identified as primary issues leading to burnout (Horner, 1993; Malach-Pines & Yafe-Yanai, 2001).

Self-psychology has looked at the issue of the therapist self-care by addressing the therapists' need for "mirroring." Guy (2000) incorporates Kohut's self-psychology in maintenance of a healthy sense of self and recommends that therapists seek mirroring from their close relationships (and not their clients) as a way of preventing professional burnout (Guy, 2000). Sapienza and Bugental (2001) offer an existential-humanistic model to help psychotherapists ward off burnout and remain true to self and others. Ellis (1997) tells his story of utilizing Rational Emotive Behavior Therapy (REBT) to cope with his health disabilities and avoid succumbing to adversities in his personal life.

Ironically however, while struggling with all the self-doubt and feeling sorry for myself, I also began to read on professional burnout and psychological adaptation for this chapter. This exploration helped me understand my situation better; to feel somehow validated by learning about other professionals' struggles with similar demands. I understood that I needed to reconnect with people whom I loved and cared for to get a better perspective and develop a balanced life. I needed to make connections; talk to my colleagues, family, and friends about my stress; and hear their support and validation.

My journey toward self-healing is a work in progress, but it started with an incident that forced me to accept that I had a problem. I could no longer ignore it and decided not to be a hypocrite. I mobilized my support system by reconnecting with my spouse and colleagues and benefited from their understanding as well as their help in taking off some of the load.

My children began to help with household chores, and my spouse to help with the in-laws. All this allowed us to reconnect as a family, and provided an opportunity for me to take some time off for meditative walks and catching up with past due deadlines at work. Colleagues also demonstrated great deal of support and understanding. I was able to move some of the deadlines for my projects to make them more manageable. Presently, I am working on my schemas of self-worth; I have become aware of my developmental struggles as a therapist and as woman in her early forties. I have even begun to consider going back to therapy, meaning I am willing to ask for help. I needed to consciously take the time to connect with my world rather than devoting all my time to "serve" that world, asking nothing in return.

I also learned that being a therapist is as important as doing therapy, if not more so. What I need to keep in mind is not to abandon my needs and myself as a work in progress, no matter how many other projects compete for my attention. I need to continue working on my growth by taking at least 10% of each day for myself; the other 90% can still go to others!

Although some of us may struggle before we come to terms with our needs for self-care and attention to our own needs, others may find clever and creative ways of managing stress early on. Being proactive perhaps is the best solution. So if you are not yet at the point in your career or you have not yet in a place where you find yourself overwhelmed with multiple demands and feeling overwhelmed, it is good to reflect on this as well. What has helped you in not being cornered and overwhelmed? What are your strategies to prevent such incidents? How does your way of protecting yourself against stress relate to what you do with clients or how you practice? A couple of our counselors provided good examples of adaptive problem solving and proactive planning. Kathy's (coauthor) story is one of those examples.

☐ It All Works Out

Although stress is a normal and expected part of life, there are some decades that are harder than others. The times, which were particularly challenging for me (Kathy), also forced me to develop a strategy to accommodate what became ongoing, chronic stress. Over time, I listened to what I said to clients and refined my approach to life's unexpected rough patches and unexpected twists or turns.

I started my professional counseling career many years ago as a single professional. But then, I proceeded to marry and have three children, and then return later in life for a Ph.D. Needless to say, most everyone thought this educational goal was impossible. How would I complete a demanding doctoral program with three children under the age of 7? How would my family accommodate my absence, and how would I handle the regular household chores of cooking, cleaning, and laundry when my husband travels every single week as part of *his* job? What would I do about the fact that all my children were interested in absolutely everything, from sports to art and drama?

Well, it all works out. First, faced with the overwhelming task of making it to my long-term goal of gaining the advanced degree, I had a simple mantra: "I can do anything for 15 weeks" (the length of a semester). No matter how bad "it" is, "it" is not going to last forever. Things change. This will pass. Things will improve.

Second, I realized that my kids would only be young once; I refused to miss their clever and cute moments, so I scheduled study and class time away from their most needy times. I would read and write papers after they were all in bed, or early in the morning. I joined neighborhood playgroups and co-ops so that we could trade child care even for a precious hour or two; this allowed me to concentrate in a focused way on schoolwork *or* my children (but not both at the same time!).

Third, I started to work with the ebb and flow, rather than against it. And I learned how to ask for help! When my doctoral program was out, or in between sessions, I'd volunteer for everything at all my kids' schools, and let them know I would drop out of sight when my next block of "15 weeks" would start up again.

But most important, I learned what has become my most important new skill. Faced with insurmountable problems with sick or ill children, papers due and a myriad of other demands, and with the full knowledge that there was no apparent solution, I learned to do one important thing: *wait*. In a day, some solution was revealed. Someone offered to help, a problem shifted ever so slightly, and *voila!* We steered our way out of the darkness and into the light.

And now all these years later, with a private practice, another full-time academic position, still fortunate to have my husband and three very busy kids, I practice this skill nearly every day. Rather than stressing out over finding an answer, I let go and wait. In an hour, the next morning, or in another day, I inevitably think of something or see something that was not available to me at the time of the "crisis." I have become a true believer.

My other companion strategy is to organize what I need to do first and keep my goals for every day small. I cannot take on too much, cannot say

Yes to everyone, and sometimes others have to wait for me. The years fly by, as it is. I make a point of stopping to schedule exercise, stretching, and physical activity, including laughing! I sleep regularly and eat healthy food (most of the time). In this way, I can enjoy my family and look forward to seeing my clients.

My clients often hear me ask whether something has to be decided right now, or where their sense of urgency to act, make a decision, or get busy is coming from. I feel more authentic and genuine when I can also approach things with a sense of patience and slow things down to maintain a sense of control over my own priorities. It keeps me calm and allows me to see what I might need for myself.

Does it always work? Of course not! Do I sometimes still overreact and worry that the "sky is falling," as did Chicken Little? Of course. But at least now I catch myself, apologize to innocent bystanders and then wait.

☐ Conclusion

This chapter documents and highlights the many sources of knowledge that are available to us as human beings and as therapists. We can come to "know" something by reading about it, by watching others model it for us, through conversations with friends, by listening to persons in authority or role models, or through personal experience. In all these instances, we have the opportunity to become transformed and to change our perspectives. We can create change for ourselves, just as we promote and create change for others in our professional lives.

As we pursue our goals of personal health and happiness, we are no less likely than others to deny our flaws or hide our vulnerabilities from others (especially our peers). Our role as "experts" (to whom others turn for help) makes it difficult to acknowledge that perfection is impossible or that there are no limits to our expertise. The key to detecting, preventing, and successfully treating our own issues and conflicts, however, lies in the ability to accept ourselves as vulnerable human beings who have a range of available talents.

This chapter combines theory, research, and personal stories to show how our knowledge and skills can be applied toward ourselves, not by "treating" ourselves, but by having faith in the process and principles we value for our clients. Self-care includes regular vigilance toward small signs of distress, so that problems and issues are brought into awareness. The goal is a sense of balance that enables us all to accomplish the ultimate and twin goals of working effectively and loving those who are part of our lives.

☐ References

Amundson, N. E. (2001). Three-dimensional living. *Journal of Employment Counseling, 38,* 114–127.

Coster, J. S., & Schwebel, M. (1997). Well-functioning in professional psychologists. *Professional Psychology: Research and Practice, 28,* 5–13.

Ellis, A. (1997). Using Rational Emotive Behavior Therapy techniques to cope with disability. *Professional Psychology: Research and Practice, 28*(1), 17–22.

Gladding, S. T., Remley, T. P., Jr., & Huber, C. H. (2001). *Ethical, legal, and professional issues in the practice of marriage and family therapy* (3rd ed.). Upper Saddle River, NJ: Merrill Prentice-Hall.

Grosch, W. N., & Olsen, D. C. (1994). *When helping stars to hurt: A new look at burnout among psychotherapists* (pp. 1–60). New York: Norton.

Guy, D. J. (2000). Holding the holding environment together: Self-psychology and psychotherapist care. *Professional Psychology: Research and Practice, 31*(3), 351–352.

Heery, M. (2001). A call and response to the soul. *Journal of Heart-Centered Therapies, 4*(1), 85–88.

Herlihy, B., & Corey, G. (1996). *ACA ethical standards casebook* (5th ed.). Alexandria, VA: American Counseling Association.

Horner, A. J. (1993). Occupational hazards and characterological vulnerability: The problem of "burnout." *The American Journal of Psychoanalysis, 53*(2), 137–143.

Kottler, J. A. (1993). *On being a therapist* (rev. ed.). San Francisco: Jossey-Bass.

Kottler, J. A. (1999). *The therapist's workbook: Self-assessment, self-care, and self-improvement exercises for mental health professionals.* San Francisco: Jossey-Bass.

Kottler, J. A., Parr, G. (2000). The family therapist's own family. *The Family Journal: Counseling and Therapy for Couples and Families, 8*(2), 143–148.

Kuyken, W., Peters, E., Power, M., & Lavender, T. (1998). The psychological adaptation of psychologists in clinical training: The role of cognition, coping and social support. *Clinical Psychology and Psychotherapy, 5,* 238–252.

Kuyken, W., Peters, E., Power, M., Lavender, T., & Rabe-Hesketh, S. (2000). A longitudinal study of the psychological adaptation of trainee clinical psychologists. *Clinical Psychology and Psychotherapy, 7,* 394–400.

Mahoney, M. J. (1997). Psychotherpists' personal problems and self-care patterns. *Professional Psychology: Research and Practice, 28*(1), 14–16.

Malach-Pines, A., & Yafe-Yanai, O. (2001). Unconscious determinants of career choice and burnout: Theoretical model of counseling strategy. *Journal of Employment Counseling, 38*(4), 170–185.

Pope, K. S., & Vasquez, M. J. T. (1998). *Ethics in psychotherapy and counseling: A practical guide* (2nd ed.). San Francisco: Jossey-Bass.

Rowe, M. M. (2000). Skills training in the long-term management of stress and occupational burnout. *Current Psychology, 19*(3), 215–228.

Sapienza, B. G., & Bugental, J. F. T. (2000). Keeping our instruments finely tuned: An existential-humanistic perspective. *Professional Psychology: Research & Practice, 31,* 458–460.

Sherman, M. D. (1996). Distress and professional impairment due to mental health programs among psychotherapists. *Clinical Psychology Review, 16,* 299–315.

Sherman, M. D., & Thelan M. H. (1998). Distress and professional impairment among psychologists in clinical practice. *Professional Psychology: Research and Practice, 29,* 79–85.

Spiegel, D. (1999). Healing words: Emotional expression and disease outcome. (editorial). *The Journal of the American Medical Association, 281*(14), 1328–1331.

15
CHAPTER

Leah Brew
Michael K. Altekruse

Blind Spots and Ruts in the Road: The Limits of Self-Supervision

I remember when I was completing my internship for my master's degree; I had to purchase my own video camera to record my sessions. I managed to delay the purchase for a few weeks, but eventually I had to purchase the camera if I was to be supervised by the off-campus supervisor I wanted. She was a strong believer in being able to view my counseling sessions when she supervised. Even then, I knew that telling my supervisor about my work versus her viewing my sessions would result in two very different types of supervision.

I was fairly insecure as a therapist during that internship experience, and I noticed when I just talked about my sessions, I seemed to leave the consultations feeling more competent. However, I also noticed that when my supervisor viewed my sessions on video, I found several areas in which I could improve, and I felt much less skilled. My delicate ego at the time came up with all kinds of rationalizations as to why I could not seem to bring good videotapes each week, and at the time, I truly felt that my excuses were legitimate. I may have presented videotape only about two-thirds of our supervision sessions.

Immediately after internship, I graduated and started my work as a doctoral student. Part of my course work was to learn how to be a supervisor and to supervise master's level counseling students. Everything became much clearer to me once I started supervising. I realized that when I supervised sessions without viewing them, the supervisees seemed to be doing quality work. However, watching the sessions live or on video sometimes told a different story. Some supervisees were not connecting with their clients. Some were giving advice or teaching their clients at inappropriate times. Others were providing reflections that lacked depth and resulted in a session or a series of sessions that seemed to go nowhere. I had to admit to myself that talking about sessions, rather than viewing them, was essentially self-supervision. I realized that this form of self-report supervision for beginning practitioners had the potential to be worthless at best, and dangerous at worst. I also realized that supervisors of licensure internships do not always require videotaping or audiotaping, and I deduced that many practitioners would be able to obtain licenses by essentially doing self-report supervision. It is true that supervisors can still challenge their supervisees without tapes. However, the challenge seems to be much less frequent in self-report supervision as compared with watching a tape. Often it is easier for students to justify, defend, or even modify the explanation of their performance in order to reduce the intensity of, if not completely eliminate the need for the critique. Therefore, although some confrontation can occur in self-report, it may be less intense and/or less frequent than observing or listening to sessions. Even though I still received some feedback during my self-report supervision sessions, I left feeling more competent than when I presented a videotape of the session. I became aware that if I felt inhibited about receiving good supervision to preserve my delicate ego, then others might do the same. Clearly, as a new therapist, self-report supervision was not enough to help me become a competent and ethical therapist.

As a third-year doctoral candidate, I had the opportunity to supervise first-year doctoral students. I noticed that, although the range of therapist experience varied from just out of school to 20 years of private practice, the length of experience as a therapist did not necessarily determine skill level. I wondered what made the differences in ability, because years of experience did not necessarily constitute a better therapist. I concluded that without external feedback therapists are at risk for continuing to provide the same quality of service year after year. Even if a therapist takes time to perform deliberate self-supervision, he or she may be limited by his or her own knowledge and phenomenological view of good therapy. I wondered if maintaining continuing education credits for licensure or certification along with self-supervision were enough. Self-supervision along with continuing education credits were not sufficient for some seasoned therapists in my doctoral program to be considered competent therapists by our advanced practicum instructors.

This chapter covers some of the blind spots or limitations of self-supervision. In addition, recommendations for reducing the limitations of self-supervision are included. Finally, case examples are utilized to help the reader understand the limitations more clearly.

☐ Blind Spots of Self-Supervision

Once a therapist receives licensure, supervision is no longer required on a weekly basis. Therefore, self-supervision is a reality with which we must contend. So, what are the consequences or blind spots? Blind spots can occur because of poor therapist preparation and training; the student may not be prepared or educated to self-supervise. In researching the literature about self-supervision, the topic seemed to be conspicuously missing. Consequently, it can only be assumed that self-supervision is not typically a deliberate curricular experience taught in most therapist preparation programs. Blind spots also can occur when self-supervision is used without consultation. Therapists are limited to seeing self, the client, or the therapeutic relationship through their own phenomenological biases. As a result, certain dynamics about the therapy session or counter-transferences may not be obvious to the therapist, and they may be at risk for responding inappropriately. Therefore, self-supervision is a skill that needs to be taught, but even with that skill, many potential blind spots still exist. Let us begin with the preparation of students to self-supervise.

Insufficient Education to Prepare Students for Self-Supervision

The ethical standards and guidelines of most therapists indicate that the primary goal of supervision is to promote the growth of the therapist in order to best serve the client and protect the public. Todd (1992, 1997) stated specifically that therapists must be trained to self-supervise. He listed three primary goals in which to promote good self-supervision in the future. First, identify therapist strengths and weaknesses in self-supervision. Second, a therapist should conceptualize within a theoretical framework that is congruent with self. Finally, preparing a beginning therapist to create well-formed goals and questions during supervision is an important goal for preparing students to self-supervise. It is realistic to believe that not *all* universities preparing therapists will meet *all* of these goals with *all* students. Therefore, what might be the consequences or resulting blind spots from not meeting these goals? The following are three case examples where students were not appropriately prepared to self-supervise.

Case Example: Susie

If a therapist is unable to identify weaknesses, how will the therapist know when to seek external consultation? Take the case of Susie. Susie graduated from a 36-semester-hour counseling program that emphasized a preventative developmental counseling model. She was not required to take a diagnosis and treatment class and was only required to take one three-semester-hour practicum. On graduation she took a position at a local mental health clinic. A client sued Susie, the clinic, and the university, charging that Susie had attempted to treat the client for a personality disorder. The client's lawyer said Susie's education had not prepared her to deal with such an illness and that the counselor needs to know her limitations. Susie should have consulted with an experienced supervisor before attempting to counsel a client that she was not trained to counsel. If Susie was more aware of her strengths and weaknesses, she might have never been sued.

Therapist-training programs that do not help students articulate their strengths and weaknesses are not sufficiently preparing students to self-supervise. If a therapist is not clearly aware of his or her strengths, how can she or he make use of them when evaluating sessions? If therapists are not clearly aware of their weaknesses, how can they know when to seek external consultation to protect the client?

Case Example: Bob

In order to be prepared to self-supervise, a therapist must be competent at conceptualizing his or her client. If the therapist is trying to conceptualize within a theoretical framework that does not fit, self-supervision may be difficult. Imagine that a therapist, Bob, is in a practicum where person-centered therapy is strongly valued and encouraged by a particular supervisor. Bob interjects this value and attempts to conceptualize and perform as a person-centered therapist. Imagine that Bob manages to graduate and obtain his licensure utilizing this therapeutic approach. However, Bob is naturally cognitive in his conceptualizations. He also does not seek out additional training experiences or supervision except when he runs into difficult cases. Every client can become a challenge for him as he tries to fit his clients into a conceptualization that feels artificial for him. He reflects feelings and content well enough, but does not feel like his clients are progressing quickly. He wants to be more directive in his approach, but he accepts the idea that he should be purely person-centered to be a competent therapist. If Bob only had supervisors that came from the person-centered approach, he might have been at risk for becoming a mediocre therapist. Perhaps he would have made an excellent cognitive therapist, but without realizing this option, he is unable to build a successful practice.

Bob tried to conceptualize and work within a theoretical framework that was not congruent with his natural style, limiting his ability to self-supervise. Without external supervision, Bob may not discover his true calling to be more cognitively based. His ability to self-supervise was limited by a person-centered paradigm. His therapist preparation program did not prepare him to self-supervise appropriately.

Case Example: Liz

Some therapist-preparation programs may lack in helping students to ask questions during therapy. Asking appropriate questions may happen in supervision, but to deliberately train a therapist to ask questions may not always occur. For example, Liz recently obtained her license in counseling and mastered the ability to reflect and clarify. She can frequently intuit a clear sense of the client's experience. However, because Liz clearly understands her client's problem does not always automatically mean she sees the direction that she should take. Often, a new therapist like Liz can be as confused as the client with the therapy process. When new therapists feel confused, they often defer to the supervisor for assistance. However, because Liz is no longer required to attend weekly supervision, she may not have the opportunity to learn how to ask the right questions to find solutions independently. What should Liz do? Consultation with a more advanced therapist is often helpful to beginning therapists. Or, she could keep doing what she has been doing with the client effecting no change.

Training programs need to train students to ask appropriate questions because, frequently, if a question is well formed, the answer seems to emerge on its own. For Liz, this skill was not developed as part of her training. As a result, when she feels stuck with a client, she may have a tendency to seek advice, or do nothing. She is not sufficiently prepared to self-supervise. Although seeking consultation is beneficial, a certain amount of independence should be expected of a licensed therapist.

Along with Todd's (1992, 1997) goals of self-supervision, Holloway (1999) listed the roles of supervision. He stated that there are five primary roles in supervision. These roles are: (a) monitoring and evaluating; (b) instructing and advising; (c) modeling; (d) consulting and exploring; and (e) supporting and sharing. If any of these roles are not well executed during training, therapists without external supervision may be at risk for harming clients because they may be unprepared to self-supervise. Let us look at how each of these five roles, if not properly executed during therapist training, may result in poor self-supervision once the therapist is licensed.

Monitoring and Evaluating

The supervisor's role as an evaluator during therapist training is important in preparing a therapist to self-supervise. The supervisor is responsible for reviewing sessions in a way that can result in an evaluation of the therapist's skill level. The therapist is best served by being aware of what he or she has mastered (strengths) and how much more mastery is needed in order to be considered competent. For example, if a supervisor is more interested in being liked than providing constructive facilitation, students may be able to graduate without having reached a competency level appropriate for the potentially less structured internship supervision experience. Ultimately, an individual may have the opportunity to receive a license without being fully aware of weaknesses and is ill prepared to self-supervise. Remember the earlier case of Susie? She was unaware of her weaknesses limiting her ability to self-supervise, and thus was sued for treating the client inappropriately.

Instructing and Advising

Another essential role of the supervisor is that of an instructor/advisor. When areas of weaknesses are identified, the supervisor should provide clear instruction as to how to overcome those weaknesses. In addition, the supervisor may provide a process for the supervisee to facilitate growth as a therapist. John, a supervisor, has identified that a supervisee, Kim, has difficulty working with a culturally different client. Kim may harbor unconscious prejudices about her client's culture, and it is inhibiting her client's progress. If John, the supervisor, does not help Kim increase her awareness about cultural differences, and if necessary, recommend therapy to explore her issues about that culture, then Kim may eventually cause harm to this client and all clients from the same cultural background. Supervisors should take instruction and advising very seriously because once the supervisee is working independently, the quality of or lack of instruction will affect all future clients. Without the recommendation to work on this issue, Kim is not prepared to self-supervise.

Modeling

One implicit role of supervising is modeling. If the supervisor does not model appropriate behaviors with the therapist-in-training, the future therapist may not be prepared to self-supervise. More specifically, when a supervisor models the type of behavior that should exist in a counseling session, a parallel process may occur so that the supervisee may exhibit the same behaviors in the counseling session with the client. According to Mueller (1982), a parallel process cannot be denied as a factor in training therapists. Therefore, if supervisors are not cognizant of their behaviors in the supervisory sessions, inappropriate habits may be passed down to the supervisee that are expressed in sessions with clients. Once supervisees are no longer under supervision, any inappropriate habits will likely continue throughout their career.

For example, a supervisor, Jane, is working with her supervisee, Steve. Steve is having a great deal of difficulty helping a client who has been diagnosed with depression. Steve feels frustrated because he does not know how to help the client. During supervision, Jane offers Steve some behavioral suggestions on exactly what to explore with the client. Steve subsequently gives direct advice to the client, and when the client does not comply, Steve feels frustrated. At the very least, Steve is becoming dependent on his supervisor rather than finding his own solutions. However, Steve is also copying his supervisor's style of giving advice, which may not be sufficient in helping his client with depression. If he develops advice giving as a general style of counseling when he graduates, then he will be less prepared to work with clients once he obtains his license. Self-supervision would not reveal why he might become an unsuccessful therapist and may be an inadequate form of supervision in this situation.

Consulting and Exploring

These two intertwined roles performed by the supervisor usually assume the supervisee has the capacity to arrive at conclusions fairly independently. During the advanced levels of training, supervision experiences should shift from being less detailed and more global so that therapists feel confident to seek consultation outside of the usual self-supervision experience. When supervisors work with more advanced practitioners and supervise them the same way they supervise beginning therapists, then supervisees might feel frustrated and unable to obtain what is needed in supervision. Furthermore, supervisees may be reluctant to seek consultation once in private practice, fearing another negative experience, and instead rely exclusively on self-supervision.

Consider a supervisor, Sally, who works with a new employee of the agency, Mike. Mike has many years of experience, but Sally is assigned to train him to work within this agency's culture. Instead of facilitating exploration, Sally treats Mike as if he is unfamiliar with therapy by analyzing each and every response Mike expresses. She evaluates his sessions in a detailed manner and works hard to find criticisms to help Mike improve. Mike is likely to feel frustrated rather than supported by Sally. He may experience Sally as condescending, even though she is trying to be helpful. Until Sally is able to recognize Mike's ability and work with him in more of a consultation role, the supervision sessions might be fraught with tension and defensiveness. Thus, poor consultation experiences might lead a therapist to rely exclusively on self-supervision, which is *not always* sufficient even for the most skilled of practitioners.

Supporting and Sharing

The task of being supportive to supervisees and sharing experiences that may be indicative of what supervisees are experiencing can be helpful in supervision. Many supervisees simply need encouragement with unusual or difficult cases. In addition, when supervisors share their personal counseling experiences, supervisees may gain a clearer sense of how to handle these difficult situations. If supervisors do not provide sufficient support to supervisees, the supervisory relationship may falter so that supervisees may not receive supervision well. In addition, being supportive helps supervisees learn to become self-supportive once they become independent practitioners and must self-supervise.

For instance, if a supervisor is constantly critical without providing encouragement to the supervisee, the supervisee may not be open to receiving supervision. The time spent on supervision may not be well spent, hurting the supervisee's ability to grow. On the other hand, the supervisee may become overly self-critical where self-support is not developed. This supervisee may not have the confidence to provide good services to clients if he or she lacks the appropriate level of confidence to counsel individuals. In addition, the confidence level may be so low that the supervisee, once independent of supervision, may be reluctant to seek external supervision for fear of being caught doing poor therapy. As a result, the therapist may rely exclusively on self-supervision.

Now that you have completed this section, you should have gained a clear understanding of why it is essential for the supervision experiences in training therapists to be done well. If the goals of self-supervision by Todd (1992, 1997) are not met, the therapist may be ill prepared to self-supervise. If the roles of self-supervision (Holloway, 1999) are not executed well, the therapist may have significant weaknesses in self-supervising. Therefore, it is essential that preparing a therapist to self-supervise should be deliberate. Think about your own supervision experiences in training. Do you see any weaknesses that may inhibit your ability to self-supervise?

Limitations to Using Self-Supervision Without Consultation

Now that we have explored preparing therapists to self-supervise, let's look at other potential limitation of self-supervision if consultation is unavailable. Let's assume the therapist has been trained appropriately to self-supervise. Do limitations still exist? According to Carroll (1996), several weaknesses exist for those therapists who use self-supervision without available consultation. First, he stated that the therapist might not be aware of internal feelings during the session. In addition, the self-supervised therapist might be at risk for missing important factors in the relationship with clients. Another limitation to self-supervision is that the therapist might be at risk for impulsively administering inappropriate interventions with the client. Finally, one of the greatest limitations of this type of self-supervision according to Carroll is that the therapist might be unable to see how his or her own issues are interfering with the client's progress. Following are four case examples of each of Carroll's weaknesses in self-supervision without consultation.

Case Example: Natalie

What a client presents during a session may trigger a countertransference reaction in the therapist. As a therapist, being self-aware during sessions is critical so that countertransferences do not interfere with the client's best interest. For example, Natalie's client resembled her father in looks and actions. Natalie was unaware that she had feelings for this client that were interfering with her counseling. She found that she was less active with this client and often had thoughts and feelings that were unnatural for her as a counselor. A consultant/supervisor could have helped Natalie identify these hidden feelings and could have helped her make a decision on a proper referral. However, as Natalie self-supervised, she was aware of how different this therapeutic relationship was, but alone, she was unable to articulate her experience exactly. Self-supervision was not sufficient for her to identify the countertransference reaction.

Case Example: Hank

There may be something going on with the counselor or client that the counselor is unaware of in a session. An external supervisor or consultant will often see important factors in the session that are imperative for client growth that self-supervision may not reveal. For instance, Hank would study each counseling session, looking for factors that would contribute to effective counseling. It never occurred to him that there might be factors in the session that contributed to *ineffective* counseling. Hank reflected very well but seldom with any depth. When he finally developed the ability to reflect at a more profound level, his counseling effectiveness improved. It is difficult to identify factors of weakness without external supervision and without systematic self-supervision. Self-supervision would not be sufficient for Hank to learn how to reflect deeper meanings.

Case Example: Jimmy

Some therapists may incorrectly assume they have appropriate training to perform certain techniques in the session. A supervisor/consultant would be able to determine competency when self-supervision is not sufficient. Jimmy, a new therapist, has learned about the paradoxical intention technique from a skilled practitioner who has used it successfully with phobias. Jimmy hears many successful accounts of how well this technique has worked and wants to utilize it with a new client who is afraid of snakes. With great enthusiasm, Jimmy brings a snake to the next session and demands that the client hold the snake. Because Jimmy did not have sufficient preparation and did not choose to consult, he did not use this intervention at an appropriate time or way and could have ultimately harmed his client. In this case, self-supervision was not sufficient to protect the client. Consultation might be advised before trying new interventions to benefit the client and promote success.

Case Example: The Supervisee Who Didn't Want to Feel

Therapists are limited in self-supervision to their own self-knowledge and paradigms. Each therapist has his or her own therapeutic issues that might interfere with the ability to provide good therapy to clients. Sometimes, a therapist can be so unaware of personal issues that a supervisor/consultant would be essential to help explore these issues. For example, I (Leah) have worked with a supervisee who struggled to reflect any feelings either stated or exhibited by the client. She consistently responded to the client with content reflections, in her better moments, and rough confrontations loaded with logic in her lesser moments. She could not understand why the client's behavior would not change. Through the supervision process and a variety of other circumstances, this supervisee revealed a value that feeling and expressing her emotions was merely a roadblock to her own self-growth. She believed feelings should only exist very briefly (a day at most), and then, as she put it, she needed to "get on with her life." She admitted to repressing her own emotions and had difficulty accepting that the full expression of emotions can facilitate growth. (Much of this difficulty was attributed to a cultural value difference.) How could she, then, identify or reflect the emotions of her client? She needed to do her own work in order to become a better therapist. Clearly, identifying why her sessions were not progressing well on her own (self-supervision) was unlikely. She needed supervision to identify what was in the way.

Other Limitations of Self-Supervision

One may agree that it is essential for therapists to be trained to self-supervise. One may also agree that self-supervision without consultation has many limitations that may not be ideal for serving clients. Let's assume you have excellent training and seek consultation on a regular basis. Do limitations still exist for self-supervision?

One potential limitation to self-supervision is that the therapist may not be aware of *when* consultation is needed. For example, a therapist has just started working with a client who has eating disorders. The therapist has not been prepared to work with this particular issue. He reads a book on eating disorders while working with the client and begins doing behavioral types of interventions while ignoring the possible causes of eating disorders. The client could be in a life-threatening situation without the therapist's intervention. It is essential that the therapist have a clear sense of his or her limitations and competencies so that clients are either properly referred or consultation is obtained to provide the best possible service.

Another potential problem is when counselors become overinvolved with the content rather than the process of the client's story. Some therapists become so intrigued with the details of a client's life that they are unable to ascertain the larger picture or the process. Some clients have interesting stories that may fascinate their therapists. Consequently, instead of helping the client with their issues, counselors are simulating the watching of a movie. In short, the counselor is not part of the counseling process.

Burnout is another limitation to self-supervision for therapists. Burnout can be a factor in two ways. First, therapists may work an excessive amount of hours or inefficiently for years until reaching a state of burnout. Consultation can sometimes help new therapists find efficient and effective ways of handling large caseloads. In addition, taking the time to discuss frustrations with another professional can reduce the incidence of burnout. Once therapists become burned out, they may be at risk for providing poor services to clients. When the passion for helping others wanes, then therapists may therapeutically be less effective with clients. Counselors who are constantly complaining about clients or find themselves with some type of addiction may be suffering from burnout.

Another limitation to self-supervision is that therapists may not take the time to evaluate their own skills. Time limitations may prohibit therapists from formally performing self-supervision. If a concerted effort is not made to evaluate one's work, then what indication will be given to change the direction with a client or seek consultation? How will a therapist know if he or she is doing effective work with clients? Therapists need to organize and take sufficient time to evaluate how effective the work is going with each client. The authors suspect that many therapists do not take the time to self-assess and may be at risk for providing poor services to clients.

Blind Spots of Self-Supervision

- The therapist is unaware of countertransference issues.
- The therapist is unaware of important relationship factors.
- The therapist uses interventions or techniques inappropriately.
- The therapist has too many personal issues related to the client's issues.
- The therapist is unaware of when consultation is needed.
- The therapist is so involved in the client's content that the process is ignored.
- The therapist experiences burnout.

☐ The Prevalence of Self-Supervision

Self-report supervision is probably one of the most widely used modalities of supervision for therapists. Self-report supervision is supervision without the benefit of watching or listening to a counseling session. It is just recalling what happened in a session. Self-report supervision is essentially a form of self-supervision.

Randy is in his first semester of fieldwork. The agency where he works does not have the capability for Randy to videotape or audiotape his sessions. In fact, it is against agency policy because the agency fears that taping sessions may scare away clients. So Randy, who was accustomed to having sessions watched live or on video in school, comes to supervision unprepared for what to expect. The supervisor asks Randy to talk about his sessions. Randy thinks he is doing a good job. He reports a summary, highlighting some of the better interventions he felt he made with his clients. He is brief so that he has time to report on his entire caseload of eight clients. The supervisor concludes that Randy is doing a good job. Randy may not criticize his own therapy because of fear of evaluation or he may be unaware of his limitations owing to lack of knowledge. Therefore, self-report supervision is like self-supervision, but worse if Randy has no training in how to self-supervise. So considering that self-report is quite popular, and self-report is essentially a form of self-supervision, how prevalent is it? Well, self-report occurs in practicum, fieldwork, internships, as well as with consultation.

Criticisms of Practicum Supervision

Self-supervision happens in many arenas for therapists. For example, some therapy training programs do not require weekly videotapes or audio-tapes of sessions. Most practicums have 10 students and group supervision is 1½ hours a week. Students are also required to have 1 hour a week of individual or triadic supervision. It is possible that only two or three sessions may be critiqued in an entire semester. A student may or may not bring in a tape for supervision. A student is required to have 40 direct contact hours with clients in a semester. If self-report supervision is the supervision of choice, then there is a large number of contact hours not supervised. Self-report supervision is considered the most ineffective form of supervision and is like not having supervision.

Criticisms of Field Practicum or Internship

A student in internship or field practicum is required to have 240 direct contact hours with clients. Students are also required to have 1 hour a week of individual or triadic supervision and 1½ hours of group supervision. Supervision may be with a field supervisor or faculty supervisor. A student may have had excellent supervision at the university, before internship. No matter how strong a student may be once completing practicum, more supervision is needed. The Council for Accreditation of Counseling and Related Educational Programs, the national accreditation agency for counseling programs, and the National Board of Certified Counselors (NBCC, 2001), the national certifying board for counselors, endorse this notion by requiring students to complete 600 clock hours of field-work/internship before graduation. Also, most state licensure boards for counselors (Altekruse, 2001) and social workers (NASW, 2001) require a total of 2,000 to 3,000 clock hours of post-master's internship experience before becoming licensed. Psychologists have even more stringent expectations requiring students to complete a doctorate and work an entire year prior to graduating with a psychology degree, and additional experience may still be required in order to become licensed (APA, 2001).

Once the therapist goes to an internship, many agency sites provide weekly supervision but do not have the resources for the therapist-in-training to have sessions watched or taped. Frequently, agency sites supervise purely on self-report, and even for some agencies that supervise with video- or audiotapes, it seems unlikely that even half of a therapist's sessions will be supervised. Again, self-report may be the most frequent type of supervision modality for agencies to utilize. Even those rare students who have better than average therapy skills still need more direct supervision at times.

Post-Degree Internship

Once the student graduates or is ready for post-degree internship, he or she may have a good didactic understanding of how to perform therapy. However, supervision is still required by licensure boards for internships (Altekruse, 2001; APA, 2001). Frequently, students continue from the university internship agency into their post-degree internship at the same agency. Once again, the primary modality for most agencies to utilize for supervision is self-report, in other words, self-supervision. If a therapist-in-training has primarily used self-report from the university experience up through a completed internship, as many as 2,000 or 3,000 hours have been accumulated, with many as direct client contact hours, and many loaded with opportunities for improvement that were missed.

Therapists in Practice

Once therapists have their license they are no longer required to seek supervision. The first author's experience in supervising doctoral-level students found that the years of experience as licensed therapists did not seem to make a difference in the strength of therapy provided. Both authors agree that continued supervision and/or consultation is a factor in improving and maintaining good therapy. However, supervision may still be beneficial, whether joining a therapist training organization for a particular theory or consulting with colleagues.

In reviewing the ethical standards for the American Counseling Association (ACA, 2001), the American Psychological Association (APA, 2001), the National Association for Social Workers (NASW, 2001), and the American Association for Marriage and Family Therapists (AAMFT, 2001), they all have similar requirements that would merit additional supervision. First, therapists must practice only within the limits of their competence. As any therapist knows, once a license to practice is obtained, the therapist is not sufficiently prepared to handle every client situation and needs to continue learning. Furthermore, all therapists are required to obtain continuing education to maintain their license or certification. In learning new techniques, therapists may need to continue to get supervision before becoming fully competent. In addition, therapists are ethically bound to seek consultation if a client's case becomes too challenging or ethical questions exist. Therapists are busy people and may no longer be accustomed to or have the time to either record or view sessions. Once again, self-report, a version of self-supervision, becomes the modality of choice, even with all its limitations.

Where Does Self-Report Self-Supervision Occur?

- University practicum classes
- Agency fieldwork experiences
- Internships
- Licensure internships
- Private practices or clinics

Self-Supervision Research

In researching the topic of self-supervision, we only found four resources that mentioned it, all in marriage and family publications, and two were from the same author (Carroll, 1996; Steiden, 1993; Todd, 1992, 1997). The popular supervision textbook by Bernard and Goodyear (1998) did not contain any information on how to teach supervisees how to self-supervise. Even the publication by the Association for Counselor Education and Supervision, a division of the American Counseling Association, did not instruct supervisors how to teach self-supervision (Borders & Leddick, 1987). Nor was anything beyond the four listed resources found in *Psyc Info*, the database for most published psychological works. Finally, many of the ethical standards required for therapists mention that the purpose of supervision is to improve the performance of the therapist, but none of them suggest learning to self-supervise as a method of enhancing performance (AAMFT, 2001; ACA, 2001; APA, 2001; NASW, 2001). So even if learning to self-supervise would reduce our anxiety about self-report supervision, it seems the existence of teaching students this skill is sparse, at best.

☐ Recommendations to Reduce the Limitations of Self-Supervision

The next session provides recommendations for supervisors to train supervisees in self-supervision; for therapists on methods of self-supervision; and to reduce the limitations of self-supervision. Perhaps these recommendations will not alleviate the blind spots of self-supervision, but rather reduce the blind.

Recommendations for Supervising Therapists-in-Training

Todd (1992, 1997) has several recommendations for supervisors of thera-pists-in-training to prepare them for self-supervision.

1. Self-supervision should always be a goal of supervision. If the supervi-sor keeps in the foreground that the supervisee will eventually self-supervise, the supervisor is more likely to supervise in a way that facilitates growth and self-awareness.
2. Todd (1997) stated that the supervisor should help the supervisee take inventory of the assets and skills of the supervisee. As stated, with an awareness of strengths, the supervisee is better prepared to utilize these strengths with clients once in private practice or an agency.
3. The supervisee should develop an understanding of his or her own learning style. Having a greater understanding of learning style can be utilized as therapists begin to work with new and different client situ-ations.
4. The supervisee needs to be well developed in conceptualizing the cli-ent and take the time to do so. Being able to conceptualize a client's situation can frequently provide guidance as to how to move forward with therapy.
5. It is important for supervisees to learn how to ask good questions. Frequently, knowing what questions to ask will lead the therapist to find the answers.
6. Supervision should not be a mysterious process by which the supervi-see is a passive receiver, but an active participant with the greatest possible understanding of the process. With supervision, knowledge can be very powerful in the development of a therapist.
7. Supervisors would best serve their supervisees if they provide alterna-tives rather than advice. Advice can be dangerous in generating de-pendence on the supervisor. In addition, modeling advice giving can be passed down as a style of therapy through the parallel process that is not usually indicative of good counseling.

Recommendations for Evaluation in Self-Supervision

Todd (1997) stated that therapists could utilize their clients in the self-supervision process. Evaluation forms or verbal discussions about the client's experience of therapy can be an effective way to obtain feedback. If a relationship with a client is well established, the client may be willing to talk about what is or is not working in session. Moreover, because much of therapy is learning how to be more effective interpersonally, the client also can benefit from this process by learning how to be more assertive and by evaluating his or her responsibility in the therapeutic process.

Kagan's (1976) Interpersonal Process Recall (IPR) method also could be utilized in self-supervision. In his original model, a third party interviews the client regarding a counseling session. A supervisor and supervisee watch a video of the feedback session of the client and pause to discuss interesting or questionable interchanges. The same method could be used in self-supervision. The therapist can simply watch a video of the session as objectively as possible to evaluate the therapeutic process. Kagan also suggested using specific questions to organize the way in which the session is evaluated. With self-supervision, the therapist can easily ask him- or herself the same questions. A supervisee also could use the same questions with the client to receive some feedback on their therapy. Using Kagan's model may be helpful to provide some structure for the therapist to evaluate the session.

Steiden's (1993) discourse analysis is another method that could provide some structure in self-supervision. She suggested at least listening to, watching, or ideally transcribing a session and analyzing the session to find patterns in speech that may have not been obvious during the session. Patterns can include the use of words, the phrasing a client uses, exchanges between the client and therapist, or frequency of talking. Once the patterns are discovered, she suggested exploring different ways in which to interpret the patterns to seek new understandings about the client. Therefore, using discourse analysis may be a helpful tool for improving the effectiveness of sessions as well as creating a structure for self-supervision.

Finally, Altekruse (Altekruse & Brown, 1969; Altekruse, Brown, & Coy, 1999) created a brief method of supervising that could be quickly utilized in self-supervision to evaluate sessions. Counselor Self-Interaction Analysis is a way that a therapist can identify each response and track response patterns. This is a systematic method of self-supervision that gives the therapist an analysis of their responses. All responses are placed in one of eight categories and two client categories. A therapist can see the relationship between their responses and client responses and consequently, make changes based on this self-feedback.

Recommendations for Self-Evaluation

- Client feedback
- Kagan's IPR model
- Steiden's disourse analysis
- Altekruse's counselor self-interaction analysis

Other Recommendations to Reduce the Limitations of Self-Supervision

One effective way for a therapist to reduce the risks that may be associated with self-supervision is to seek consultation. As stated, many ethical standards for therapists state that consultation is an option for therapists to utilize as long as the person with whom the therapist is consulting is competent (AAMFT, 2001; ACA, 2001; APA, 2001; NASW, 2001). The guidelines specify that one of the goals of consultation should be to encourage self-direction (or self-supervision) by the person seeking consultation. Thus, the use of consultation on a regular basis does not seem to be encouraged by the guidelines. However, therapists may want to use consultation on a regular but infrequent basis to ensure that the client is receiving the best possible services. Seeing a different perspective of the client may help to keep sessions with clients fresh and reduce the chances of burnout. At the very least, consultation should be used when the therapist experiences difficult or unusual situations. Finally, to prevent the risks associated with self-report, recording sessions and reviewing those recordings with your consultant could be far more beneficial.

Many new graduates of counseling programs may think their education is completed once they receive their license. However, the educational process should just be beginning. Another method for reducing the risks that may be associated with self-supervision is to make use of continuing education. Although continuing education is required of all licensed therapists (Altekruse, 2001), licensed psychologists (APA, 2001), and certified counselors (NBCC, 2001), there is a potential that therapists may not take full advantage of this requirement. As therapists come in contact with different or more diverse client situations, they may need to go to workshops or programs at conferences that deal with these issues to enhance the sessions. Moreover, a therapist can obtain training to work with new populations in order to expand his or her practice. Learning new material may help the therapist see all clients in different ways in order to facilitate the best possible service to a client.

Finally, one of the most effective ways to reduce the risks associated with self-supervision is for therapists to continually do their own work. At the very least, therapists could benefit by exploring countertransferences with clients and work on increasing awareness about those issues that facilitate a reaction. At best, attending sessions as a client may be necessary intermittently throughout a therapist's career to work on personal struggles, discuss therapist burnout, or anything else that might interfere with the ability to provide the best service to clients. In a way, personal therapy can be self-supervision for a therapist as he or she begins to explore personal issues.

To Reduce Limitations of Self-Supervision

- Seek consultation.
- Seek continuing education.
- Seek your own therapy; be a client.

In conclusion, self-supervision is a reality of most therapists, and not doing it well may run the risk of providing mediocre if not poor services to clients. Therefore, learning to self-supervise should be an important and deliberate component during the educational process for new counselors. In addition, therapists who are no longer in training should be conscientious about self-supervising and not allow time constraints to interfere with this essential task. Self-supervision should be deliberate and may be best accomplished with the use of formal or structured tools. Finally, because self-supervision cannot always be sufficient, therapists need to be self-aware in order to self-supervise effectively. Being self-aware, therapists will know their limitations and seek consultation or additional education when necessary. After all, according to ethical guidelines, the primary responsibility of therapists is to always maintain the welfare of the client (AAMFT, 2001; ACA, 2001; APA, 2001; NASW, 2001).

☐ References

Altekruse, M. K. (2001) *Counselor portability*. Keynote Address at the American Association for the State Counseling Board, North Reddington Shores, FL.

Altekruse, M. K., Brown, C., & Coy, D. (1999). *An instrument to measure and improve counselor effectiveness*. Paper presented at Association for Counselor Education and Supervision National Convention, New Orleans, LA.

Altekruse, M. K., & Brown, D. (1969). Counseling behavior change through self-analysis. *Counselor Education and Supervision*, 8, 108–112.

American Association for Marriage and Family Therapy (AAMFT). (2001). http://www.aamft.org/

American Counseling Association (ACA). (2001). http://www.counseling.org/

American Psychological Association (APA). (2001). http://www.apa.org/

Bernard, J., & Goodyear, R. (1998). *Fundamental of clinical supervision*. Needham Heights, MA: Allyn & Bacon.

Borders, L., & Leddick, G. (1987). *Handbook of counseling supervision*. Alexandria, VA: Association for Counselor Education and Supervision.

Carroll, M. (1996). Forms of supervision and presentation in supervsion. In *Counselling supervision: Theory, skills, and practice* (pp.128–147). New York: Cassell.

Holloway, E. (1999). A framework for supervision training. In E. Holloway & M. Carroll (Eds.), *Training Counselling Supervisors* (pp. 8–43). London: Sage.

Kagan, N. (1976). *Influencing human interaction*. Mason, MI: Mason Media.

Mueller, W. J. (1982). Issues in the application of "Supervision: A conceptual model" to dynamically oriented supervision: A reaction paper. *Counseling Psychologist*, 10, 43–46.

National Association of Social Workers (NASW). (2001). http://www.naswdc.org/

National Board of Certified Counselors (NBCC). (2001). http://www.nbcc.org.

Steiden, D. (1993). Self-supervision using discourse analysis: Playing with talk about talk. *The Supervision Bulletin, VI*(2), 2.

Todd, T. (1992). Self-supervision? A goal for all supervisors. *The Supervision Bulletin V*(1), 3–4.

Todd, T. (1997). Self-supervision as a universal supervisory goal. In T. Todd & C. Storm (Eds.), *The complete systemic supervisor: Context, philosophy, and pragmatics* (pp.17–25). Boston: Allyn & Bacon.

Jeffrey A. Kottler
W. Paul Jones

Final Thoughts

When we first conceived of this project, we envisioned it as an opportunity both to provide helpful information to other therapists and to confront some of our own blind spots and clinical weaknesses. The contributing authors have shared a wealth of information. Each chapter, from a different vantage point, has addressed features associated with a common need, maintaining and enhancing clinical skills.

The extent to which the first of the objectives was accomplished is in your hands. Without question, we can report that the suggestions and warning signs provided by the authors have stimulated reflective thought on our own areas of practice.

Not wanting to repeat or inadvertently dilute the topics that have already been addressed, we've decided instead to conclude by sharing some thoughts about the steps to facilitate incorporating this information into your work and life.

☐ The First Step

The first step, logical but often ignored, is to admit that we don't already know it all. This might sound rather obvious, but if you listen to yourself, and your colleagues, you will find that a lot of the time we are pretending to know and understand a heck of a lot more than we really do. If it is not safe to admit to your supervisors and coworkers that you are lost, that you are sometimes clueless, that you don't even know what you did wrong, much less how to fix it, then it is that much more difficult to work on improvement.

In working with our clients we've learned to identify this as the move from the precontemplation to the contemplation stage, and it applies equally well when applied to ourselves. The first step of any self-help effort is to acknowledge one's limitations.

We've probably all experienced sitting in workshops about therapy in which the presenter is speaking with total authority and confidence about *the way things are*. First we hear, "This is what's going on with this couple." Then, "And this is why things turned out the way they did." Followed by, "And this is what needs to be done to improve the situation." No hesitation—no room for doubt—just absolute certainty and assurance.

Any feelings of awe toward colleagues who speak this way about their work should be tempered by even stronger feelings of mistrust. Pick any area of human endeavor, including therapy, and consider what it would be like today if the world had been populated in the past by persons with this attitude. Avoiding sabertooth tigers might well be your primary daily activity. The truth is that all of us are just scratching the surface of what we are capable of doing; there is always room to get better.

As therapists, we may be particularly at risk for developing exaggerated feelings of self-importance. We were probably taught that it was important to convey an image of expertise. Our clients expect us to be near perfect. Managed care administrators demand perfect outcomes in predetermined time periods.

How important are you? For any who might feel that the limitations described just don't apply to you, we encourage a simple test. From your kitchen, get a cooking pan, and fill it with lukewarm water. Immerse your hand in the water. Remove your hand from the water. Carefully inspect the water. If the imprint of your hand remains in the water, you undoubtedly are a superior being (and probably should ask for a refund of the price of this book). For the rest of us, we are not perfect; there is still room to grow.

☐ You'll Never Be Good Enough

The second step is also an exercise in humility. Try as hard as you might, devote every waking moment to your growth and development, and you still won't put a dent in everything there is to learn. There will always be skill deficiencies. There will always be lapses in your judgment. There will always be gaping holes in your knowledge. You will always be impaired in one area or another. You will always have your blind spots, your biases and prejudices, the kinks in your armor. You will never be perfect.

Traditional supervision can help, but there are inherent limitations. There are multiple functions that compromise the relationship. There is a fear of judgment. Access is limited to certain times that don't often coincide with need. It is necessary, of course, even imperative for healthy professional functioning, but it is still not enough.

Self-supervision, our theme here, can also help. It, though, is also not a magic bullet. It offers many advantages as have been described by the contributing authors, and it overcomes some of the limitations of traditional supervision. But, there probably are some inherent limitations in the capability of a biological organism to observe itself. Self-supervision is better than no supervision. The combination of self-supervision and traditional supervision is better than either one alone. Even if diligently applied in combination, gaps and deficiencies will remain.

☐ You Can Be Better Than You Are

We believe that these admonitions are "good advice." But, if the strong suggestions to recognize our limitations and admit that perfection is not a reasonable goal result in feelings of helplessness or hopelessness, then we have failed the first test of good practice, do no harm. While accepting the reality of the "you are not perfect" statement, we both are tempted to insert a parenthetical thought (but I will be some day). If taken to an extreme, this belief is harmful. To the extent that it results in trying just a little bit harder each day working a little more carefully, and devoting a little more time, we believe it is a worthy goal. The stakes are high for both you and the clients you serve.

"Doing perfect" is not a reasonable objective. "Doing better" is a viable option with high stakes and tangible benefits for the clients we serve and for ourselves.

We believe that the contributing authors, in a variety of contexts, have provided essential content for development of self-initiated and self-moderated internal structures to facilitate your ability to:

1. Identify skills and knowledge deficits.
2. Recognize difficulties *as they are occurring* in sessions.
3. Notice recurrent themes and unresolved issues in real time.
4. Become aware of blocks interfering with progress.
5. Rekindle passion and curiosity.
6. Access intuition and creativity.

To the extent that these capabilities are incorporated into your practice, we believe you will be "doing better" with gain for all involved.

A story is told about two therapists who were attending a retirement party in honor of a colleague. When the speaker noted the retiree's 30 years of experience, one therapist leaned over to the other and whispered, "He didn't have 30 years of experience. He had 1 year, 30 times."

Our hope and objective in this book has been to avoid any such closure on our careers. Unlike many professions, we have the opportunity as therapists for our last year of service to be our best year.

INDEX